MEMOIRS

ALFRED ROSENBERG

Ostara Publications

Memoirs
By Alfred Rosenberg

Ostara Publications
http://ostarapublications.com

ISBN 978-1507690161

Contents

Introduction...v

Part One: Youth..1
    Youth in Baltic Russia

Part Two: Russia and the Bolshevik Revolution...............................7
    Move to Moscow; The Bolshevik Revolution

Part Three: Germany and the Early Party Days...............................18
    The Move to Germany; First Days in Munich; First
    Meeting with Dietrich Eckhart; Help from German-
    Russian Émigrés; Meeting with Gottfried Feder; The
    Jewish Communist Revolution in Munich; Meeting with
    Anton Drexler and the German Worker's Party; First
    Meeting with Adolf Hitler; An "Anonymous Scribbler"

Part Four: The Years of Struggle..33
    The 25 Points of the NSDAP; The Spirit behind National
    Socialism; The Elimination of Class War; The Story
    of Kurt Lüdecke; The Völkischer Beobachter; Storm
    Troopers Organized in Response to Communist Violence;
    Editor of the Völkischer Beobachter; Ludendorff Comes
    to Munich; The Kapp Putsch; The Battle of Coburg; First
    Major Speeches; Becoming a German Citizen; Death of
    My First Wife; First Major Writings for the NSDAP

Part Five: The 1923 Putsch and Acting Leader of the NSDAP...........47
    The November 1923 Putsch; NSDAP Outlawed, Hitler
    Appoints Rosenberg Leader; The Hitler Trial; Internal
    Party Schism; NSDAP Refounded

Part Six: The Myth of the Twentieth Century is Published.................57
    Christianity and National Socialism: The Myth of the
    Twentieth Century; Hitler's Concordat with the Vatican;
    Publication of Myth of the Twentieth Century the Reason
    for Rosenberg's Exclusion from Hitler's first Cabinet;
    Attacked by Christians; Interest in Cathars

Part Seven: Race and Racial Theory...69
1939: Ordered by Hitler to Secure Unification of
National Socialist Philosophy; Racial Respect Required
between Races; The Jewish Question; Jewish Terrorism
in Palestine; Prediction of the Racial Dissolution of
America; Study of Ancient India; Christianity Aids and
Abets Miscegenation; Race and Racial History; Racial
Theory and Science

Part Eight: Policy Considerations.......................................82
Euthanasia Program: Justified but Badly Implemented;
Democracy and Form of Government; Oswald Mosley's
Mistake in Choosing the Word "Fascist"; Foreign
Translations of Myth of the Twentieth Century; The
Nordic Society; Martin Mutschmann and Saxony;

Part Nine: Internal Party Conflicts.......................................90
Alfred Meyer and Westphalia-North; The Strasser
Brothers and Conflict within the Party; Clashes with
Doctor Robert Ley; The National Socialist "Training
Castles"— Ordensburgen; Strength through Joy Vacation
Ships; The Volkswagen; The Spa at Rügen; Cultural
Community Competition

Part Ten: Clash with Dr Joseph Goebbels..100
Troubled Relationship with Dr. Joseph Goebbels; Hitler's
Willingness to Forgive his Enemies   ; Complaints to
Hitler about Goebbels

Part Eleven: Himmler and Political Control over the Police............113
Dislike of and Clashes with Heinrich Himmler; Himmler
Founds Ahenerbe; Debate over Use of "Nordic"; Mistake
to Let Police Fall under Political Control; Over 300
NSDAP Members Murdered by Communists During
Kampfzeit; Unable to Foresee the Future; Time Needed
to Resurrect the Ideal from the Rubble of the Reich

Part Twelve: Bormann, Axmann, and the Alpine Redoubt..............123
Martin Bormann's Career; Alliance between Bormann
and Himmler; The Hitler Youth; Axmann and the Alpine
Redoubt; Bormann's Death in Berlin

Part Thirteen: Adolf Hitler, Man and Myth......................................130
Cannot Judge Adolf Hitler Yet; Hitler a Principled
Politician; Hitler Sought Alliance with England; Hitler
Should Have Taken Control of Weaker Party Leaders;
Hitler Supported the Wehrmacht When Others Did
Not; Ernst Röhm, Homosexuality, and the SA; Hitler
Tried to Get Party Factions to Compromise; Hitler
and the Wehrmacht; Hitler and Hindenburg; National
Socialism and the Military; Important to Keep Army out
of Politics; Artistic Side of Hitler Led to his Downfall in
Foreign Affairs; Hitler, Art, and Architecture; The Plans
for Berlin and other Cities; Hitler as a Disciplinarian and
Bohemian; Origin of the Swastika Flag; Mass Rallies as
a Cultural Phenomenon; Hitler as Chancellor; Hitler as
Military Strategist; Hitler Self-Educated; Hitler Rejected
Christianity

Part Fourteen: The Collapse of the Reich...161
Did Hitler Risk the Existence of the Reich by Going to
War?; The Cause of the Collapse of the Reich; Hitler
Overrated Italian Fascism and Mussolini; Germany
Needed Shrewd and Sober Leaders, Not Artistic
Personalities; Hitler Summarized

Part Fifteen: The Occupied Eastern Territories.............................166
Eastern Policies; Richard Walther Darré and Himmler;
Reich Commissioner for the Occupied Eastern Territories;
Attempts to Stem Anti-Slavic Attitude

Part Sixteen: The End of the Reich......................................178
    Hitler Made Same Mistake as Napoleon in Russia; End
    of the Third Reich—End of a Career; The Last Meeting
    with Hitler; Home is Bombed;
    Ministers Ordered to Leave Berlin; Arrival in Flensburg;
    Arrested by the British; British Sergeant Who Attended
    Nuremberg Rally

Part Seventeen: My Political Testament............................187
    Only Hitler Could be Supreme Leader: Next in Line
    Would Have to Have Been Elected; Hitler and Wotan's
    Tragedy

Introduction

Alfred Ernst Rosenberg (January 12, 1893–October 16, 1946) was born in Reval in the Russian Empire, a town today called Tallinn, the capital of present-day Estonia. He studied at the Petri-Realschule in Reval and went on to study architecture at the Riga Polytechnical Institute and engineering at Moscow's Highest Technical School, completing his PhD in 1917.

During the Russian Revolution of 1917 Rosenberg supported the counter-revolutionaries. Following the Bolshevik victory, he immigrated to Germany in 1918. Upon his arrival in Munich, he became friends with Dietrich Eckart, and started writing for the then small newspaper, the *Völkischer Beobachter*.

In 1919, he joined the German Workers' Party (*Deutsches Arbeiterpartei,* or DAP), which later was transformed into the National Socialist German Workers' Party (*Nationalsozialistische Deutsche Arbeiterpartei,* or NSDAP), becoming a member even before Adolf Hitler joined the party.

He was also an early member of the Thule Society (*Thule-Gesellschaft,* originally the *Studiengruppe für germanisches Altertum,* or "Study Group for Germanic Antiquity") along with Eckhart and other early leading DAP members. After the *Völkischer Beobachter* was purchased by the NSDAP and became their official party organ in December 1920, Rosenberg was eventually appointed editor in 1923.

In 1923, after the failed Beer Hall Putsch, Hitler, who had been imprisoned for treason, appointed Rosenberg as a leader of the National Socialist movement, a position he held until Hitler's release.

He continued to play a leading role in party affairs, founding in 1929 the Militant League for German Culture and several organizations devoted to the study and promotion of Nordic affairs. He also formed the "Institute for the Study of the Jewish Question," dedicated to identifying Jewish influence in German culture and to recording the history of Judaism.

He was elected to the Reichstag for the NSDAP in the 1930 elections, the same year he published the book for which he is best known, *Der Mythus des 20. Jahrhunderts* (*The Myth of the 20th Century*). While dealing with a large number of issues, it was the remarks on Christianity in that book which drew the greatest opprobrium. The

Sanctum Officium of the Catholic Church in Rome recommended that *The Myth of the 20th Century* be put on its *Index Librorum Prohibitorum* ("forbidden books list") for "scorning and rejecting all dogmas of the Catholic Church, indeed the very fundamentals of the Christian religion."

Once Hitler was appointed Chancellor, Rosenberg became leader of the NSDAP's foreign political office, and spent much of his time trying to promote an alliance between Germany and Britain. In January 1934, Rosenberg was responsible for the spiritual and philosophical education of the NSDAP and all related organizations. In 1940 Rosenberg was made head of the *Hohe Schule* ("high school")—the center of National Socialist ideological and educational research.

Following the invasion of the USSR in June 1941, Rosenberg was appointed *Reichsminister für die besetzten Ostgebiete* ("Reich Minister for the Occupied Eastern Territories"). Rosenberg followed a policy designed to encourage anti-Communist opinion among the population of the occupied territories, and was largely responsible for the very large flow of recruits to the German military effort against the Soviet Union, drawn directly from peoples formerly under the control of the Communist state.

Amongst many other measures, Rosenberg announced the end of the Soviet collective farms (kolkhoz) and issued an Agrarian Law in February 1942, annulling all Soviet legislation on farming, and restoring all family farms.

At the end of the war, he was arrested along with other major leaders of the Third Reich, and put on trial in Nuremberg. There he denied any knowledge of the alleged "holocaust," telling the court that he had only heard of the claims at Nuremberg but that he didn't believe them.

"I would assume that in such a gigantic struggle there would be many victims but I still don't believe this part where you allege to prove that deliberate mass extermination was practiced in this manner. I did, of course, know that in connection with our struggle there were many executions. I did not know anything about mass extermination to the extent and in the manner as you say."—Interrogation of Alfred Rosenberg, conducted by Major General Alexandrov, Nuremberg, Nov 5, 1945, International Military Tribunal records, pp. 16–18.

It was during this trial that he wrote his memoirs, the book the reader now holds. He was sentenced to death and executed with other condemned co-defendants at Nuremberg on the morning of October 16, 1946. Although no specific crimes could be attributed to him, he was generally held responsible for creating the National Socialist ideology, and it was clear that his execution was for this "crime" alone.

Rosenberg was married twice. He married his first wife, Hilda Leesmann, an ethnic Estonian, in 1915; after eight years of marriage, they divorced in 1923. He married his second wife, Hedwig Kramer, in 1925; the marriage lasted until his execution. He and Kramer had two children; a son, who died in infancy, and a daughter, Irene, who was born in 1930.

Writings:

Die Spur des Juden im Wandel der Zeiten, 1920. München: Deutscher Volksverlag (*The Track of the Jew through the Ages*).
Unmoral im Talmud, 1920, Ernst Boepple's Deutscher Volksverlag, Munich (*Immorality in the Talmud*).
Das Verbrechen der Freimaurerei: Judentum, Jesuitismus, Deutsches Christentum, 1921 (*The Crime of Freemasonry: Judaism, Jesuitism, German Christianity*).
Wesen, Grundsätze und Ziele der Nationalsozialistischen Deutschen Arbeiterpartei, 1922, Ernst Boepple's Deutscher Volksverlag, Munich (*Being, principles, and goals of the National Socialist German Worker's Party*).
Pest in Russland. Der Bolschewismus, seine Häupter, Handlanger und Opfer, 1922, Ernst Boepple's Deutscher Volksverlag, Munich (*The Plague in Russia. Bolshevism, its heads, henchmen, and victims*).
Bolschewismus, Hunger, Tod, 1922, Ernst Boepple's Deutscher Volksverlag, Munich (*Bolshevism, hunger, death*).
Die Protokolle der Weisen von Zion und die jüdische Weltpolitik, 1923 (*The Protocols of the Elders of Zion and the Jewish World Politics*).
Der Mythus des 20. Jahrhunderts, 1930 (*The Myth of the 20th Century*).
Dietrich Eckhart. Ein Vermächtnis, 1935 (*Dietrich Eckhart: A Legacy*).
An die Dunkelmänner unserer Zeit. Eine Antwort auf die Angriffe gegen den „Mythus des 20. Jahrhunderts", 1937 (*The Obscurantists of Our Time: A Response to the Attacks against 'The Myth of the 20th Century'*).
Protestantische Rompilger. Der Verrat an Luther und der „Mythus des 20. Jahrhunderts," 1937 (*Protestant Rome Pilgrims: The Betrayal of Luther and the 'Myth of the 20th Century'*).

Part One:
Youth

Youth in Baltic Russia

For 200 years after the beginning of the 18th century, the Balticum[1] had been under Russian control. Most solemnly Czar Peter[2] had guaranteed to the Germans their special privileges for all time, a fact which caused many of the later differences between the Balts and the Russian government.

The majority of the Czars were benevolent—and their realm certainly profited by that benevolence—until a growing Slavophilism began to oppose westernization, and proceeded with particular harshness against Balts as the protagonists of this leaning toward the west.

A wave of Russification ensued. Professors who had taught in German were forced to learn Russian during their summer vacations. The harbingers of the coming oppression rushed over the land. However, these early storms died down again. In spite of everything the Russian determination accomplished, a true foundation was still lacking, namely a really Russian population.

As a substitute large Russian garrisons and groups of government officials were brought in. But more often than not the offspring of these functionaries simply became Balts.

My earliest memory of my grandfather is a brown top hat with which I always wanted to play, something he laughingly permitted. He stands before my mind's eye as a tall old man in a brown dressing gown, sharp features and a small mouth, with narrow eyes that looked a little tired.

---

[1] A now archaic term referring to the Baltic countries, from the Latin name for the Baltic Sea, *Mare Balticum*. Here meant to specifically refer to Estonia, Latvia, Finland, and Lithuania.
[2] Peter the Great (1672–1725), Emperor of Russia from 1682 to his death. Due to his young age at his ascension, he initially co-ruled with his brother.

My grandfather no longer had sufficient money to permit my father to study. Thus he entered life as a merchant's apprentice and became, after a comparatively short period, the head of the Reval[3] branch of a rich German commercial house.

When, later on, I became active in Germany, I was amazed at the ever present opposition to the teachers. In many of my fellow students this broke through quite openly and crassly. In the youth movement, the Prof was referred to with great acerbity. Of our own teachers at the same type of school in Reval I can only speak with the greatest respect.

Petersen was a naturalist. He owned a large butterfly collection, wrote on the geological history of Estonia, and corresponded with many of the scientific institutes of the Reich. I believe it would have been easy for him to have obtained an appointment in Germany. But his love for the homeland, and probably the feeling that he was more independent there, held him back. His only son, however, was sent to Jena where Haeckel and Eucken were making this university world famous. This son died shortly after he had finished his studies.

A small thin mannequin with a tremendous mustache and a beard, the sense of duty personified, who presupposed in us boys practically Spartan virtues. From behind the pince-nez which he never took off, dark blue eyes looked sternly out at the class. His delivery was without warmth, but easily understood and to the point, so that we carried home, if not enthusiasm, at least knowledge.

However, Spreckelsen contained himself strictly within the framework of everyday discourses, and never went beyond an unquestioned rehashing of Russian concepts. Our official history textbook was his standard, too.

But after the bell tolled, he spoke German; and though he never paternally patted us on the shoulders, he conversed with us as if he were talking to understanding adults. We felt for him no particular reverence, but never denied him our complete respect. His free time was devoted to the care of the Reval Museum and other historic institutes.

Once he asked if anyone cared to accompany him on a prehistoric expedition. I volunteered with two of my fellow students. In a graveyard we discovered and excavated a stone urn. We also unearthed some pitchers, armlets, and rings. For the first time Spreckelsen told us

---

[3] Today known as Tallinn, the capital and largest city of Estonia. The city was known as Reval from the 13th century until 1917, and again during the German occupation of Estonia from 1941 to 1944.

about the great migrations of nations that had taken place long before those recorded in writing.

I was promoted every year and was *primus* (class president) up to my senior year. A *primus* in our school was not the student with the highest grades. Others were much better at that sort of thing than I. A boy was made *primus* because the authorities expected him to be a good influence on the rest of the class.

As *primus* I had the keys to the cabinet where examination papers, chalk and so on were kept. I used it also to hide my own textbooks in because I was too lazy to carry them home.

For any of the oral exams I simply studied during recess. Only the most important things were taken care of at home. As a net result I was not very good in mathematics. My fellow students often helped by explaining things to me, and I remember with particular gratitude the Pole, Tscheskesski, who helped me solve many an algebra problem.

During the regents exam I, in turn, dictated his German thesis to him. During all those years I always feared that someday a terrible exposure would certainly come. But in the end everything turned out all right.

In my class, consisting of about forty pupils, there were four Russians, three Poles, two genuine Estonians and two who later posed as such. All the rest were Balts. I do not remember that we ever had heated nationalistic discussions. With the Russians we talked German or Russian, as the case might be, and the same with the Poles. The two Estonians, for reasons of their own, kept to themselves.

But conflicts that might well have been possible never occurred. In spite of the nationalistic attitude of the country itself, our school remained an exemplary oasis of peace for the youths of such varied national origins. This still strikes me as being something pleasant and promising.

The battle these children and their horse Begard waged against Charlemagne impressed me greatly, but I was especially touched by the fate of the horse itself. The noble animal would not sink even under the heaviest load. As long as his master kept on looking at it, the beast could always hold itself above water.

But then Reinhold was forced to turn his tear-filled eyes away, and Begard sank. I cried when I thus first discovered how fidelity is rewarded in this world. And now when I remember that quiet, great experience of my youth, tears again rush to my eyes, and not merely because of Begard's fate.

Here, and later also in the suburb of Reval where she lived, Hilda[4] came into more immediate contact with Russian customs than I, and accepted them with appropriate sympathy. Besides, she had an adopted sister, Johanna, who, at the Petersburg Academy of Art, had met and married the son of the Rector. This association also helped her to become acquainted with the Russians.

To be sure, the opinions of this man were quite revolutionary, so that the differentiation between Russia and the hated Czarist regime became ever more pronounced. Provoked by these theories, I read Tolstoy's *War and Peace* and *Anna Karenina*. They impressed me greatly and remained for me the great novels of European literature.

In the course of time I had a chance to visit Hilda. She played for me—she played well even then—Russian compositions: Borodin and Rimsky-Korsakov. These, too, were beautiful and gratifying, so in a roundabout way I learned more about Russia than most other Balts did during these years.

One day Hilda brought a book to the train which I simply had to read. It was Nietzsche's *Zarathustra*. I immediately tried to absorb the entire work, but something about it struck me as alien.

That was, as I realized later, the overly pathetic, even theatrical element which, to me, appeared willful rather than perfect. I then read two books about the author. Even these did not enlighten me any further. So I returned *Zarathustra* somewhat shamefacedly.

An artistic success of my own came during my senior year. In Woesso I had practiced drawing, not only with pencil but with chalk on grey art paper; the highlights were touched up with white. In this way the stroke of the pencil did, indeed, lose some of its immediacy, but the finished product, in turn, gained plasticity.

Now I impudently sketched the cottage of Peter the Great. In the center, the sunlit house, the walls brought out in white, the roof tiles done in pale cinnabar. As a study it was not too bad. In the great hall of the so-called firehouse, all the students' drawings were exhibited and were viewed by Inspector Krutchenko among others. He liked my drawing so well that he declared it could not possibly have been done by a student without the aid of the teacher.

---

[4] Hilda Leesmann, an ethnic Estonian, who became Alfred Rosenberg's first wife.

In any case, he had it gorgeously framed and presented to the senior class. When, at the occasion of a visit to Reval as Reich Minister for the Occupied Eastern Territories, I inquired about the drawing. I learned that it was still there. That was thirty-two years later.

The social center of the Germans was the Riflemen's Park, a large, fenced-in garden at the center of the city, with restaurants, tennis courts, and so on, belonging to the three German corps. This was a rendezvous for all German youth, during the summer in the park, during the winter in the ballroom. Admission was only on a pass, since the Riflemen's Guild, as the owner, had a right to select its guests.

This fact, however, gave the whole thing both a nationalistic and a caste-like character which was undoubtedly noted by the others with slightly mixed feelings. Riga's society definitely felt more advanced than that of Reval.

Whereas the former was dominated largely by university professors, the latter was dominated by mere high school principals. Riga students were not at all liked in Reval.

The nobility in particular was considered especially overbearing. The tension between the barons and the bourgeois in Riga was for this reason quite apparent, except among those who had intermarried with the nobility, or who considered an intimate association with it a distinction.

However, it could not be denied: what was closest to my heart—art and philosophy—had the short end of this sort of student's life.

Look here, Fred, when we suddenly disappeared during the revolution, and when we returned afterwards, we were unable to work. We had to agree among ourselves to educate the younger people like yourself in order to raise another generation of Balts for our homeland. I can understand you, but you too must understand.

You have spent years in their company, and they have given you a great deal. You have been accepted into their comradeship, something that may be a help to you for the rest of your life. Do you really want to leave now? What would happen to our homeland if all of us thought as you do?

I faced the decision of my life. Study in Germany meant freedom and broadening of horizons, but also loss of my Russian citizenship. At home, camaraderie, yes; but narrowness, even though it was home. What to choose? Would I have chosen differently had I kept silent and had my elder brother not shown me my obligation toward my homeland? I shook his hand. You are right; I would be ungrateful; I'll stay. I returned to the university and asked the first secretary to return my resignation.

She had finally convinced her parents that her decision had been right. They realized it indicated a serious will to work; and so Hilda returned to Paris. She took dancing lessons from the well-known Professor Landosse, as well as rhythmic gymnastics. Jules d'Udine, a friend of Dalcroze, wanted to make her a professional dancer. She had looked into things of which I as yet had not even become aware. I was still a freshman, unfortunately forced to take part in a children's ballet, and, clad in a medieval uniform, to help represent the people in Wallenstein's camp.

In the meantime Hilda had become a favorite pupil of Jules d'Udine and was assisting him in his teaching. I watched him once in an amphitheater-shaped building. His rhythmic method seemed an excellent way to gain control over the body; toward other applications of it, however, I remained cold. Whether rightly so, I am unable to say. At the Café de la Rotonde, on the corner Raspail-Montparnasse, where I breakfasted daily and where the artists of the vicinity met, the atmosphere was always congenial. At that time it was still a comfortable old French place, not the monster it turned into later.

Hilda's name was already fairly well known; the Russian Ballet had approached her regarding a possible tour. Thus I gained an insight into Hilda's work and world. As for the future, I was sure we would find a way together.

That the promise of Peter the Great, guaranteeing the Balts their privileges for all time, could not be taken any too literally in the face of developments, must have been obvious even to the most stubborn land-holder. Nevertheless the Balts were perfectly justified in their claim that they had a right to be heard in connection with certain changes, and in their refusal to be the objects of frequent, purely inner, political attacks.

Part Two:
Russia and the Bolshevik Revolution

Move to Moscow

The retreat of the Russian armies from Germany forced the government to transplant important industries on a large scale. My father-in-law's canning factory had to move to St. Petersburg. The technical university also had to go.

For its new location Moscow had been selected. It was supposed to move with all its material possessions, all its books, and the entire student body, to the center of primordial Russia. While these transhipments went on we retired to the country for the summer. We found shelter and board with the lessee of an estate. Once again I was able to read and paint in peace. In 1912, I had received as a gift Chamberlain's *Goethe*. To me it seemed the best thing Chamberlain had ever written. I read the entire book to Hilda, who listened patiently to much that cannot be grasped immediately.

That fall she joined her parents in St. Petersburg, and I went to Moscow. Thus my home vanished behind me. War and revolution tossed people and fates about. In my heart remained the love for the homeland which lived on, unconcerned with human destiny.

In all honesty I must confess that the social question in Russia did not begin to interest me until much later. In the beginning I simply saw the big city quite innocently through the eyes of a young man—noted its palaces and galleries, and was hardly aware, in spite of 1905,[5] of how far advanced the internal crisis already was.

---

[5] In 1905, mass unrest erupted throughout the Russian Empire which led to the establishment of limited constitutional monarchy, the State Duma of the Russian Empire, the multi-party system, and the Russian Constitution of 1906.

Only the outbreak of the war brought the real situation to my attention. There were tumults shortly before the war, overturned trolley cars and street brawls. Whether these were isolated incidents or part of a planned conspiracy, I cannot say. They stopped when the Czar made an appeal for general unity before an immense crowd that sank on its knees in front of his palace and prayed for Russia.

From a childless couple I had rented a room close to the suburbs where some of my fellow students lived. It was a rather simple abode facing a court, but quite comfortably furnished.

The man worked somewhere in a store. The woman, as is the custom in Russia, served me tea every morning and evening. Since I had to husband my means—Riga had cost more than anticipated—we ate dinner with a Russian family. At a table covered with oilcloth in a room that also served as a bedroom, we had soup and whatever else happened to be available.

Once every week, however, we went to the center of the city and had a real dinner with pastries such as only the Russians can make. Sometimes we were able to buy beer—two percent beer. At ten o'clock everybody was ready for bed. Occasionally we listened to music at the Savoy, a hotel of old-fashioned magnificence; otherwise we sat around in cheap restaurants along the Tverskaya.

Real comradeship was, of course, out of the question. Only small groups living close to each other, or meeting at school, got together regularly. The Riga Technical College was housed in several different buildings, so that it was often necessary to make long trips to get from one lecture to the other. Some of the classes for draftsmen were temporarily held in hallways, and the streetcars were always crowded. I particularly like to remember one large drawing of the Freiburg Cathedral which I copied from a small original.

All the wealth of this edifice I traced lovingly with a hard pencil. We did a great deal of drawing and painting from models. This was not enough for me, so I took additional private lessons in portraiture. I found that I was unable to do a portrait quickly, but that the results were passable only if I had time enough to concentrate. Which soon satisfied me.

The merchant Shtchukin was a Maecenas[6] for modern painting.

[6] Gaius Cilnius Maecenas (68BC–8BC) was a political advisor to Octavian Augustus and the most important patron for the Augustan poets, including both Horace and Virgil. His name has become a byword for a wealthy, generous and enlightened patron of the arts.

He must have gone to Paris regularly, for his villa, which could be freely visited, was filled with every conceivable product of French art: Picasso, Guérin, and especially Henri Matisse. The latter had an entire room to himself. Chiefly still-lifes. Quite light: which, blue, pink, with occasionally interesting coloration, smoothly and ably painted; but altogether, mere surface and a straining for effect. Great art could not possibly be achieved in this way.

Most characteristic, to my mind, was the obviously revolutionary mood. Though they all sewed shirts for soldiers, they were sure that most of these gifts never reached the right address, but were diverted and sold instead. They swore, for example, that markers they themselves had sewed in were often found on things they later bought in the open market. The adolescent brother claimed to be a member of the Cadets.

In fact, large parts of the municipal intelligentsia did belong to that organization which was well supported by the press. Unsatisfactory though Gorki's Night-lodging had once seemed to me, when it was performed here it showed up human misery and suffering, in the very midst of which there was again and again a ray of renewed hope, of belief.

That, too, is part of life, more than most of us think. My landlord occasionally invited me to tea. With the great liberal Moscow paper, *Ruskoye Slovo,* always before him, he invariably referred to the government as those ruling scoundrels. In other words, among the lower middle classes, too, one heard very outspoken references to an institution which, while resting on a great tradition, had turned into something that everybody had begun to find repulsive.

Outside of my work, the suburb of Shednya offered me yet another solace: Goethe. B. had a beautiful edition of his collected works. Now I picked up volume after volume. Once again, *Poem and Truth* and *Wilhelm Meister;* then the scientific essays, and especially the *Farbenlehre.* From many of his works I copied excerpts in an oilcloth-covered memo-book which I later reread frequently with great enjoyment. Then came a long list of Balzac's novels, since I had discovered that, in order properly to appreciate this man, one cannot rely on single works, but simply must read the entire *Comédie Humaine* to feel the whole impact of his accomplishment.

Balzac wrote much claptrap; he frequently had to work for bread, and so often concocted much which his own better judgment would hardly have passed. But Balzac was a demoniacal artist equaled by few

9

other novelists. Then came Tolstoy and Dostoyevski. The letters by the author of *War and Peace* greatly disappointed me. Was this the same man? Had not an entirely different one risen from his innermost core to damn Europe's art and culture, yes, even its work?

And, withal, were not his theses always confined to the same narrow circle of constantly repeated arguments? Soul-shaking, on the other hand, was the Brothers Karamazov, that powerful description of the Russian provinces, yes, and in many instances of the Russian soul itself.

Where should one secure an insight into the soul of another people if not from a great analyzer of souls? Thus I read with particular interest the Diary of a writer, which gives a precise analysis of Dostoyevski's own political and social opinions. St. Petersburg and its Balkan policy of the day, Russia's mission in Europe, Bismarck's policies, the life of the Russian intelligentsia and the Russian peasants.

All this gave a good picture of the attitude of Dostoyevski who, despite his one-sidedness, was one of the giants of his people. Side by side with all this went much else, some of it accidental, some of it searched out, so that I might be permitted to say that never before had I been as immersed in work and reading as in Shednya near Moscow in 1916–17.

The Bolshevik Revolution

At this time the Russian Revolution occurred.[7] If I attempted to give here a description of its causes and the forces involved, I'd run the risk of including knowledge which I acquired only much later through the memoirs of Russians and Englishmen (Buchanan, his daughter, and Sir Samuel Hoare).

What I knew at the time was primarily that the Czarist regime, due to the many failures of the Russian troops, became ever more isolated. There were rumors that Russian soldiers were forced to attack with sticks instead of guns in their hands, that in the Carpathian Mountains they had been sent boots with paper soles, and similar things.

Russian industry was unable to meet the requirements of the Great War; traffic became snarled; genuine support on the part of the people was lacking, in spite of the protestations of even the liberal-

---

[7] The Russian Revolution was actually a series of uprisings in 1917, which culminated in the overthrow of the Tsar and the establishment of the Soviet Union.

revolutionary party that they were ready to fight the war to a victorious end.

Among those fighting against Czarism the Cadets were the ones who wanted to stay in the war alongside their Entente allies because they feared that, in the face of the general situation, a separate peace for Russia would deprive the Revolution of most of its impetus. In his great winter speech of 1916 their leader, Milyukov, openly attacked the sinister forces at court, meaning Rasputin and the advocates of a separate peace with Germany.

He was answered stiffly but shrewdly by the Conservative, Markov, who predicted the most terrible consequences for Russia if a change in the traditional regime occurred. Milyukov's banned speech was secretly printed and distributed throughout Russia, though it must be admitted that Markov's speech accompanied it. I was able to look over both of them in E.'s house.

The organization for their distribution was based on the existing local relief organizations. Government officials were unable to master unaided the problems posed by the war, so the Czarist regime, willy-nilly, had to depend upon help from the country at large and from local administrations. Now this great charitable organization, through its leaders, became the spearhead of the democratic-revolutionary movement.

Their president, Prince Lvov, in due course became the head of the first revolutionary government. Moscow itself underscored its belligerent attitude by ostentatiously honoring the British Ambassador who, if memory serves me correctly, at this occasion received the freedom of the city.

In contrast to the apparent vacillation in St. Petersburg, Moscow thus tried to prove itself the real capital, the true heart of Russia. I did not witness the first days of the successful March uprising. No doubt, long-suppressed public opinion boiled over. Strangers embraced and congratulated each other. The new government issued an appeal for nation-wide unity.

But it soon became apparent that, though they all were opponents of the overturned regime, they were far apart in their political and social demands. The provisional government declared that a National Assembly would make the decision regarding the future fate of the country. The various parties were given a free hand with their propaganda. And even now the first newspapers of the opposition began to put in an appearance. With some dismay I read the *Vörwarts* newspaper.[8] The vituperations they indulged in made almost anything likely to happen, since no consideration whatever was given to Russia's actual position.

Withal, this paper was merely the voice of the Social Democrats, in other words, not yet that of Communism which, in due time, in its organ *Pravda*,[9] demanded all power for the gradually developing Workers' and Soldiers' Councils. But above everything—peace! This became the slogan for millions, much stronger in its appeal than all the speeches about treaty obligations, war until victory, and so on.

Later on I accidentally overheard a conversation between two Russian officers in a railway car on this topic. The one said resignedly: What do you want? A soldier thinks primitively: what good does my newly won freedom do me if I can't enjoy it? So—home as quickly as possible and make sure that my freedom isn't taken away again. . .

At this time I began to work for my diploma in earnest. In Riga a hilly plot of land had been set aside for a crematory. This I was to take as the proposed terrain upon which to base my design. The technical prerequisites were quickly enough established, and I went to work. It turned into a central hall, with Romanesque vaults and a large colonnade, as well as an adjoining graveyard.

So far as the actual construction and work were concerned, this problem was not a particularly difficult one. But who, in these days, was able to think of a really great task! Thus my work proceeded until I heard that Hilda was ill. She went to the Crimea to recuperate, and wrote me from there.

The air of St. Petersburg had begun to have its effect, and the growing scarcity of food had done the rest. I decided to interrupt my studies and resume them again in the fall. At the end of the semester I went to the Crimea myself. The way led through the Ukraine. Endless fields, tremendous plains. You felt the whole immensity of the Eastern land in your own body, so to speak, as you traveled into this infinity.

[8] *Vorwärts* ("Forward") was the central organ of the Social Democratic Party of Germany, founded in 1876. It ceased publication in Germany in 1933, but was refounded in 1948 as the *Neuer Vorwärts* ("New Forward") and in 1955 renamed *Vorwärts* again.

[9] *Pravda* was the official newspaper of the Soviet Union's Communist Party which originally began publication in 1912. After the collapse of the Soviet Union in 1991, it was sold off to a private company, but was purchased by the Communist Party of Russian Federation in 1997 and still serves as that party's official mouthpiece.

From Simeis I watched the whole political and military turmoil with great interest. It became ever clearer that Kerenski[10] would be unable to keep the aroused spirits in check much longer. The desire to return home had taken hold of the Russian soldier; entire divisions fell apart and disappeared. There were reports of desperate attempts to form a center of resistance made up entirely of officers.

Certainly, desperate sacrifices were being made. But in vain. In vain, too, were Kerenski's speeches; even his charge that these soldiers were, after all, not the banner carriers of freedom but merely mutinous slaves, failed to make an impression. Came a report that German troops had landed on Ösel. Then even I began to doubt that I could stay in the Crimea any longer. I went to the commandant to get a *laissez-passer* for Reval. To join my family, I told the officer. He replied: *I'd like to go myself!*

In St. Petersburg, political tension, frequent difficulty in securing food. The bread contained a great deal of straw. In Reval we lived at first with our Aunt Lydia (we had been long since forced to sell our old house), later in the evacuated furnished apartment of a departed Russian engineer.

Hilda's health grew worse, the doctor diagnosed tuberculosis. To bed immediately, or else you can order a coffin! This was terrible; a new worry that was never to end. Hilda lay in bed and was spoiled. I read to her, kept on working for my diploma, painted pictures after studies I had made in Shednya, or else I went back to the old courtyards and attics of Reval and drew subjects well known to me of old.

In Russia, communism was victorious over the attempt to create a democratic republic. I would be lying if I were to say that I understood the immense consequences of this occurrence.

On the contrary, I was of the opinion that in the long run the combined troops of the Russian generals would eventually be victorious over the unorganized Bolshevik regiments. But what was lacking was a leader, a slogan for the future; for the return of those who had been overthrown, nobody wanted to fight. And Holy Russia, for whom so many in the south still did fight, was a symbol, to be sure, but one that in these days of revolutionary upheaval no longer carried enough weight.

---

[10] Alexander Fyodorovich Kerensky (1881–1970), who served as Minister of Justice in the democratic Russian Provisional Government after the February 1917 revolution. In July he became the second Prime Minister until it was overthrown by the Bolsheviks in the October Revolution.

In Reval there was still comparative quiet, but everywhere soldiers' councils under the domination of sailors. All exits from the city barred; in other cities the same. I learned that a friend had managed to get to Ösel by boat from Hapsal. I went to the sailors' headquarters and asked for a laissez-passer to Hapsal. I was refused; even the rouble failed.

Let me add here that I did not put too much energy into this attempt, for what was I to do with my wife? There was still hope, after all, that the Germans would march into Estonia. But the year passed and nothing happened.

But I faced what was for me a decisive change. The work for my diploma was finished. Was I to break off almost seven years of study without a final examination, or was I to undertake a trip to Bolshevik Moscow in the bare hope that I might be granted, in the middle of a semester, the privilege of passing my state exam? I decided in favor of the latter.

Trains were still more or less running on schedule, and I arrived safely in Moscow. Many professors and fellow students from Riga were missing; they had been at home when the Germans marched in.

Nevertheless classes still met, professors from Moscow having replaced those from Riga. They were benevolent: the exam was passed. Directly afterwards I had a very cordial conversation with Professor Klein. He asked me quite suddenly: Wouldn't you like to stay on in Moscow as my assistant?

Under different circumstances such an offer would have enraptured any young architect. To be called, fresh from the exam and on the same day, by the examiner himself and offered a position as architect for central Russia—nothing could have been more auspicious for a career. But I didn't hesitate for a moment. I thanked him very much, but I simply had to return to Reval. I left the same evening.

About a fortnight later German troops marched in. Before then Reval had seen dangerous days. The Reval Soviet proposed to fight the Germans. Fear that armed bands might rob their houses prompted the Balts and Estonians to organize a secret home guard. Every house from then on was guarded by its male inhabitants, each carrying a gun. Thus I met again my old teacher Laipmann who lived in the same house with us. Grown old, but still the fiery Estonian national revolutionary.

On the eve of the occupation there was a rumor that the sailors were coming up from the harbor. We stood around on the street in groups.

But the threat passed. On a clear, cold winter morning German soldiers marched through the suburb past Czar Peter's monument. They were Hannoverian chasseurs with the Gibraltar stripe on their sleeves. On bicycles.

Where the roses suddenly came from was a riddle; in any case, the German chasseurs were showered with them and welcomed with tear-filled eyes as saviors of a city in dire distress. I shook hands with many of them and asked questions. The commanding general, von Seckendorff, reviewed the parade. A new regime began in old Reval.

But I had only one thought: if I had made the resolution to go to Moscow only twenty days later than I did, I would have been stuck in Soviet Russia, would have been sunk forever. . .

After a while I went to the commandant to ask whether they would accept me as a volunteer. I was turned down—after all, this was occupied territory. Could I give any references in Germany? No? In that case it couldn't be done.

Thus my home life went on at its old pace. I was restless. To be sure, I did meet some officers at the home of a lady who lived in the same house, and with them I was able to discuss many problems, but all this could not satisfy me. When the German schools were opened I applied at three of them for a position as art teacher.

As an architect I entered only one competition. A furniture company, well known for its specialities, had started a prize contest for a set of living room furniture. Since I had nothing to do anyway I made two sketches and submitted them, with the result that no first prize but two second prizes were given, both of them to me.

There was also an art exhibition to which I contributed drawings from old Reval, almost all of which were sold. Thus I earned a little money, the one and only time that my artistic activities brought in some cash. In the meantime my sick wife had secured permission to go to Badenweiler for treatments. I taught rather unwilling youngsters the art of drawing and went to teachers' conferences, while in the outside world the German fate took its course without our even being aware of the most decisive changes.

When I mentioned some time ago that for one of my teachers, as for so many Balts, Weimar was what Athens had once been for Weimar, I merely paraphrased the primarily cultural feeling with which all of us were imbued.

We honored old Prussia and Bismarck's edifice, and watched the rise of the Reich; but since the Balts could not actively participate in it, we concentrated largely on the psychological values of the arts and sciences. After all, the Reich was the birthplace of German culture in its entirety, and looked, as everything great does from a distance, still greater in its personalities and effects. Now the Reich was embroiled in the most desperate battles and crises. I wanted to go there, just then, after my rejection by the army, in order at least to share Germany's fate; I did not want to stand any longer between the fronts.

When the conditions for a truce came, I was thrown into despair. When the revolution came,[11] it destroyed the old order and allowed the rise of the most sinister figures. In the army of occupation little of all these changes was outwardly noticeable. Rumors made the rounds. It became ever clearer to us that, all protestations to the contrary, the German army was getting ready to return home.

I was still undecided as to what I should do. An emptied space indicated the possible foundation of an independent state of Estonia of unpredictable shape, possible with the Soviets, or else an immediate attack by the Bolsheviks on Estonia. I did not intend to carry on my future life between the fronts, probably alternately Estonian and Russian. I wanted to go to the Reich. Now no homeland was holding me any longer, since it would soon be in alien hands anyway.

I drove to the commandant and begged the officer of the day for a travel permit to Germany. He asked me whether I had ever worked for the Germans and might therefore expect trouble after the German troops left. I mentioned my profession. It looks sad in Germany, too, he remarked, but he did issue the permit.

Then he sent for the representative of the Soldiers' Council. The man came, stood at attention, agreed with the officer, and I was told that if I wanted to get away I'd have to leave that same evening with the military transport from this or that station at eleven o'clock sharp.

This was on November 30, 1918. Once I had pictured a trip into Germany somewhat differently—as a journey into a great country full of energy, full of ambitious, striving men; a country of art and science and the will to live. Now I journeyed into a broken life, into the most terrible conflict between parties in the face of a cruel political fate dictated from abroad.

[11] The German Revolution started in November 1918 and only ended in August 1919 with the overthrow of Germany's imperial government and its replacement with the Weimar Republic.

And yet, exactly at this hour there was something I wanted to find. From a practical standpoint I had put my stake on zero; but at least I had made a decision in a time that was growing ever more chaotic. Once again that mysterious something called free will had entered the picture. What if I hadn't casually overheard the remark of a colleague about these travel permits? If I had sat at another table? Would I still have gone to the German commandant?

That, of course, is difficult to say, even though I had considered going to Germany for a long time. And, after all, others had heard these identical words, too, without being affected by them in the same way. Thus the real decision in the midst of all kinds of causative mechanics had to be mine alone.

The train left Reval. Behind me Russia fell away with all her memories, with all her unpredictable future; behind me my student days in Riga fell away, and the camaraderie of the *Pulverturm*;[12] behind me fell away the city of my youth with her towers and old streets and all the men with whom I had once lived there. I left my homeland behind me in order to gain a fatherland for myself.

---

[12] Literally, the "Powder Tower"—a reference to a specially constructed tower used in Europe until the late 20th century for the storage of gunpowder. The *Pulverturm* in Riga still stands, and today houses the Latvian War Museum. During Rosenberg's time, it was regarded as a symbolic center for German nationalism.

Part Three:
Germany and the Early Party Days

The Move to Germany

It took us several days to reach Berlin. Strange how empty memory can be sometimes, in spite of all attempts to remember certain details. I can recall no specific episode of the trip, no conversation. The landscape passed by slowly, the days were grey and cold, the thoughts clung to the past and were busy with the future. We merely saw to it that our stove was provided with coal; even the old pastor didn't consider it theft when we replenished our supplies occasionally from the piles along the railroad station.

How we ate I don't quite remember either. Only this much I remember: that our entrance into Berlin was sad, that the houses looked twice as grey, and that at the entrance to our hotel revolutionary pamphlets were immediately pressed into our hands.

And then I still had time to experience the most moving interlude of these days: the return of the German troops along Unter den Linden. I had little difficulty finding room to stand at the crossing of Friedrichstraße and Unter den Linden.

They came, slow and serious. With frozen features the soldiers sat on their gun carriages. From almost all the balconies and windows women and children were waving white handkerchiefs. A few almost inaudible shouts of welcome—all of them knew what an entrance like this meant. At that moment the great sorrow of the German people came upon me. This is a picture I have never forgotten. Later I heard that a while before Ebert[13] and Scheidemann[14] had talked to the soldiers on Pariser Platz. We back there couldn't hear anything since loudspeakers were not yet in use at that time. Years afterward we heard that the corps of General Lequis[15] had been standing ready near Berlin waiting for an order to overthrow the new government. But the order never came. Nor was that an accident—there simply wasn't anybody left who could have given orders.

Thus I came to the Reich. Originally a man completely devoted to art, philosophy and history, who never dreamed of getting mixed up with politics. But I had observed the present, and that too would be history some time. I had seen many forces pushing to the fore, and in Russia had watched the course of a revolution which, in my opinion, represented a terrible danger to Germany if, on top of all this tremendous sorrow, it ever hit the delicate structure of her industry, commerce, and population. So life pulled me, and I followed. I saw myself amidst the interplay of forces with all their confusing aspects. This was my journey to Germany in the darkling November of 1918.

First Days in Munich

I had brought along my good paint box from Reval. In my boarding house I now painted from memory the enlarged sketches I had made at Shednya. Not without some naïveté I thought that they might find favor in spite of the worries of the day. I took them to a book-shop on Odeonsplatz, but they were rejected after a mere cursory examination: they had all they wanted of that sort of stuff.

With my article on *Form and Forming* in my pocket, I frequently loitered around the entrance to the publishing house Callwey, even

[13] Friedrich Ebert (1871–1925), first Social Democratic Party of Germany (SPD) President of Germany from 1919 until his death in office in 1925.

[14] Philipp Scheidemann (1865–1939), a Social Democratic Party of Germany (SPD) politician who proclaimed Germany a republic on 9 November 1918 and subsequently became the second head of government of the Weimar Republic.

[15] General Arnold Lequis (1861–1949), a military leader of German forces during World War I. During the "November Revolution" of 1918, Lequis was ordered to carry out a coup against the republican revolutionaries, but failed to carry out this order, mainly because of large scale desertions by his troops. Lequis was then sworn in by the Ebert government as temporary military governor of Berlin, and played a leading role in suppressing Communist riots in the capital city in December 1918. He was then appointed to head of infantry for the much diminished *Reichswehr,* or army of the Weimar Republic, a post he held until his retirement.

though I really wanted to think it all out for myself before putting it up for discussion and permitting it to be talked about to shreds. In order to familiarize myself with the general trend of those days, I attended a meeting of revolutionary artists held at the German Theatre. On the stage, a table for the committee. The main speech was made by someone called Stückgold, I think. He praised the times which, he said, were even then liberating the arts, and giving the creative artist his chance.

But, then, hadn't Munich always been the spot where, artistically speaking, almost anything was permitted anyway? Here the *Art Nouveau* had been born, as well as the literary cabaret, the *Simplizissimus*, and *Wedekind's*. The eleven executioners' literary cabaret.[16] Those who were meeting here were obviously the artistically short-changed who hoped to secure fame and fortune by riding a new wave.

During the speech Kurt Eisner[17] appeared on the stage, was greeted as *Herr Ministerpräsident,* and took his seat at the table. That's the only time I saw him, with shaggy grey hair and beard, his pince-nez askew. What his real name was has never been established. He had been a contributor to the *Vörwarts* magazine. As members of the opposition later told the story, the entire editorial staff had gone into convulsions when they heard that this man, of all people, had become Prime Minister of Bavaria. Now he praised international Marxism and the great patriot Clemenceau.

Of the other speeches I remember nothing; they were on the same spiritual level as the above. During the afternoons, I usually took a walk through the streets. On such occasions I studied the advertising pillars to see what was playing at the various theaters and to keep posted on other events. Then one day I unexpectedly read: Dances.

---

[16] *Die Elf Scharfrichter,* or the "Eleven Executioners," was Munich's first cabaret, founded in 1901. The Executioners rented the back room of an inn and decorated it with paintings and etchings by their contemporaries from *Jugend* and *Simplicissmus,* as well as an impressive collection of torture instruments. The cabaret's most striking and influential figure was writer, performer and enfant terrible of Munich's *avant garde,* Frank Wedekind (1864–1918), whose sexually-explicit works scandalized contemporary society.

[17] Kurt Eisner (1867–1919), a Jewish Communist who organized the Socialist Revolution that overthrew the Wittelsbach monarchy in Bavaria in November 1918. He declared Bavaria to be a "free state" and became its first premier, but was defeated in the first elections held in 1919. While on his way to hand in his resignation, he was assassinated in the streets of Munich, an act which resulted in a Communist uprising and the establishment of the short-lived "Bavarian Soviet Republic" until its suppression by the army and private *Freikorps* militia a short while later.

Edith von Schrenck. Miss von Schrenck had worked with my wife in St. Petersburg.

True, I had never met her personally, but I wanted to speak to her, anyway, if for no other reason than to be able to write about it to my wife, who happened to be in Arosa at the time. In the course of our conversation, I told Miss von Schrenck about my trip and about my intention to write something on Bolshevism and the Jewish question. She told me she knew an author who shared my beliefs and who published a magazine devoted to the discussion of such problems: Dietrich Eckart.[18]

First Meeting with Dietrich Eckhart

The following day I called on him. This was the first fateful contact I made in Munich, From behind a desk covered with papers rose a tall figure. A shaved head, a high, lined forehead, dark-rimmed glasses shielding blue eyes. The nose slightly curved, somewhat too short and fleshy. A full mouth, a broad, rather brutal chin.

After a brief sarcastic remark about Miss von Schrenck, whom Eckart had met at the sanatorium of his brother-in-law in Thuringia, he listened to me attentively. Yes, he could use contributors like me. Here was the first number of his magazine, *Auf Gut Deutsch*. I gave him a few articles on my observations in Russia.

Next day Eckart called me. He liked my stuff and wanted me to come over immediately. He received me very cordially, and together we walked to the restaurant Alt Wien on Bayrerstraße.

On the way we talked of many things. I told him about my artistic interests, and suddenly veered off into a discussion of the Gothic period. He stopped, listened carefully, and then began to speak about his own philosophical opinions. Thus the first contact was established. Merely because of the personal impression I had made, Eckart accepted me wholeheartedly, introduced me to his friends, and offered me, a stranger in dire need, an opportunity to work and, yes, even to live.

Eckart had a checkered past. Studying medicine, reporting for the

---

[18] Dietrich Eckart (1868–1923), a German journalist and politician and, with Adolf Hitler, was one of the early key members of the NSDAP. Hitler officially dedicated his book, *Mein Kampf,* to Eckart.

Festspiele at Bayreuth,[19] going hungry in Berlin, writing comedies and dramas which were actually performed. His love of *Peer Gynt*,[20] and the inadequacies of existing interpretations and translations, encouraged him to do an excellent poetic translation of his own which had begun to appear on many stages, bringing in royalties that helped allay some of his early financial worries.

Eckart saw in *Peer Gynt* not a Norwegian adventurer, but rather a symbol of earth-bound man attempting to shed his fetters. Educated on Goethe and Schopenhauer, Eckart had entered public life as a poet. He did not see the entire circumference of the great problems, but he did grasp certain details with amazing perspicacity.

During the First World War he had observed developments, particularly the profiteering that ate into the very substance of life, with no power strong enough to conquer it or even to dam it up. And on top of this, a world of different parties which, in the face of an ever harsher fate, talked themselves ever farther apart instead of uniting in a closed front. Thus he decided to speak up for everything he recognized as true regardless of public opinion and party platforms.

One night he woke his wife to tell her that he would found a magazine: I'll call it *Auf Gut Deutsch,* he declared, and it will speak openly and frankly. His first article was entitled Men, and was addressed to all whose honest convictions were similar to his. At his own expense he mailed out 25,000 copies, and waited for an echo. That was all he wanted. There weren't many responses, as he admitted in the second issue, but some sympathetic persons, touched by his frankness, did write. Even a little money to help cover printing costs came in.

Help from German-Russian Émigrés

From home I received rather disquieting news. In the beginning the Bolshevists had declared that every one of the peoples of Russia would have the right to complete self-determination, including the right of

---

[19] The Bayreuth Festival (*Bayreuther Festspiele*) is a music festival held annually in Bayreuth, Germany, at which performances of operas by the 19th-century German composer Richard Wagner are presented. Wagner himself conceived and promoted the idea of a special festival to showcase his own works, in particular his monumental cycle *Der Ring des Nibelungen* and *Parsifal.*

[20] *Peer Gynt* is a five-act play in verse by the Norwegian dramatist Henrik Ibsen. Written in the Bokmål form of Norwegian, it is one of the most widely performed Norwegian plays.

separation.

The Baltic states had been formed. Though still insecure itself, the Soviet Union now attempted to absorb them. The people fought against that; the Finns had sent some troops to help Estonia, and Germany, too, had organized a Baltic regiment.

Now the question arose as to whether I should return. I wrote the Baltic Committee in Berlin describing my situation and mentioning the fact that I had to take care of a sick wife. I received a reply that I would not be needed.

In Munich a committee had been founded to help German émigrés. Thus I got a free room with a retired army doctor. He and his wife harbored me most amiably for some time, and I have always remembered them gratefully.

Taking along my own spoon, I now went daily to the soup kitchen. On the corner of Theresienstraße and a cross street to Kauffingerstraße many stepchildren of fate sat quietly, shoulder to shoulder, eating cabbage soup with dumplings. This helped stretch my means. Occasionally Dietrich Eckart paid for my articles, but not enough to safeguard me for any length of time.

Meeting with Gottfried Feder

That was the situation shortly after I met Eckart. At about the same time a man appeared on our horizon who later acquired some influence, the engineer, Gottfried Feder.[21]

He maintained that the great economic crises were entirely due to what he termed interest slavery into which every nation in the world had gradually fallen because of mobile loan and finance capital. He made a clear distinction between that and the earth-bound industrial capital whose protection, he said, was definitely one of the tasks of the state. How could money multiply itself? How could capital increase without working, merely through the endless accruing of interests? To

---

[21] Gottfried Feder (1883–1941), an economist and one of the early key members of the NSDAP, serving as the party's economic theoretician. It was a lecture of his in 1919 that initially drew Adolf Hitler into the party. In February 1920, together with Hitler and Anton Drexler, Feder drafted the famous "25 points" which summed up the party's views. In 1936, he was appointed a professor at the Technische Hochschule in Berlin, a position he held until his death.

save, yes, that was the result of work. But coupon-clipping, no! Hence, gradual reorganization, and the eventual end of interest slavery and the entire system of interest economy.

In these unsettled times such an idea intrigued a great many people. Some of his theories were indubitably correct, and in fighting usury we had, after all, no intention of doing away with a national industry.

Eckart took them up with enthusiasm and proclaimed the idea of government control of the entire credit system, saying if anybody protested that this would cause the collapse of the entire world, well, then let this world collapse. Feder himself spoke at many meetings of an organization, founded by him to abolish interest slavery, and later made contact with the growing National Socialist German Workers' Party.

Like many others who concentrate on a mere symptom of the totality of events, Feder's development was rather like that of a sectarian who considers himself the very hub of things. In later years his unfortunate conceit got quite out of hand, inasmuch as he came to believe his program was the very core of National Socialism.

This conviction went hand in hand with an unpleasant tendency to make a good thing out of it by not only asking large fees for his speeches, but by insisting upon payment in advance, something which the embattled and frequently broke National Socialist German Workers' Party considered, to say the least, somewhat strange, and which gradually lost him all sympathy.

But Feder's ideas turned out to be not entirely original when someone produced a copy of Theodor Fritsch's *Hammer,* a magazine containing verbatim, and as early as 1917, much of what Feder later promulgated, without bothering to mention his source. In any case, these thoughts were stimulating enough to cause the examination of quite a few other theories, even though, in practice, no clear differentiation could be made between the various capitalistic systems.

Still, there were tangible values inseparably bound up with the people and the soil, and others that were much more mobile. That government supervision of the latter was necessary seemed obvious to many of us. These talks spurred Eckart on to public action of his own. He published a leaflet, *To all workers,* in which he called them to arms against usury, and which he signed with his full name and address. He printed quite a large edition, and hired two taxicabs from which we scattered them on the streets of Munich. Since many such pamphlets were printed and distributed in these days of revolutionary fermentation, Eckart at first had no difficulties. In fact, when he was about to be arrested during the *Räterepublik*,[22] and placed among the hostages, this pamphlet may very well have saved his life, for his own janitor and the men who came to arrest him declared with one accord that the author of such a leaflet could not possibly by a reactionary. He went free.

One day I was coming down the stairs in Kühn's boarding-house, carrying Schlaginweit's huge tome on India under my arm. Several people suddenly came rushing in, shrieking that Eisner had been murdered. They saw me on the stairs, obviously took me for a reactionary student, and forced me to follow them back to my lodgings. There my neighbor, whom one of them knew, opened the door. Who was I? Why, someone who quietly worked for himself all day. Well, in that case everything was all right. The men left without searching my room.

If they had found my temporary identification papers—the German translation of a Russian passport—they would probably have considered me a White-Russian immigrant, and what might have happened to me in this hour of general excitement is not difficult to imagine.

During the afternoon automobiles carrying armed men rushed through the streets. Revenge for Eisner! Matters now began to come to a head in Munich, after the first Communistic uprising had been quelled in Berlin at Christmas time.

The Jewish Communist Revolution in Munich

One day we in Munich woke to find ourselves in the midst of a Red republic. The great radical Marxist undertaking that had been successful in Russia was now to be repeated here, no matter at what cost. It was a beautiful, cool day. Everywhere on the streets of Munich

---

[22] The German term for the Communist Bavarian Soviet Republic, the short-lived attempt to establish a Soviet state in Bavaria. Led by a number of Jewish Communists under Eugen Leviné, the Bavarian Soviet government took civilian hostages from its enemies, including Prince Gustav of Thurn and Taxis, and executed them. In May 1919, a force of 9,000 regular German Army soldiers, backed up by a 30,000-strong private *Freikorps* militia, attacked Munich in a bloody street battle which over 1,000 Communists were killed and the Bavarian Soviet suppressed. The Jewish leadership of the *Räterepublik* was later used as evidence of the Jewish nature of Communism by the NSDAP.

were enraged groups, among them men who had never before been visible in the center of the city. It was toward evening. I joined in the discussion of a group of men near the Marienplatz, declaring that it was sheer insanity to bring Bolshevism to Germany. Its victims in Russia itself were already numerous enough.

The excitement all around me was growing, and someone called for a public demonstration of protest. Then we found ourselves in a wine restaurant near the old City Hall, asking for a piece of cardboard. *Long live the German worker! Down with Bolshevism!* was the inscription. Did I write that? I don't know to this day.

We left the restaurant. I told the excited men that all this was senseless. But they insisted that I simply had to speak to a larger group of people. The *Mariensäule*[23] in front of the City Hall is surrounded by a stone balustrade. On this lovely clear evening it was also surrounded by a few thousand people. And suddenly I found myself addressing them, telling them about my observations in Russia, about the insanity of advocating a dictatorship for a Germany already in such jeopardy.

Some applauded; otherwise, quiet attention. I stepped off my platform and found a quiet spot below the colonnades of the City Hall. Next to me stood a man who wanted to know details. We chatted for a while. From the stone balustrade around the pillar someone else was now speaking in favor of the social revolution. Slowly I turned toward home. The man asked me whether he might accompany me. Yes, why not? But I began to be suspicious. In any case, I said goodbye in front of a house door not my own, and waited for a while—at that time I was already living on Ottingerstraße—before I actually went home. The following day Mrs. Osann reported that she had heard that speeches against the *Räterepublik* had been made on Marienplatz the day before. I confessed.

During the next few days I, who was completely unknown in Munich, was repeatedly saluted on the streets. In the beginning I failed to understand why, but then I remembered my speech, and began to feel slightly uncomfortable. In the meantime Eckart, too, had had some dubious adventures, and suggested that we leave the city for a while. We drove to Wolfrathshausen in the Isar valley.

A few days later I returned to Munich. From my house, I heard the

---

[23] The Marian column on the Marienplatz in Munich. Marian columns are religious monuments built in honor of the Virgin Mary, and the one in Munich was built in 1638 to celebrate the end of Swedish occupation during the religious Thirty Years' War.

boom of cannon in the northern suburbs, and later witnessed the entry of the liberating troops under von Epp.[24] A short while before, the murder of the hostages, ten or twelve members of the Organization Thule, had shaken not only Munich but all of Germany.

Chief of the Munich *Räterepublik* was Doctor Leviné, who had been sent there from Russia. Beside him was one Doctor Levien. Also a Doctor W. Adler from Austria, who was more of a café Communist. And in addition, Mühsam and Toller. Following the example set by Russia, Leviné planned to use terror. The first victims were selected from the Organization Thule,[25] which devoted its attention to early Germanic history, and opposed Jewry without, however, being politically active.

Among those murdered were the secretary of the organization, who held a small position in the post office, and others—all little people, not one capitalist. This was the first time in history that hostages had been murdered in Germany; it showed what kind of spirit dominated the opposition. As was proven later, this original terror was to have been succeeded continuously by more terror. Doctor Leviné was arrested and shot. Doctor Levien managed to escape. I happened to be present when, a few days before von Epp's entrance, a speaker standing on top of one of the lions in front of the Wittelsbach Palais declared that it was slander to claim that Doctor Levien had absconded with stolen money.

Toller[26] was eventually found, but was pardoned after he served a short term in jail. Later he wrote plays and was a contributor to the *Berliner Tageblatt.*[27]

---

[24] Franz Ritter von Epp (1868–1946). An officer in the Imperial German Army during World War I, he founded the *Freikorps* Epp, a private paramilitary made up of war veterans in 1919. His Freikorps played a major part in the crushing of the Bavarian Soviet Republic in Munich. Epp became a member of the German parliament for the NSDAP in 1928, a positon he held until 1945. He served as head of the NSDAP's Military-Political Office from 1928 to 1945. Suffering from a heart condition, he was hospitalized at Bad Nauheim at the end of the war. On 9 May 1945, a clerk at the hospital alerted agents from the US Counter Intelligence Corps that von Epp was a patient there, and he was arrested and sent to a prison camp in Munich to await trial at Nuremberg. He died in detention without ever being charged.

[25] The Thule Society, originally the *Studiengruppe für germanisches Altertum* ("Study Group for Germanic Antiquity"), was a German nationalist group in Munich, named after a mythical northern country from Greek legend. The Society is notable chiefly as the organization that sponsored the *Deutsche Arbeiterpartei* (DAP), which was later reorganized by Adolf Hitler into the National Socialist German Workers' Party (NSDAP).

[26] Ernst Toller (1893–1939), a Jewish Communist playwright who served in 1919 for six days as President of the Bavarian Soviet Republic, and was later imprisoned for five years as a result. In 1933 Toller was exiled from Germany, and committed suicide in New York.

[27] The German "newspaper of record," of the time, published by the Jewish-owned media

Meeting with Anton Drexler and the German Worker's Party

At this time one Anton Drexler,[28] member of a German Workers' Party, completely unknown up to then, called on Dietrich Eckart. And this visit marked the turning point in my entire life, from that of a private individual to that of a political entity. I did not meet Drexler on the occasion of his first call on Eckart. I learned, however, that he told Eckart a German Workers' Party had been founded in one of Munich's suburbs. It had been started because of the general graft that went on during the war, because people were dissatisfied with other workers' organizations and were looking for an entirely new approach, faced as they were with the great national need. His fellow workers, Drexler said, had read our articles, and wanted Eckart to speak to them sometime.

Drexler was not any too well acquainted with economic problems, but he was a man with a simple, direct heart. As a toolmaker foreman in one of the machine shops of the German railroads, he had personally experienced a great many of the sorrows and cares of the German workingman, and understood that any solution to the problem depended upon the unity of the entire people.

Later he described his career in a modest little book, *My Political Awakening*. He didn't think very much of the old parties, nor did the *Reichstag* seem to hold out much hope for social rebirth. Everything seemed to be bogged down. And those who preached revolt merely collected bands of the despairing around them without giving a thought to the oneness of fate.

What to do? Drexler was genuinely worried. He was a tall man with a well-shaped head. From behind his spectacles his eyes frequently looked out in honest despair. One of the many, many thousands searching for a way out of the chaos, though they often stood on opposite sides of the barricades.

company Mosse.

[28] Anton Drexler (1884–1942), one of the founders of the *Deutsche Arbeiterpartei* (DAP) which was later changed into the *Nationalsozialistische Deutsche Arbeiterpartei* (NSDAP). Drexler served as mentor to Adolf Hitler during his early days in politics and was the one who invited Hitler to join the DAP. Hitler eventually replaced Drexler as party chairman. After the 1923 putsch, when the NSDAP was outlawed, Drexler became a Reichstag member for a smaller nationalist party, and only rejoined the NSDAP after Hitler had come to power in 1933.

They were workingmen who felt cheated; soldiers of the *Freikorps* torn loose from all the old traditions; officers who had lost their supreme commander; students desirous of a future, and some nationalistic writers.

First Meeting with Adolf Hitler

After some time I heard about one Adolf Hitler who had joined the German Workers' Party and was making remarkable speeches. He, too, called on Eckart, and during one of these visits I met him. This meeting changed my entire personal fate and merged it with the fate of the German nation as a whole. Munich itself became the focal point of the new political movement led by Hitler.

Everything that I had up to then thought, seen, learned and done, had, after all, been egocentric. Practicing my art had enriched me, and had sharpened my faculty to differentiate between the genuine and the imitative. The study of history and philosophy had brought about a widening of the horizon and, in spite of all gaps, an unquenchable desire for, and a persistent inner compulsion toward, fruition.

My carefree youth had laid the groundwork for experiences beyond the merely subjective; the comradeship of my student days had made it impossible for me to stand apart as a mere theorist. On top of all this came the influence of the variegated world around me: the national tension in my homeland, the generosity of St. Petersburg, the quietude of our forests and the beauty of the sea, the stirring up of greater possibilities by the war, the strangeness of Moscow, the huge space in the East. Then the German occupation, the collapse, the journey into the Reich, and the tattered picture of the German people.

My meeting with Eckart had already constituted an emergence from the narrow confines of the experiencing ego; but whatever I had said or written so far had, after all, been done with and for a small group. Only a slightly enlarged reading circle had, so to speak, participated. True, more and more people joined Eckart, and in all likelihood he would have kept on collecting an ever growing group of followers around himself. But Eckart was essentially a poet, a confessor rather than the shaper of a political movement.

Besides, there always came, after days full of energy, these pauses during which he retreated into himself, simply refusing to consider

29

outward occurrences important enough, while he wrote poems about the most beautiful and delicate things (as, for example, Grünewald's Altar, *Ecce Deus*). And I was, after all, a stranger in Bavaria.

Eckart himself had accepted me without question, as had his friends. But I had inhibitions. True, I had come to work somehow for Germany and could not understand how others dared come to this land to engage in destructive activities; yet even then I felt that I still didn't have the full right to speak publicly.

Besides, I was not yet a German citizen. Soon after my arrival I had made an application to be admitted to citizenship and permitted to stay on in Munich.

A gentleman at the City Hall questioned me. He was primarily interested in knowing whether I was wealthy. When I said no, he grew noticeably cooler and declared that, after all, Munich was crowded and I could really live just as well somewhere else in Bavaria.

This shocked me particularly because my leaving Munich would have deprived me of all opportunities, and would have put the Government Library beyond my reach. I told the official that I had to work constantly at the library to finish a book for the publishing house of J. F. Lehmann. And even though he didn't seem to like that name much, he declared that, under the circumstances, he didn't want to interfere with any chances I might have. But he wanted some proof.

Now, I had actually called on the firm of J. F. Lehmann and had talked to Mr. Schwartz, a partner. He had read a manuscript of mine on Bolshevism, and had spoken about the possibility of publishing it in their magazine, *Germany's Renewal*. Now he was kind enough to give me a letter confirming the fact that I was working with their house, and so I was allowed to stay on in Munich. On this thin thread of permission by an alderman hung my entire fate at that time.

An "Anonymous Scribbler"

However, I had not become a citizen, a fact which hampered me daily in the course of the first few years. It wasn't until 1923 that my application, thanks to some friendly intercession, was favorably acted upon. Up to then I could easily have been deported as an undesirable alien.

The fact that a Doctor Leviné could come from St. Petersburg or Moscow to take over command of a Communistic revolution upset me more than it did the Bavarian people. But this did not lessen my desire to work for the Reich in spite of my own lack of legal status.

Nevertheless I refused to write under a pseudonym, something Eckart—who had jokingly suggested this very thing to me at one time—understood particularly well, inasmuch as he had quoted Schopenhauer's harsh words about anonymous scribblers more than once.[29]

I met Hitler at Dietrich Eckart's. I would be lying if I said I was overwhelmed by him and forthwith became his unconditional adherent, as so many others claimed after he already had a name and accomplishments to his credit.

We had, as I remember, a short enough talk about the danger of Bolshevism, and in the course of our conversation he referred to conditions in ancient Rome. He claimed that, just as Christianity had been victorious at that time, Communism might actually have a real chance now.

What Hitler meant was that in heavily populated living spaces there are invariably so many individuals who are discontented and disinherited that an all-embracing precept can easily find favor among them. A basic difference lies in the fact that the Romans themselves gradually diminished in number, whereas in Europe the old population, in spite of wars and pestilence, remained more or less constant.

What made the situation on the continent dangerous was that most peoples had been completely uprooted by the war, their leadership was vacillating, and the number of the discontented, the hungry, and the despairing had grown tremendously.

Hitler spoke to several small gatherings of the party, which was now no longer called the German Workers' Party, but the National Socialist German Workers' Party. This change indicated the union of a cleansed

---

[29] "What the pathetic commonplace heads with which the world is crammed really lack are two closely related faculties: that of forming judgments and that of producing ideas of their own. Both these are lacking to a degree which he who is not one of them cannot really conceive, so that he cannot easily conceive the dolefulness of their existence. It is this deficiency, however, which explains on the one hand the poverty of the scribbling which in all nations passes itself off to its contemporaries as their literature, and on the other the fate that overtakes true and genuine man who appear among such people. All genuine thought and art is to a certain extent an attempt to put big heads on small people: so it is no wonder the attempt does not always come off."—Arthur Schopenhauer, *Parerga und Paralipomena,* 1851.

nationalism and a purified socialism.

I heard one of the speeches at the Inn Zum Deutschen Reich on Dachauer Street. About forty or fifty people were present. Hitler postulated that, just as before Luther everyone had been dissatisfied with the old forms until his words struck fire, so millions today felt that new thinking on all levels was essential. All we needed was courage. He spoke well, and from his heart.

I agreed with him completely, filled with joy to discover that a clever, impassioned man of the people, an ex-soldier, had the courage to undertake single-handed such a battle for the weal of the German nation. During the following weeks Hitler spoke before gradually growing audiences until, on February 24, 1920, he formulated and read the program of the party in the great hall of the Hofbräuhaus.[30]

---

[30] Munich's most famous beer hall in the city center.

Part Four:
The Years of Struggle

The 25 Points of the NSDAP

I did not participate in the preparation of the program, but I think that besides Hitler and Drexler, Feder was called upon to help settle a dubious point. Demands were proclaimed which, after some hesitation, probably most of us would have approved. Instead of class and professional interests, the interests of the entire productive population were placed at the center of all thinking. Perhaps on more mature consideration some points would have been formulated differently; perhaps the succession of individual paragraphs was not altogether memorable (Hitler himself admitted as much at a later date); but in view of the general situation it was best to have at least a skeleton to which life might cling.

It will remain forevermore necessary to start with a symbolic day in German history—November 9, 1918. This day marks the collapse of the German Empire and the foundation of the November Republic based on the dictates of Versailles. Large sections of the population considered the action taken on November 9 a dagger thrust in the back.

Peace negotiations were under way, the armistice conditions had been accepted, and it was now a question of keeping Reich and army intact. November saw Germany deprived of her last important asset, the army, and left completely defenseless. This, at the time, was considered treason. Later, this concept was unexpectedly confirmed by Lloyd George when he visited the Führer after the latter had taken over. He declared that the Entente, too, had been at the end of its rope; only a few more weeks and it would have offered Germany reasonable peace proposals.

This was followed by the loss of all colonies, the loss of Reich territory, disarmament, reparations, and finally the inflation that wiped out

Germany's savings and working capital. Growing hopelessness gripped the population.

Certain separatist groups cropped up in Bavaria and the Rhineland. And in response to all this came the equally desperate endeavors of activist national organizations: the Free Corps in the Balticum, in Silesia, in Bavaria and in the Ruhr. Meanwhile, all the old parties began to reassert themselves, strengthened by two left-wing groups of the Social Democrats: the Independent Socialists and the Communists. The German Nationalists remained monarchists in principle, but still wanted to have a hand in the governing of the new state.

The German People's Party took a similar stand, only to enter after a while into closer connections with the Republic. The Democratic Party identified itself with them. So did the Centrists, with some philosophical reservations. Barring a few incorrigible reactionaries and alien politicians, millions of honest Germans were either tied inextricably to the middle classes, or to various Marxist groups.

Party strife began, and continued unabated for years. It did not display a picture of a clear will, nor one of position and opposition but—if I may anticipate the developments of later years—a fight of all against all. In the end the parliamentary system was represented by forty-nine different parties, each one trying to present its own particular problem as the most important of them all, irrespective of whether it was concerned with revaluation, farmers' interests, or rent ceilings.

German development was conditioned by the princely states which remained in existence even after the founding of the Empire, thus preserving court traditions and a certain unity of the nobility, something that up to the very last gave many of the most important government offices their noble face. At the universities, membership in certain Corps and Rings was a prerequisite for the scions of nobility and others completely subservient to them, if they aspired to a career in the Foreign Office, or in the army.

Prussia herself was a creation of the soldiery, and her military leadership was recruited exclusively from families belonging to the rural nobility who had once been settled there by grateful Prussian kings. They and the royal house constituted an entity and, as such, represented certain economic interests that often were opposed to the new industrial age.

Thus the guidance of the Reich was monopolized by rather exclusive groups, even though a few breaks in the impenetrable wall had been made. The owners of great fortunes maneuvered between the camps. They kowtowed before the monarchy, but wanted to get the old fogies out of leading positions in order to open the road to world-economic enterprise. In any case, advancement from the broad, healthy ranks of the masses was extremely difficult.

Thwarted ambition had driven many members of the intelligentsia into the arms of the opposition, even though that opposition by no means represented what they really wanted. In view of all these contradictory forces and developments, Adolf Hitler, who had encountered such problems in Austria, before serving for four and a half years as a soldier in the German army, not only recognized the necessity of national unity above everything else, but was also willing to press to the hilt the demand for social justice.

The Spirit behind National Socialism

The National Socialist Party entered the battle. Adolf Hitler became its leader. The point of departure of his way of thinking was this: If so many honest men stand in each of the two opposing camps, no matter how their individual programs look, they must be impelled by decent motives.

But if the totality of the bourgeoisie and the totality of the proletariat are such bitter enemies, there must needs be spiritual, political and social causes that prevent understanding, to say nothing of co-operation in regard to all great tasks confronting the Reich.

Without going into economic details, National Socialism affirmed the demand for justice for the working classes. But the conviction that social justice could be secured only within the national framework became ever more firm.

And here basic dogmas barred the way, dogmas which had been taught only too well to a people more often than not inclined to place veracity above practicality. The class war was looked upon as something factual, and Marxism had not been able to offer anything beyond still more class war—an eye for an eye, a tooth for a tooth.

It could be accepted as actuality conditioned by the times; but to accept it as a principle of national life was anathema to anyone for

35

whom the German Reich was both home and idea—anyone who knew of the sacrifices that had been made in the interest of the growth, shape and spiritual contents of the Reich; anyone, *in fine,* to whom the people appeared as a psychological-biological-historical entity.

On top of all this was the pacifist-spouted propaganda—which did not display any desirable love of peace, but insisted instead upon the right to treason—an idea frequently expressed in 1918 and later years.

Eventually the protest against private ownership led to renewed demands for government ownership, a demand which could not help but meet with violent opposition, particularly among peasants to whom inherited property was the very breath of life. True, events had apparently smoothed out a great many problems; labor unions were devoting their attention to essentials, but politico-philosophical difficulties kept cropping up. It was Adolf Hitler who declared war against all this.

In Austria, with her various peoples, he had realized that nationalism was something that had to be defended ever anew; now he saw that it also would have to be defended in the Reich even though here it was a birthright. In the Sudetenland a small National Socialist party was already in existence—yet another reason why he should found his own. Hitler had come to the conclusion that a just socialism had, *per se,* nothing to do with class war and internationalism.

The Elimination of Class War

To perpetuate class war was wrong. It would have to be eliminated. Thus he became an opponent of Marxism in all of its manifestations, and characterized it as a philosophy of government inimical to both the state and the working class.

As far as the workers were concerned it was, therefore, a question of renouncing this doctrine as well as their opposition to both the farmer and the property owner. The middle classes, too, had every reason to revise their attitude. They had failed to provide the working classes in their hour of dire need with leaders conversant with their requirements and had left them to the tender mercy of international propagandists.

German nationalism, Hitler believed, was hemmed in by the nobility, while an entirely false conceit separated the middle classes from the broad mass of the productive population.

The bourgeoisie would have to shed its prejudices before it would once again be entitled to leadership. To end Germany's fratricidal strife he proposed to gather together all active nationalists of every party, and fighters for social justice from every camp, to form a new movement.

From Bavaria, and other countries also, people begged for additional information. Now Hitler began to propagandize outside of Munich, too: in Rosenheim, Landshut, Ingolstadt. Everywhere new cells were formed. He was not at all like the representatives of other parties. Where the latter appealed to the interests of their listeners, who all belonged to a certain definite group, by promising to press their interests before all others, Hitler invariably spoke for the absent ones.

In other words, before an audience of Red workers he spoke about the need for a healthy farmers' class, or he defended the German officers. Facing officers he criticized the attitude of the intelligentsia which had ignored the workingman and left him to his fate. The time for self-criticism had come, he would say, and the way from man to man had to be found despite all obstacles. Then the famous huge red posters began to appear in Munich, placards that not only advertised meetings, but also carried a few lines of text intended to arouse interest and curiosity.

Since these posters required police permits, the attitude of Police President Pöhner became important. Evidently, he said to himself that he and his police alone could not keep Communism in check; and if idea, will and resistance arose from among the people themselves, it was to his advantage not to interfere. The memory of April, 1919, was still very green.

The Story of Kurt Lüdecke

Here I want to devote a few words to a person who began to be active at about this time—Kurt Lüdecke. He had money, foreign money, in fact, and placed some of it at the disposal of the party. He even outfitted, at his own expense, a troop of the Storm troops. He impressed people as being somewhat extravagant, was always clad in the best custom-made suits, and otherwise well groomed. I always got along well with him, and believed in his honorableness and good will. But someone, perhaps the police themselves, warned Hitler against him—Lüdecke's foreign money might be of French origin. In view of

37

the general situation, Hitler had to be careful.

Therefore, he banked the money in the presence of witnesses, to leave it untouched until the situation could be clarified. Later on Lüdecke was arrested. Secret entries in his pocket diary were held against him. He was able to prove his innocence and was freed. But the breath of suspicion had brushed him; he felt it and was depressed. He did, however, participate in the march on Coburg. Later he returned to America, where he married.

Lüdecke was then doing some outside work for me and the *Völkischer Beobachter*,[31] and, after the taking over or power, he returned to the Reich to offer his services. He was active in my sphere of interest and had undertaken the task of bringing about an understanding between America and Germany. But then misfortune hit him a second time.

Denounced by a collaborator, he was arrested in the Chancellery. While under arrest he was permitted to visit me twice. The second time I told him that I expected to see the Führer within a few days, and would then discuss his case and try to bring about a solution. Lüdecke was extremely depressed. A few days later I heard that he had escaped, first to Prague, and then to America.

I actually did see the Führer about this, feeling somewhat guilty, as if I myself had helped Lüdecke to escape, and told him that I didn't think Lüdecke should have been treated as he was. The Führer expressed his regrets. He obviously had known nothing about the arrest. But things couldn't be changed, nor would Lüdecke, in all likelihood, have returned.

The work accomplished by women merits special mention. They came to us less because they admired some of the points in our program than for sentimental reasons. The man who had dared take a stand against the entire welter of parties around us had captured their fancy, and as a speaker he fascinated them. Quite a number of women came regularly to our meetings in Munich, and always brought along new ones to attend the next. They offered their help and made sacrifices wherever they could. The same was true in other cities.

There was a great deal of courage, will to sacrifice, and readiness to act, that found expression in the young movement—the secret of all future success.

---

[31] The *Völkischer Beobachter* ("Folkish Observer") was the newspaper of the NSDAP from 1920 onwards.

The *Völkischer Beobachter*

The *Völkischer Beobachter* now appeared twice a week. There were hardly any contributors. Frequently I was forced to fall back on the petty politics of the day. In any case, here was a mouthpiece that could be used throughout the Reich to propagate the continuity of our program. Hitler wanted a daily, of course. And here a wealthy woman helped out. She owned, if I am not mistaken, shares in some Finnish paper mills, and of these she gave the party a sufficient number to make it possible for us to run the risk of getting out a daily.

Since Eckart was simply incapable of any sustained effort, I had taken care of all routine work from the very beginning, and relieved him of most of his editorial duties. When the problems of starting our daily became acute, Hitler went shopping with me. I was to select a desk. I picked one with a roll top, since my untidiness made this desirable. Hitler was almost childishly pleased. Another step forward! It filled him with new enterprise.

Gradually the newly founded organization in Munich became well known. Visitors attended Hitler's meetings and talked about them back home. After having thought things over, many of them volunteered as helpers. Nationalist organizations and clubs offered to join forces. Many a member of the Free Corps wanted to know what was going on in Munich.

Hitler and Eckart, too, had innumerable callers and held hundreds of conferences. And even if I did not participate in these meetings, I naturally met some of the callers. From Westphalia and Saxony came itinerant prophets. One of them, a poor devil carrying a huge knapsack, said: Just give me propaganda material and explain things to me. I'll return home immediately and shall go from village to village to distribute your stuff. Another one produced a filthy manuscript and said: If I could make these things come true, Germany would be saved. Letters containing suggestions, programs, poems, arrived constantly in an endless stream. They probably weren't kept.

Occasionally all this turned our offices into a sort of a spiritual torture chamber—and yet, what a wealth of suppressed love was here, that merely could not express itself! How much need and despair, anxious to find something to cling to!

Storm Troopers Organized in Response to Communist Violence

Hitler could not go on with his public meetings without a fight. What he demanded was no more than an equal right to that freedom of speech which the Social Democrats and Communists claimed as their prerogative. In return he promised freedom of debate. In answer, attempts were made to prevent him from speaking, and to break up meetings by force. Infuriated gangs appeared on the scene armed with lead pipes and blackjacks. There were bloody heads on both sides.

Hitler began to organize his Hall Protection corps. Its members were recruited from the S.A., our defense organization.

Political life in Germany found expression not only in parliamentary speeches, but particularly in the fact that the extreme Marxists arrogated the right of having the streets to themselves, preventing anybody else from holding public meetings. The new state was unable to do anything effective to protect the proclaimed general freedom of speech.

Thus the organization of the Storm troopers, now a part of every one of our branches, represented no more than an act of self-defense on our part. They were trained by officers from the Brigade Ehrhardt. And eventually Hermann Göring offered his services to Adolf Hitler.

Editor of the *Völkischer Beobachter*

In the beginning few people I knew called at the editorial offices of the *Völkischer Beobachter*. I myself contributed only an occasional article. When matters didn't go any too well with Eckart, he decided to discontinue his own magazine, transferred his subscribers to the *Völkischer Beobachter,* and became editor in chief.

I retired to the editorial department located in the house of the printer, 39 Schellingstraße, and remained there until the end of 1932. During these years Hitler had gained my respect and loyalty. I saw in him a man continuously wrestling for the soul of a people.

I witnessed his maturing, saw how he constantly thought and brooded, only to be ready suddenly with amazingly apt answers to whatever questions arose. Thus, time after time, he gave evidence of sound instincts and natural cleverness.

Eckart spoke of him with growing veneration, and that meant a great deal. Eckart had managed to acquire a house, or rather, part of a house, in a settlement on Richildenstraße in Nymphenburg. I found a furnished room nearby.

There Eckart attained the peace he needed to be able to devote himself to his poetry. Pacing to and fro in his small garden, he pondered over his ideas, and frequently emphasized the rhythm of some nascent poem by thrashing around with his hands.

Occasionally, when I went to see him in the morning, he would meet me on the stairs and read me his latest effort right then and there. These are the poems which were printed in his magazine in 1920. Or else, Eckart might just have come across another beautiful passage in his beloved Schopenhauer, which he would insist upon reading to me on the spot.

He was particularly impressed by what Schopenhauer had to say about the German language. For this, too, I owe Eckart my thanks.

The Balts lack a peasant class that acts as a perpetual spring of rejuvenation for the language. They write a literary, slightly bookish German, but use entirely too many foreign words. Eckart undertook the task of cleaning up many of my articles, and in doing so gave me many an excellent stylistic hint—though I did occasionally protest timidly when he attempted to point up one of my articles somewhat too dramatically.

Ludendorff Comes to Munich

Ludendorff,[32] too, had come to Munich. One of his followers had offered him a house in Prinz-Ludwigs-Höhe on the Isar, and Ludendorff had accepted. We had sent him some of our printed material, and he had answered with a few lines of appreciation. His entire life had been spent in military service, and he accepted state and church in their entirety as established institutions without feeling obliged to concern

---

[32] Erich Friedrich Wilhelm Ludendorff (1865–1937), the famous German general who was victor at Liège and at the Battle of Tannenberg during the First World War. He took part in the 1923 Putsch, but after the banning of the NSDAP, represented the *Deutschvölkische Freiheitspartei* ("German Völkisch Freedom Party") in the Reichstag. He retired from active politics in 1928.

himself particularly with the problems of the day. That he left to others.

However, the war forced General Headquarters to pay at least some attention to the politics of the Reich. That there should be frequent clashes between personalities as divergent as those of Ludendorff and Bethmann-Hollweg was inevitable.

To Ludendorff it seemed that not enough consideration was being given at home to the demands of the army. But in spite of everything, all parties were quite unanimous in their conviction that Germany had found in Ludendorff a great field marshal and a man of untiring energy. Now he was retired, embittered, subject to daily attacks by political parties, and was finishing the writing of his war memoirs.

Somehow it was made possible for me to call on him. He received me very amiably. He possessed a strangely high voice, something he had in common with Bismarck and Charlemagne, and spoke very calmly about our fate. Nothing of the bitterness against Wilhelm II and Hindenburg, which he later expressed so brusquely, was noticeable at the time. He didn't say a single word about his dismissal.

Now Ludendorff was catching up with what he had neglected so far: he studied the history of politics and diplomacy. Suddenly things that heretofore had seemed unequivocal and clear took on problematical aspects.

And as occasionally happens to men who have a successful past behind them, he did not look for illumination from clear thinkers, but instead came under the influence of a primarily sectarian crowd.

Doctor Mathilde von Kemmnitz[33]—who in private conversations praised the Field Marshal to the skies—made contact with him. For her the history of the world was merely a matter of secret conspiracies.

The Kapp Putsch

The practice of basing sound judgments on official sources turned into the very opposite, and Ludendorff's shining name as a soldier was to shield much that was more than merely regrettable. One day we suddenly heard that a counterrevolution led by Kapp had broken out in

---

[33] Dr. Von Kemmnitz became Ludendorff's second wife and together with him, set up the *Bund für Gotteserkenntnis* ("Society for the Knowledge of God"), a small society of Theists which blamed the world's problems on Christians (especially the Jesuits and Catholics), Jews, and Freemasons.

Berlin. Ebert and his government were supposed to have fled, General von Lüttwitz was said to be in Berlin.

We waited feverishly to see what would happen in Bavaria. To begin with, the inhabitants were called to arms. And, as once before in Reval, I had to go on night patrol duty armed with an unfamiliar rifle.

I was stationed on the Nymphenburg Canal. There I met a young comrade by the name of Diebitsch, a descendant of the German-born Russian general who had once closed the Convention of Tauroggen.[34] Hitler and Eckart had flown to Berlin. When they arrived there after a terrible trip, the whole undertaking had gone on the rocks.

A general strike had checkmated Kapp, who was also threatened with foreign intervention. Kapp probably couldn't and wouldn't institute a dictatorship by brute force.

And when he found no help in the provinces, he gave up and fled to Sweden. This was the famous Kapp Putsch, an attempt to turn fate about, explicable only by the fact that things in Germany were in desperate shape.

The Battle of Coburg

Meanwhile our work in Munich went on its appointed way. Several *völkische* organizations had arranged a so-called German Day in Coburg. They had secured the necessary permission only by promising that they would meet indoors; in other words, there was an interdict against non-Marxist organizations holding meetings in the open.

Hitler was invited. He accepted, declaring, however, that the streets of Germany belonged to all Germans. He chartered a special train, and we went to Franconia accompanied by about 600 Storm Troopers. What followed, Hitler has described in his book.[35]

Those who were waiting for us with lead pipes and nail-studded, heavy sticks, were not strong enough to break up our parade. On the contrary, whenever they attacked, they were beaten back without

---

[34] The Convention of Tauroggen was a truce signed 30 December 1812 at Tauroggen (today called Tauragé in Lithuania; then part of the Russian Empire), between General Ludwig Yorck von Wartenburg on behalf of his Prussian troops, and by General Hans Karl von Diebitsch of the Russian Army. Yorck's act is considered a turning point of Prussian history, triggering an insurgency against Napoleon in the Rheinbund.

[35] *Mein Kampf,* Volume 2, Chapter 9.

mercy. Hitler himself left the ranks several times and used his stick. I had been slightly naïve and didn't have a stick, only a pistol in my pocket, which, under the circumstances, naturally couldn't be used. After all, we acted merely in self-defense. In any case, in Coburg, for the first time in our party's history, we captured the streets, a symbolic act that made quite an impression on Germany as a whole. Later we sat up there in the fortress and looked far out over the land.

First Major Speeches

In the meantime I began making my first speeches in and outside of Munich. Once I was asked what I thought of the Jesuits. I gave my personal opinion, but added that this was hardly a subject to be discussed just then. As it turned out, my attitude—it happened in Rosenheim—was obviously correct. Two listeners demanded almost immediately that religious questions be eliminated from the discussion.

This incident showed me how sensitive people were on that particular subject. Later, whenever I felt I had to say something about it, I always said it by way of the printed word. I have never talked in public about the Jesuits or the Catholic Church *per se,* about the latter's metaphysical dogma, nor that of the Protestants. Nor did I ever speak publicly about my principal book, published some years later. As critical as I might have been of certain prelates who were the leaders of the Centrist Party, I preferred to let sleeping dogs lie.

At a big Munich handicraft exhibition a carved crucifix was on display along with many other objects. It was so painfully distorted, with stupid, popping eyes, that we considered it blasphemous. Hitler referred to it in one of his speeches, whereupon the authorities came to a similar conclusion and had it withdrawn. In other words, the young party, in spite of its freethinking, stood ready, if necessary, to fight all mockery—most often originating in Berlin—not only of national, but also of religious symbols.

But this willingness to work hand in hand with religious circles, at least in some respects, was summarily rejected by them, not only at that time, but even more emphatically later on. This automatically led to a growing retaliatory enmity on the part of many of the followers of the National Socialist German Workers' Party. To us, however, it seemed as if the two churches missed an important moment in history.

Becoming a German Citizen

In February, 1923, I finally had in my pocket official confirmation that I had been granted German citizenship. And in spite of the fact that this, after all, was no more than a formality, it gave me that definite feeling of belonging which I had not had before.

During the last few months, Eckart had not bothered to come to our editorial department at all. He frequently entertained guests from Northern Germany, and talked often about a humorous novel he planned to write.

Hitler told me one day that, since I did all of the work, I might as well get credit for it. I called Eckart and told him that I was now a full-fledged German citizen, and that all our former caution was now superfluous. I thought he had understood me, and announced in the *Völkischer Beobachter* that I had taken over the title of editor-in-chief. But when I met Eckart shortly thereafter, he told me that mutual friends had asked him whether we had had a falling out, whether he had given up his job without even a word of explanation, and so on.

At first, he said, he hadn't thought much about it, but then he began to wonder whether I had acted quite decently.

This gave me a nasty jolt: to be accused of ingratitude by Eckart was terrible! I told him as much, and he seemed satisfied; but some resentment remained, at least with me, ever after. To have published an official article in appreciation afterwards would have merely made things worse.

Death of My First Wife

In the meantime my wife had returned from Switzerland, and was looking for a cure in Germany. We had agreed to separate. She said that at first she might have been able to help me a little, but now I had found my way. She was sick, she said, and probably would have to rely on other people for the rest of her life. The divorce was granted in the spring of 1923. Later she joined her parents in Reval, went to France in a last attempt to find a cure, and died. In other words, the first Mrs. Rosenberg, who had hoped to imbue the German Balt with an all-embracing European culture, had at last given up.

First Major Writings for the NSDAP

We were approached from many sides with the request for further elucidation of our program. I wrote a brief outline and discussed it with Hitler. In doing so I remembered how important he considered old-age pensions.

A carefree old age after a life of honest toil seemed to him to be a most important social necessity; the casualties of labor should be considered no less worthy than the casualties of war, and officials pensioned by the government.

Wesen, Grundsätze und Ziele der Nationalsozialistische Deutsche Arbeiter Partei[36] certainly was by no means a mature piece of work; it had all the earmarks of both a youthful author and a youthful movement, but it was in any case an outline which each individual could enlarge upon according to his knowledge of, and experience in, special fields.

---

[36] "Being, principles, and goals of the National Socialist German Worker's Party", Rosenberg's work published in 1922.

Part Five:
The 1923 Putsch and Being the Acting Leader of the NSDAP

The November 1923 Putsch

In November, 1923, the first storm broke. Munich was rife with plotting, and Hitler had to make some sort of a decision lest he become the object of the politics of others rather than the master of his own and the party's destiny.

Thus the October days were crowded with ever more conferences between the Führer and his Storm Trooper deputy leader. Approximately a week before the fateful day, Adolf Hitler, Göring, Röhm,[37] and I met at the apartment of Doctor von Scheubner-Richter.[38]

Naturally we discussed the coming action, its possibilities, and its chances of success. The general opinion was that we simply had to bring matters to a head in some way. At this occasion Röhm laughingly told us that while he was cleaning his revolver, it suddenly exploded and drove a bullet into his bookcase, hitting, of all books, *Die Spur der Juden im Wandel der Zeiten*.[39] To a superstitious mind this may have seemed indicative of something or other.

---

[37] Ernst Julius Günther Röhm (1887–1934), an officer in the Bavarian Army and co-founder of the *Sturmabteilung* ("Storm Battalion" or SA), the NSDAP's militia set up to ward off the Communist Party's violent attacks on party meetings. An active homosexual, Röhm was also part of a far left clique within the NSDAP which, upset at Hitler's refusal to implement the more socialist economic parts of the party program after coming to power, plotted a "Second Revolution" with fellow party members Gregor and Otto Strasser. This plot was suppressed in 1934 during the "Night of the Long Knives" and Röhm was among those executed without trial at that time.

[38] Ludwig Maximilian Erwin von Scheubner-Richter (1884–1923), an early member of the NSDAP. During the 1923 Putsch, he was shot in the lungs and died instantly, at the same time dislocating Hitler's right shoulder.

[39] "The Track of the Jew through the Ages", Rosenberg's first book, published in 1920.

When we started for the Feldherrnhalle, party member Müller said to me: Don't go along, Herr Rosenberg; this is pure suicide. In an hour like that, however, one no longer thought about whether it would be suicide or not. I joined the second row and we marched off, Hitler in the lead.

After November 8 and 9, I went back to the office of the *Völkischer Beobachter*. There I found my editorial assistants, together with Eckart and Feder. The premises still had not been searched. An elderly lady suggested that I take shelter in her house, an offer which I gratefully accepted.

During the ensuing months she mothered me in a most touching fashion. The others, we heard, had either been arrested or had fled to Austria. Each night I rode to town, standing on the dark back platform of the streetcar, my hat deep down over my eyes, to meet some of our comrades.

NSDAP Outlawed, Hitler Appoints Rosenberg Leader

Shortly before his arrest, Hitler had written many brief notes. I received this penciled message: "Dear Rosenberg. From now on you will lead the movement." I was rather surprised. Hitler had never taken me into his confidence as far as organizational matters were concerned, and now I was to assume control at this critical moment!

The party was outlawed. Anyone who tried to revive it would face a heavy jail sentence, and Germans, more particularly Bavarians, were certainly not the sort who gloried in conspiracies. It soon became apparent, incidentally, that a thoroughly organized party in the true sense of the word had never really existed, but at best had consisted of certain isolated groups with a growing number of adherents.

Nevertheless, public opinion was definitely in our favor, so much so that the Bavarian government desisted from making mass arrests, apparently satisfied with taking the leaders into custody, and making only a cursory search for the rest of us. Even when the foundation of a *Grossdeutsche Volksgemeinschaft E.V.*[40] was announced—it was the brain child of one of the section leaders of the party—it received the necessary official sanction without much ado, probably because its

---

[40] The "Greater German Peoples' Community" or CVG, a front organization for the NSDAP after the latter's banning following the 1923 Putsch.

existence would facilitate official supervision, and also help disperse the comparatively large number of party members. The idea was sound enough, since many rumors were in circulation concerning the actions of some of our men who had either fled abroad or were under arrest and thus unable to defend themselves. In my retreat I heard only fragments of this gossip.

Whenever I met party members I tried to reassure them, but human nature being what it is, it took some talking to calm them down. The pettiness of human nature became rather painfully apparent both then and in 1924—that and the lack of a responsible attitude toward the serious turn of events as well as toward the young party. Those who had found sanctuary in Austria heard all this thrice exaggerated, as is usual among emigrants.

It was suggested that I cross the border to reassure the people in Salzburg. I agreed and went to Reichenhall where I called on a designated person. That night I crossed over into Austria. The way led through a forest deep in snow, then across a vast plain. At about 3 A.M. I reached Salzburg.

The National Socialists in Austria were naturally very much upset over the things that had happened in Munich, but had cared for the fugitives in a most exemplary manner, and had even collected funds to aid those in Munich who had lost their positions.

I talked to one after the other of our comrades, trying to give them renewed courage and to dispel all senseless rumors.

The next day Herr von Graefe arrived in Salzburg to discuss future collaboration. Graefe, together with some other representatives, had left the German-National faction of the *Reichstag*, and had founded the *Deutsch Völkische Freiheits Partei*. This party embraced some of the more radical bourgeois elements, but had little influence.

Graefe had long since been in contact with Hitler, and on November 9, he actually accompanied us to the Feldherrnhalle. The goal of this northern German group was to take over the leadership in the north, and to get the local National Socialists to join them. I was asked to give my permission to a merger of the provincial organizations. The conference lasted until late at night.

In order to bring about at least a semblance of unity, we were willing to make certain concessions—all except one. That, I suggested, we discuss the following day, and went to bed. Then I heard that my

49

supposed agreement had already been publicized throughout the Reich.

Naturally I protested against this attempt to confound me with a *fait accompli,* and denied their claim, much to the satisfaction of our National Socialists, but this understandably led to a worsening of our relations with Graefe and his followers.

In broad daylight I was conducted back to the German border where I was observed by an Austrian revenue man; my companion returned home on skis.

At the border control station I explained matters to the official and begged him to be reasonable—all I had done was visit a few friends from Munich. He allowed me to go on, and since nobody bothered me on the Bavarian side I reached Munich without further incident. One thing called for an almost immediate decision: were we to participate in the coming elections for the Landtag[41] and the *Reichstag*? My considered opinion was that an underground party was sheer foolishness, and that any hope of resuming the activities of the National Socialists rested squarely on participation.

But against this stood the fact that our chances weren't any too good, and that we had not tried and true human material, and very little money at our disposal. Should we give up altogether the plan of building up a true people's movement untrammeled by the party strife of the *Reichstag*? During our conferences in Munich, opinion was quite unequivocally for participation. However, some of the motives for coming to this decision displeased me considerably.

A few of the party leaders obviously already saw themselves as representatives, making lasting impressions with the speeches they intended to deliver, and sunning themselves in the anticipated comforts of personal security. Through his attorney the question was put to Hitler. He declared himself violently against any participation in the elections.

In due course he wrote me a letter enumerating all the points that spoke against our entering parliament. I replied that, even though certain dangers could not be denied, our participation in the elections was the only possible way for us to become active again. To leave our adherents without action of any kind was, in my opinion, the worst thing we could do. Thus I felt that I had to speak out for our

---

[41] A state legislature, in this case, the governing body of the state of Bavaria.

participation, and begged Hitler to make me personally responsible for this decision. Related organizations were grouped together under the name *Der Völkische Block*; and in the other provinces usually under the name *Völkisch-Sozialer Block*.

The *Grossdeutsche Zeitung*[42] became our newspaper, thanks primarily to a wealthy family that wanted to help Hitler during his trial. All the discussions concerning candidates, and so on, were rather painful for me, since they so frequently brought to the surface the all-too-human side of human character.

Hitler had taken our decision in his stride, but now he wanted me to run for office. That was one thing, however, I refused to do under any circumstances, and for the following reason: I didn't want to risk being accused at some future time of having been in favor of our participation merely because I wanted to get into the *Reichstag* myself.

Members of the *Reichstag* were entitled to free transportation on all railroads, received 500 to 600 marks per month, and enjoyed political immunity, so that they could hardly be brought before a court because of their political speeches.

All this would have given any future accusation a somewhat unpleasant undertone. It so happened that just at this time I was visited by a National Socialist from an Upper Bavarian city. He told me he esteemed me highly, but that the mentality of the Bavarians was such that only men known to them, natives of Bavaria itself, could be suggested as possible candidates for the Landtag and as political leaders.

The man was absolutely right, but nevertheless it hurt me. After all, I was still not deeply enough rooted, and the realization of this fact strengthened my decision not to allow my name to appear on the lists. I hoped that Hitler would eventually understand.

How to arrange the elections, under what name, with what candidates—all this had to be discussed. Our correspondence was camouflaged by printing the names of nonexistent firms on our envelopes. At first I signed as Schulz, until my assistant, who took care of most of the routine work, made up the name Rolf Eidhalt from the letters of Adolf Hitler's name, and this was used as a signature from then on.

---

[42] The "Greater Germany Newspaper" appeared between January 29 and May 22, 1924 as the voice of the *Grossdeutsche Volksgemeinschaft E. V.*

The Hitler Trial

The mood of Munich had gradually become normal again. The Hitler Trial was about to begin. From all one heard, it was apparent that the Bavarian government had no intention of being particularly severe. Partly because of Ludendorff's fame, but also to avoid creating any martyrs in the face of the indubitable public sympathy for the accused.

On trial with Hitler were Colonel Kriebel, Police President Pöhner, and Doctor Weber, the leader of the organization Oberland—all of them highly esteemed personalities. The trial itself resulted in a pronounced victory for Hitler. His speech moved even his enemies. The sentence of five years incarceration with the recommendation for parole after a year, was a mere formality against which no one protested. In view of these developments, I had settled down in the city again. The police invited me to a brief informal talk, but after that left me alone.

I was able to see Hitler on Blutenburgerstraße in Munich while we made our preparations. He was now in accord with us as far as our participation in the elections was concerned; he had also heard that our meetings were well attended. Only the electoral organization, *Völkischer Block,* brought forth some derisive remarks from him. I told him that under the name National Socialist German Workers' Party preparations could not have been made in time.

We simply had to wait until we could reorganize our party on a legal basis. Ludendorff was all for the fusion of the National Socialist German Workers' Party with the *Deutsch-Völkische Freiheits Partei.* But much as I favored occasional co-operation during elections, I was strongly opposed to such a mechanistic theory of amalgamation.

Once we went together to visit Hitler at Landsberg. The Führer was of the opinion that there would be less danger of a fight if the fusion were brought about, but that all this should first be thoroughly discussed. Satisfied, Ludendorff listened only to the first part while I took particular note of the second part of this sentence.

Our entire *Reichstag* list of thirty-two or thirty-four names, was victorious. This was a rather remarkable success, undoubtedly harking back to Hitler's attitude during his trial. All the rest of what went on in 1924 under the general heading of discord in the ranks of the nationalists is so unimportant that it is superfluous to go into details.

Internal Party Schism

Only, as far as I am concerned, I ought to make this much clear: in a difficult hour Hitler had entrusted me with the leadership of what splinters remained of the party; but party members who happened to be my adversaries had also been received by him and thereupon posed as his special confidants. So I wrote Hitler, asking him for the sake of my honor to cancel his order, and recommended in my stead Gregor Strasser.[43]

Thereupon Hitler declared publicly that nobody was entitled to speak for him since he was personally unable from his place of confinement to survey the general situation. The leadership of Ludendorff-Graefe-Strasser ensued. I had withdrawn from the actual leadership of the party and had kept close contact only with Strasser, whom I knew to be both active and honest.

The *Grossdeutsche Zeitung* had folded in the meanwhile, but two other papers had been founded. For one of them, the *Völkische Kourier,* I became a regular contributor. Following the suggestion of my publisher, I also issued the *Weltkampf* as a monthly. Besides that, I again devoted considerable time to my research work at the State Library.

Hitler's year of incarceration had in the meantime come to an end, the proposed parole became effective, and he was welcomed back by all of us with joy. He was satisfied now with my arbitrary decision regarding the elections, even though he had certain reservations concerning its actual execution (without ever mentioning them to anyone).

[43] Gregor Strasser (1892–1934), a prominent figure in the early NSDAP until his resignation in 1932. Part of the "leftist" wing of the NSDAP, Strasser was, like his brother Otto, far more focused on the socialist economic platform than Hitler, and although important within the party organization, always clashed with the leadership over economics. He took an active part in the unsuccessful 1923 Putsch and was sentenced to prison in April 1924 to one-and-a-half year's confinement in the Landsberg Prison. He was released only a few weeks later after being elected as a member of the Bavarian state parliament for the NSDAP front party, the *Völkischer Block*. In December 1924, Strasser won a seat in the Reichstag the *Deutsch Völkische Freiheitspartei*. He remained a member of the Reichstag until December 1932, when the then Chancellor, Kurt von Schleicher, offered Strasser the offices of Vice-Chancellor and Prime Minister of Prussia in the hope of splitting the NSDAP. Schleicher's plan failed because of Hitler's intervention, and instead resulted in Strasser's resignation from all party positions. By 1934, he had become actively involved in the plot to overthrow Hitler hatched by the "leftist" faction of the NSDAP, and was arrested and executed during the "Night of the Long Knives" in June of that year.

In the course of the year 1924, a few party members had considered it necessary to suspect me of various things. After overlooking this for some time, I eventually made an official complaint.

Hitler asked me not to go through with it, however, and promised to write me a letter which, he said, ought to give me greater satisfaction than a trial. Nobody doubted my integrity, he said, and all this was due to no more than the general nervousness. In the interest of the party I agreed and, in time, received the promised letter.

NSDAP Refounded

On February 24, 1925, the party was legally organized anew. Hitler addressed a big crowd and again called for unity. Many who had once fought each other bitterly, shook hands. Since I loathed such public gestures, I had stayed away. I have always done whatever work seemed necessary at the time, but have always shunned anything that smacked of the theatrical.

Dietrich Eckart was gone. He had been arrested. The sudden collapse of the party and his confinement had aggravated an old liver ailment. To prevent his dying in jail, the government set him free. I heard about it—this was in the middle of December, 1924—and called on him late one night at the house where he had found shelter.

He was tired and shriveled, but his kind old smile returned when I offered words of encouragement. Later he returned to his beloved Berchtesgaden where he died on December 26.

The *Völkischer Beobachter*, our central organ, a daily, had exactly four editors, a few contributors, and practically no local representatives anywhere. It had to rely on occasional contributions from readers. This inevitably led to many careless words, complaints, and, by way of an occasional unjustified accusation, court actions.

As the legally responsible editor, I frequently had to shoulder the blame. Invariably this meant a few nerve-shattering hours in court, since I was held responsible for articles that I myself had not even written.

Usually there were fines which, as a matter of principle, I had to pay out of my own pocket, but which as a rule were refunded to me by the publisher.

Twice I was sentenced to jail for contempt of court. A National Socialist newspaper had started proceedings against someone. Shortly before the trial the editor telephoned the presiding judge to find out whether it was true that he had had supper with the attorney for the opposing party. Whereupon the newspaper was confiscated. The report reaching the *Völkischer Beobachter* said, in part, that this shamelessly wilful act would certainly find its sequel in court. The sequel for me was four weeks in jail. This sentence, combined with another, sent me to Stadelheim for six weeks. I was assigned to the cell which had been occupied some time before—for *lèse majesté*, I think—by Ludwig Thoma, and after that by Dietrich Eckart.

It was a little larger than the others, and boasted of huge opaque windows. In other words, it was one reserved for political miscreants. I was permitted to write, and got novels from the jail library, so that I managed to pass the time. But the memory of this solitary confinement has always been unpleasant.

That the National Socialists came to power legally, that a great revolution came about without civil war, barricades, guillotines, and so on, was our pride. Certainly, a few bloody local skirmishes did occur where enemies had lived side by side for years. I heard about some of these clashes without getting details; but they must have been infinitesimal in comparison to the huge upheaval.

Later on we heard that the former Social Democratic president of the *Reichstag* had resumed his job as a printer without being molested, that former Secretary of the Interior Severing was living quietly in Bielefeld and receiving his secretary's pension. Throughout all these years I never heard one word of protest against all that. On the contrary, only words of praise for the generous attitude of the Führer.

Hitler rarely came to my editorial offices; he traveled through the Reich a great deal to meet important people and to make speeches. Gradually he had surrounded himself with a small circle of companions who went with him on these trips, and to whom he had become accustomed.

Once I asked him to take me along, since there was danger of my getting out of touch with political reality in the regions beyond Bavaria if I had to spend all my time behind my desk. He promised, but never asked me to go along. We made only one journey to Berlin together, accompanied by Frau Ritter, a granddaughter of Richard Wagner's. I know that he kept me away intentionally. He probably couldn't forgive me for having decided against his expressed will upon our basic course after November, 1923, although he later agreed to our participation in the elections, permitted himself to be praised for these tactics, as supposedly invented by himself, and even claimed them as such.

He also knew that I had my own ideas about the inter-party strife of 1924, particularly concerning Esser,[44] Streicher, Dinter, and Hanfstängl.[45] Later on, he himself was forced to eliminate Esser from all political activities because of his obvious lack of ability, entrusting him instead with the management of the Central Bureau for Foreign Travel; he had to kick out Dinter and give Streicher a leave of absence.

Hanfstängl he treated so shabbily that he practically forced him to go abroad—something which even I, who hated Hanfstängl, had to admit was unworthy. A clean and clear-cut decision in 1925 would have saved us a lot of future trouble.

Occasionally I talked with Hitler in the restaurant Viktoria, since we both—I only temporarily—lived near the May Monument. But he was seldom at my office, so that, as far as the treatment of political themes in the *Völkischer Beobachter* was concerned, I had to rely upon my own judgment.

---

[44] Hermann Esser (1900–1981), editor of the *Völkischer Beobachter,* Reichstag member and in the early history of the NSDAP, a *de facto* deputy of Adolf Hitler.
[45] A reference to an early power struggle involving party members entangled with the Strasser brothers and the economically socialist "left wing" of the NSDAP.

Part Six:
The Myth of the Twentieth Century is Published

Christianity and National Socialism: *The Myth of the Twentieth Century*

At the focal point of all spiritual-psychological discussion stands Christianity, its personages, its relationship to the peoples and to the problems of our epoch.

Was my attitude wrong, then, in the face of existing realities, in the face of the dignity inherent in durable historic figures? Or possibly even harmful, perhaps because existing social ties really should be preserved in these days of great fermentation, in contrast to my own persistent opposition to the churches and Christian dogma?

As indicated in the beginning, a certain heretical attitude grew up in me quite early, particularly during the confirmation lessons. But it received its strongest impetus, as was the case with so many others, from Houston Stewart Chamberlain's *Grundlagen des 20. Jahrhunderts.*[46] The interminable discussions constantly carried on by European thinkers were a sign of inner truthfulness, that is, they were engaged in by genuine seekers of the truth.

Nor is it important whether these people merely wanted to go back to the simple evangelical teachings, or whether, as scientists, they declined to accept the entire edifice of dogma.

What is important and significant is their attitude as such, which ties the Albigensian Count de Foix to Luther, Goethe, and Lagarde. And even though Protestant believers, together with the Roman Church, have done their best to brush aside the following paragraphs as superficial rationalism, Copernicus' discovery still spells the end of

[46] "The Foundations of the 20th Century," first published in 1899.

the creed. The theological opponents of my *Mythus*[47] have attacked me with all the weapons of antiquated dialectics. They have discovered ten single errors; I would be more than happy to admit others. The work was conceived during a busy time of political strife without the aid of a comprehensive card index. So memory misled me in connection with some historical dates; and the description of one incident or the other may also permit of a different interpretation than the one I gave.

Besides, I frequently used drastic adjectives that simply had to hurt. In my old age I half intended to revise my *Mythus,* eliminating everything time-conditioned in order to strengthen its basic concept. But the more I search my heart, the less reason I can find for retracting anything.

Since then the problem of Christianity has interested me. On a hike I came to the Monastery Ettal and looked over its church. Under the cupola I saw all around me, in glass showcases, skeletons clad in brocade gowns. On the skulls, bishops' mitres and abbots' caps; rings on the bony fingers. I hardly trusted my eyes and asked myself whether I was in Europe or somewhere in Tibet or Africa.

A few days later I looked over the church on the Fraueninsel in the Chiemsee. Just as I passed a confessional, a blond peasant lad of about twenty, and more than six feet tall, fell on his knees next to me and propelled himself toward the confessional three feet away to start his whispering.

And then I asked myself: Is that what you have turned a proud people into, that it no longer understands the indignity of such an act?

After I had left the monastery church at Ettal, I sat down at a wooden table in front of an inn across the road. Next to me sat a big, strong peasant with his little son whose nose hardly reached above the table top. The peasant drank his measure of beer, cut off huge pieces

[47] A reference to Alfred Rosenberg's most important book, *The Myth of the Twentieth Century* ("Der Mythus des 20. Jahrhunderts"), first published in 1930. Regarded as the second most important book to come out of Nazi Germany, *Mythus* is a philosophical and political map which outlines the ideological background to the Nazi Party and maps out how that party viewed society, other races, social ordering, religion, art, aesthetics and the structure of the state. The "Mythus" to which Rosenberg refers was the concept of blood, which, according to the preface, "unchains the racial world-revolution." Rosenberg's no-hold barred depiction of the history of Christianity earned it the accusation that it was anti-Christian, and that controversy overshadowed the most interesting sections of the book which deal with the world racial situation and the demand for racially homogeneous states as the only method to preserve individual world cultures.

of sausage with his pocket knife, stuffed some of them into the boy's mouth, and also gave him a few sips of the liquid bread of Bavaria. This powerful, earthbound figure quieted me down a bit, but actually brought home to me what later became the content of my religious-philosophical treatise: the fateful interrelation between an Oriental cult of revelation, and the German peasantry. Two wars had brought them into contact—the first at the time of the peasant's growth, the second, when his old gods lay dying—and both sides have attempted to create a union.

The churches stirred Germanic ingredients into the acid of their own teachings, but they proved insoluble—harsh as the methods they used might be.

I have never used political power to undo my adversaries, though, after 1933, they made me the target of their harshest polemics. In my works I postulated that I was against all propaganda for leaving the Church, since Christianity is ennobled by the beliefs and the deaths of so many generations. Nobody can expect more tolerance. Basically, the National Socialist movement was obliged to be tolerant; but each single individual could claim for himself the identical freedom of conscience which the churches apparently consider their exclusive property.

Hitler's Concordat with the Vatican

In 1933, Hitler concluded the concordat with the Vatican. Though personally not a participant, I considered this treaty completely justified. I always differentiated between spiritual battles among individuals or institutions and churches, and the attitude dictated by reasons of state. I studied the text of the concordat carefully and, because of my heretic way of thinking, occasionally shook my head; but eventually I came to the conclusion that this was, after all, just as much of a compromise as the Four Power Pact[48] was, and as every foreign political treaty always will be.

I must confess, however, that I never bothered to learn in detail if and when the Führer broke this concordat, because I was aware of

---

[48] The Four-Power Pact, also known as a Quadripartite Agreement, was an international treaty signed on July 15, 1933, in Rome between representatives of Britain, France, Germany, and Italy. It was intended to ensure peace between the four nations and to facilitate the settlement of international disputes. The French parliament, then under the control of socialists, refused to ratify the agreement and it was never implemented.

the fact that, after the initial overwhelming revolutionary surge had passed, bishops had begun a rather remarkable counter-propaganda campaign against the basic laws of the new Reich by way of sermons as well as Episcopal letters. That they sorely missed their worldly arm, the Centrist Party, was quite obvious. Thus I was not particularly inclined to believe that the Führer had planned from the very beginning to break an agreement which, after all, had been made quite cold-bloodedly. The concordat was primarily intended to help break through the foreign moral-political boycott ring, and it would have been positively idiotic to make this newly gained success illusionary by breaking the concordat itself, an act which merely would have added new opponents to those already so numerous. I am unable to give an opinion on the beginning of the controversy.

Frank,[49] who is sitting next to me in the prisoners' dock,[50] is of the opinion that it was probably due to our own negligence, since he himself had gone to Rome for this very reason. In all likelihood—as I am forced to conclude now—it was here that Heydrich's[51] *Sicherheitspolizei*[52] intervened by following up Himmler's personal investigations. How far Heydrich went I don't know; but these Episcopal letters, following historical precedent, seemed to me no more than attempts on the part of a church no longer in power to stage a comeback in the guise of persecuted religion.

Publication of *Myth of the Twentieth Century* the Reason for Rosenberg's Exclusion from Hitler's first Cabinet

Be that as it may, if Hitler concluded the concordat for reasons of state, he simply had to overlook, for the same reasons, attacks in letters, occasional speeches by bishops, and so on. I had carefully refrained

---

[49] Hans Michael Frank (1900–1946), was Hitler's personal lawyer who was appointed Germany's chief jurist and after the war broke out, was appointed Governor-General of occupied Poland's 'General Government' territory.

[50] This manuscript was written while Rosenberg was on trial at Nuremberg.

[51] Reinhard Tristan Eugen Heydrich (1904–1942), SS-Obergruppenführer (General) and General der Polizei, chief of the Reich Main Security Office (including the Gestapo, Kripo, and SD) and *Stellvertretender Reichsprotektor* (Deputy/Acting Reich-Protector) of Bohemia and Moravia. Heydrich served as President of Interpol (the international law enforcement agency). He was assassinated by agents from the British intelligence services in Prague.

[52] *Sicherheitspolizei* or SiPo, which consisted of the Gestapo and the criminal police detective forces (Kriminalpolizei; Kripo), from 1936 until 1942.

from interfering with the execution of the concordat, conscious of the fact that, as looked upon from the perspective of high political expediency, I was somewhat of a burden to the movement.

True, I had given Hitler the manuscript of my *Mythus* before it went to press, had clearly characterized the book in its introduction as a personal confession, and did not have it brought out by the publisher of the party, but rather by an affiliated house.

However, it did have the effect of a bombshell on a heretofore completely secure Centrist Party. The Centrists knew full well that the Social Democrats had to rely on the prelates to remain in office. The German Nationalists, in turn, were hoping for a coming reorganization of a bourgeois regime which, again, could be accomplished only with the aid of the Centrists.

Thus both these parties were careful not to publicize either their atheistic or Protestant attitudes.

This apparently securely balanced situation was rudely shaken by the *Mythus,* particularly since I was no longer completely unknown; and such an open demand as this for the right to freely express an opinion at variance with the one accepted by the Church was considered nothing short of sacrilegious.

No use going into further details; all I want to say here is that I understand completely why the Führer did not add me to his cabinet. He was right, in spite of his promise that I was to join the *Auswärtige Amt*[53] as an Under-secretary of State, and to wait for developments from then on. In view of my position I never reminded the Führer of his promise.

Attacked by Christians

When the *Mythus* was published in October, 1930, it was greeted with enthusiastic applause on the one hand, and by extraordinary attacks on the other.

In Catholic regions doubts arose even in the ranks of the party. I told everyone that freedom of the spirit embraced not only the Catholic and Protestant confessions, but also such confessions as I had made, and pointed out in the personal, and thus non-party, aspects of the book.

---

[53] "Foreign Office."

The situation was particularly difficult for some of the Catholic clergymen who were in accord with quite a few of the social demands of the party. This was especially true for good old Abbot Schachleitner. He called the attention of several party functionaries to the fact that, in his opinion, I was endangering our entire movement.

Thereupon I wrote Hitler a letter asking him to ignore my person completely, and to dismiss me from the service of the party if this seemed desirable. He replied—if memory serves me correctly, on the same sheet of paper—that he wouldn't think of it. Thus the book made its way through edition after edition. By 1944, a million copies had been distributed.

Hans Schemm was a teacher totally under the spell of Bayreuth's music, and particularly, as I found out in 1924, of *Parsifal.* In 1933, he became Bavarian Secretary of Education, and started out on a consciously Christian course. His old motto, *"Our politics are Germany, our religion is Christ,"* was honorable; but in its official tone he went far beyond the tolerance agreed upon.

However, I do want to emphasize here that I never quarreled with Schemm, that I naturally granted him his freedom of conscience, just as I insisted upon the right to my own, and recognized that the new world we visualized could come into being only after a complete change of heart, something that certainly wasn't a matter of years but of generations.

Why the Führer permitted the Heydrichs to change our course by brute force, until pressure and counter-pressure were no longer distinguishable from each other, is a question which only the future may answer. True, there were reasons aplenty for defending our political and spiritual positions. I am not even thinking of the Center's participation in the November revolution, nor of the separatist activities indulged in by the head of the party, Prelate Doctor Kaas.

Actually I was much more upset by some of their public utterances, since these characterized the very essence of their entire attitude. At the Catholic Day at Constance, in 1923, it was said: Nationalism is the greatest heresy of our times, a statement which was later frequently repeated—at a time when Polish supernationalism was directed in the most vicious fashion against Germany—primarily by Catholic priests.

Another one came from Doctor Moenius, the editor of the *General Review*, a newspaper distributed in Bavarian schools, who wrote in his pamphlet, *Paris, the heart of France:* Catholicism will break the backbone of all Nationalism—a deliberate lie, considering Poland and Spain. What bearing this had on Germany was made clear by his dictum that the Catholic segment of the population was located like a pole in the flesh of the nation, and would make the formation of a nationalistic state completely unthinkable.

In this atmosphere Abbot Schachleitner who, in spite of his complete Catholic integrity, was a National Socialist *Gauleiter* (provincial leader) was forbidden to preach and read the mass; the deceased Catholic Gmeinder was denied a religious burial.

In 1933, Cardinal Faulhaber cancelled the interdict against Schachleitner who, in the meantime, had become a veritable focal point of veneration and who, after reading his first mass, was solemnly escorted home from his church by Storm trooper men. The *Völkischer Beobachter* published his picture, and also published the directives for Bavarian teachers by Schemm to preserve the Christian spirit in their teachings.

Joseph Wagner, *Gauleiter* of Bochum, and his family, were ardent Catholics who violently rejected my opinions on religion. Actually, as I learned, he was all for reducing my book to pulp.

For my part, I left Wagner thoroughly alone, and had absolutely no feeling of satisfaction when, for reasons unknown to me, he was later dismissed from his post under circumstances which proved that Hitler was already on a dangerous road.

Before some sort of *Reichsleiter*[54] or *Gauleiter*[55] conference, he read a letter of Wagner's (or of his wife's) in which he (or she) forbade their daughter to marry an S.S.-Leader because he wasn't a good enough Catholic. Hitler declared that, in spite of all his tolerance, he would not permit such intolerance. He dismissed Wagner from his post, leaving to further investigation the decision as to whether he should be permitted to remain a member of the party. That, to me, seemed a dubious procedure. The outcome of the investigation, carried on by six *Gauleiters*, was said to have been favorable to Wagner because Himmler had supposedly misinformed the Führer. So had Röver.[56]

---

[54] Reich leaders.

[55] Provincial leaders.

[56] Carl Georg Röver (1889–1942) was Gauleiter of Weser-Ems and Reichsstatthalter of Oldenburg/Bremen. Röver acted as Gauleiter in Oldenburg, which was already ruled by the NSDAP before January 1933. He is most famous for the so-called "Kwami affair"—an

Ley,[57] with his eternal, whining motto: *The Führer is always right,* was reported to have declared that the investigation was dragging on too long anyway, that the letter had been no more than a subterfuge, that the Führer had the right to appoint or dismiss as he pleased, and so on. Röver refused to convict. But the entire affair, though unknown to me in detail, was altogether unpleasant. Wagner, I believe, remained in the party and was assigned to some other post.

One man with whom I was always on comradely terms was the *Gauleiter* of Westphalia-North, Doctor Alfred Meyer, captain during the First World War, prisoner of war in France, laborer, and clerk in his native city. A National Socialist since 1923, he was the first National Socialist alderman in his Westphalian home town. Not the heavyset, broad-shouldered type, but a man of medium height, slender, dark-haired, with quiet blue eyes behind glasses. A cautious, thoughtful person who, although firm, never went to extremes, and who certainly led his Gau exemplarily.

It was his misfortune that his district was also the home of one of our bitterest enemies, Bishop Klemens August Count von Galen. Count van Galen, the future Cardinal, who died in 1946, shortly after he assumed the office conferred upon him in appreciation of his war against us, was one of those strong personalities whose choice of an ecclesiastical career had been due not only to tradition but also to the hope that he might rule some day.

In Münster each stone reminded him of one of his ancestors who had ground every damned heretic under his heel, and who was such a great warrior that even Louis XIV spoke of him with respect. This Prince of the Church was by no means quiet and scholarly, but enraged over the fact that he could no longer command bodies as well as souls.

Following the old tried-and-true method, he began to complain about persecution. Each tiny incident of these revolutionary times was put under a glaring spotlight; that a new generation, following the dictates of its own conscience, might think and act differently, was

---

incident sparked off by the church council of Oldenburg's decision to use the St. Lambert Church in that city for a sermon by the African Pastor Robert Kwami, who came from Togo. Röver demanded that the church council to cancel the sermon, but it proceeded as planned, earning considerable local and foreign media coverage. Röver died from a stroke in May 1942. Hitler attended his funeral and Alfred Rosenberg delivered the eulogy.

[57] Robert Ley (1890–1945), head of the German Labor Front (*Deutsche Arbeitsfront*, DAF) from 1933 to 1945. He committed suicide in custody rather than be subjected to the Nuremberg Trials.

blasphemy to him. Completely without a sense of humor, he faced a new world with gnashing teeth. When I was advertised in 1935 as one of the speakers at a Gau conference, he wrote a letter to the president of that Gau demanding that my speech be forbidden, since it would result in the persecution of Christians.

That was indeed an impudent challenge, but at least it threw light on his real attitude—an attitude which, if given power, is utterly unwilling to honor any other opinion but its own, and invariably calls upon the worldly arm of the Church to annihilate heretics, atheists, and so on. The Church, after all, is not so completely innocent of blame for what has happened in Germany. Unfortunately, the Himmler-Heydrich police answered this challenge, as has become clear in the meantime, in a most unworthy manner.

Interest in Cathars

On a trip to the Bretagne, I felt the desire to go even farther south, to the country of the Albigenses. The struggles and fate of this huge sect of the Cathars[58] had always interested me and, on closer acquaintance, moved me deeply.

A strange movement, combining the religious desire for freedom of will and character which was essentially West Gothic, with the late Iranian mysticism that had reached France by way of Italy after the crusaders had come in contact with the Orient. Since the Cathars, that is, the *pure ones*, wanted to remain Christians, they chose from among the various epistles that of John.

Against the religion of the worldly power of the Church of Peter they upheld the teachings of the Baraclete, the Merciful Savior and God of Mercy. They rejected the Old Testament, avoided the use of any and all Jewish names—a significant attitude, different from that of the later Calvinists and Puritans who also searched for the pure teachings—and shunned even the name of Mary. The crucifix to them appeared an unworthy symbol since, they claimed, nobody would venerate the

---

[58] Catharism (from the Greek "the pure ones") was a Christian dualist movement that thrived in some areas of Southern Europe, particularly northern Italy and southern France, between the 12th and 14th centuries. Cathar beliefs varied between communities because Catharism was initially taught by ascetic priests who had set few guidelines. The Cathars were a direct challenge to the Catholic Church, which denounced its practices and dismissed it outright as "the Church of Satan."

rope with which a human being, even though he be a martyr, had been hanged. They dedicated themselves to charity and taught religious tolerance, but did eventually introduce a certain social order with various religious ranks and deacons, and the saving consecration (*Consolmentum*) by the laying on of hands.

The former military chaplain, Müller, was appointed Reich Bishop. He had originally been a chaplain in the navy, and had later joined General Blomberg in East Prussia when the latter was military commander of that district. This appointment was, in a manner of speaking, a vote of confidence for the army.

To be sure, it soon became dubious whether or not he was the right person for the job. Little known, personally, he considered orthodox religious circles the opposition, and was later, without actually being demoted, treated rather shabbily by Church Secretary Kerrl.

Finally, the Führer himself definitely forbade any further attempts to help the Protestants organize, and simply let things drift. To bring about any sort of religious reform is one thing he never attempted. He always insisted that politics and the founding of religious organizations were two entirely different things. Besides, he added, our movement is too closely identified with the smell of beer and the rowdyism of tavern brawls. Nor can anyone breed a reformer by speeches and articles. If one exists, he will certainly call public attention to himself by growling and thundering.

At that time it was by no means true that the Wehrmacht was being seduced spiritually and religiously by the party, something that came about much later (under Himmler and Heydrich), and a goal toward which Bormann, as is obvious today, always steered.

Thanks to influences already mentioned, the situation was actually just the reverse. It was primarily the matter of Sunday church attendance that caused such bad blood, and which, handled as it was, left an unpleasant taste in my mouth. Those who later complained, perhaps with some justification, about religious intolerance, considered it their undeniable prerogative to order soldiers to attend church even though they were no longer communicants. That was considered part of their duties as soldiers.

Beliefs at variance with those of the two official confessions were not recognized, and anyone who protested against this attitude in the name of the very religious freedom that had once been upheld by the Protestants themselves, was subjected to all kinds of chicanery. Since most of the National Socialists were not church members, the reactivated reactionary officers who, as a matter of fact, really owed their promotions exclusively to the National Socialists, found revenge for their former political defeats by meting out particularly harsh treatment for our young men who had joined the Wehrmacht so enthusiastically. This attitude was perpetuated even during the 1920s by openly snubbing these young men whenever their name came up for promotion. I received many complaints, all of which I passed on to Hess.

In due time, and with great difficulty, we finally enforced a ruling that nobody was to be coerced into attending church. In retaliation, we learned the soldiers in question were made to scrub floors and perform other unpleasant duties. And in spite of an order forbidding these good Christians to persist in their chicanery, we kept on getting complaints. This was one of the causes of many future conflicts, as well as the springboard for Bormann's counteroffensive which eventually deprived the Wehrmacht of almost all right to any spiritual supervision of its members, an attitude quite as narrow-minded as that of the officers themselves.

The only point of view completely in accord with National Socialist theories would have been that of allowing every individual to seek and find religious consolation wherever he chose. Nobody should be forced to look for it among the existing confessions.

To uphold his own religious beliefs is up to the individual; neither political nor police power must ever be used for or against any given conviction. Adolf Hitler always supported this dictum and, as Field Marshal Keitel told me, rejected all of Bormann's attempts to interfere. The confessional staff of the Wehrmacht was to be kept intact at whatever strength was required, a rule that was observed to the very end.

An officer in whom I recognized an attitude in accordance with the finest Prussian tradition, a man I saw quite frequently, was the future General Field Marshal Hans von Kluge. I had met him during some of my visits to Westphalia. A medium-sized, erect man, with a high forehead, slightly curved nose, cold blue eyes. Reserved and generally sparing of words, but especially so with me. I knew, of course, that I wasn't held in particularly high esteem by the officers' corps; indeed, I could hardly expect anything else from such a religion-conditioned group. My *Mythus* had met with considerable disapproval. I know, for example, that copies of the collective attack made against me by the Roman Church (it was entitled *Studieste*) had been sent by the various bishoprics to all higher military posts in an effort to do away with me scientifically. But I want to make it clear, once and for all, that I never used my political position to prosecute those theological adversaries of mine.

Part Seven:
Race and Racial Theory

1939: Ordered by Hitler to Secure Unification of National Socialist Philosophy

At the end of 1939, the Führer accepted the suggestion that he give me a directive, addressed to party, state and Wehrmacht, to bring about and secure a unification of National Socialist philosophy.

Odd characters had attached themselves to our various branches, and the Reich Ministry of Education vacillated considerably. I wanted to bring about a firm though non-sectarian attitude. My appointment had been agreed upon. Then, suddenly, the Führer told me that Mussolini wanted to come into the war after all, and had asked him to do nothing at the moment that might aggravate the Church. My assuming office at this critical time would cause a great deal of disquiet. I agreed that under the circumstances my appointment would naturally have to be postponed.

Much would have been different if Hitler had also used these reasons of state in connection with others who merited such treatment much more than I did. But since his feeling for Goebbels and Himmler was stronger than it was for me, these two were able to do the most unbelievable things without being restrained.

Here, in this purely human soil, is the root of Adolf Hitler's great sins of omission which resulted in such ghastly consequences—that indefinable element of inconsistency, muddle-headedness, negligence and, in the long run, injustice that so frequently nullified his own considerations, plans, and activities.

What the police did was narrow-minded, sectarian, occasionally indecent. However, some day the churches themselves will be examined to determine whether their own behavior since 1918 has been in accordance with what a great fate expected of them.

Now that National Socialism lies prostrate, they have a new opportunity to gain respect and influence through active Christian charity, thus becoming a unifying force. Until then, any philosophical discussion must, needs be, relegated to the background. No matter what the respective spiritual positions may be, today, after the collapse, the time for a final showdown between opposing philosophies has certainly not yet arrived.

In their condemnation of a police regime, the churches ought to be careful not to condemn Himmler on such general charges as those our enemies fell back upon. In view of their own past, caution should be the watchword. Great philosophical changes need many generations to turn them into pulsating life. And even our present acres of death will someday bloom again.

Racial Respect Required between Races

I have explained in many speeches that the veneration of Germanic blood does not imply contempt for other races but, on the contrary, racial respect. Since races, as the core of nations, are created by nature, the very respect for nature itself demands respect for such creations.

The purpose of the large-scale development of peoples is the juridical recognition of racially conditioned families of people in their own homelands. Style, customs, language, are the manifestation of different souls and peoples; and just as these cannot be mixed without a resultant deterioration of their purity, so men, as their embodiment, and to whom they belong organically and spiritually, cannot intermingle.

The Jewish Question

These concepts met with world-wide opposition on the part of those who, perhaps originally influenced by the generous humanitarianism of the 18th century, simply did not have the courage to face the new discoveries, or feared that any corrective measure might affect their economic status.

The great questions concerning the fate of the both century could not be discussed calmly and deliberately because one problem barred the view—that of Jewry.

The Jewish question is as old as Jewry itself, and anti-Semitism has always been the answer whenever Jews have appeared on the scene, from Tacitus to Goethe, Schopenhauer, Wagner, and Dostoyevsky. In the Germany of 1911, they had all rights, and sat in important positions.

Anti-Semitism began with war profiteering; it grew with growing usury; and it became widespread after the revolt of November 9, 1918. Their being different was admitted by all Jews. Soldiers were greeted upon their return by the Jewish professor Gumbel with the declaration that their comrades had fallen on the field of dishonor. In a theatre financed by a Jewish millionaire, the *Stahlhelm* was trampled underfoot, while a poem with the refrain: *Dreck, weg damit!* (Filth, away with it!) was recited.

Just now the explosive news arriving from Palestine[59] is certainly not only sensational but actually provides new historical symbols.

At the end of the 18th century London had replaced Paris as the center of Jewish world politics. Great Britain has always been generous in her attitude toward Western Jewry, especially since the days of Edward VII.

During the First World War, it was in London that Palestine was promised to the Jews. Despite the protests of Lords Leamington, Islington, and Sydenham, London persisted in an attitude of extreme leniency toward Jewish demands.

The Jewish agency became the Supreme council of Western Jewry. It owed its existence to the political influence of the Zionist world organization under Professor Chaim Weizmann. Since liberal, orthodox, and many other Jews refused to join the Zionist movement, this Jewish agency was founded so that Weizmann could also take over, in a sort of personal union, the leadership of the non-Zionists.

Once the official executive was firmly entrenched in London, the conspiracy against England's position in the Orient started. Today the real center is probably in New York. Weizmann was opposed by a group of radicals under Vladimir Jabotinsky, the so-called revisionists, whose followers were almost exclusively recruited from Eastern Jewry. They demanded not merely Palestine but also Transjordania, and the expulsion of all Arabs from this living space which had been abandoned by the Jews more than two thousand years ago. Jabotinsky died.

[59] A reference to then ongoing Jewish terrorist Igrun attacks against the British overseers of Palestine, which included a large number of bombings and murders, part of the Zionist attempt to seize Palestine for Jewish settlement.

Jewish Terrorism in Palestine

Several terror groups were formed and continuously fed by illegal immigrants. Among others, the so-called Stern group whose members, in 1944, murdered the British Under-secretary for the Near East, Lord Moyne, in Cairo. Now they have apparently blown up British headquarters in Jerusalem.[60] In a speech he made early in 1920, in Jerusalem, Weizmann declared: *We told the authorities in London. We shall be in Palestine whether you want us there or not. But it would be better for you to want us, otherwise our constructive force will turn into a destructive one that will bring about ferment in the entire world.*

At the Congress in Karlsbad, a broken British promise might prove more costly than the upkeep of an army in Palestine. And on yet another occasion, the Jewish question was wandering like a shadow across the world and could turn into a tremendous force for its construction or destruction. What is happening in Palestine now is ample proof of a fact that cannot be overlooked: that good will and generosity towards proven historical arrogance can no longer do any good; that even the Jews' best friends are attacked with bombs to force them into endless compliance. The British Empire, which places us on trial, has had to do much more than we did in 1933.

The Christian churches correctly claim that they opposed the anti-Jewish laws. But here, too, it must be admitted that much of that was merely petty chicanery. Today Christianity claims that under its guidance such acts could not have taken place. Maybe so, providing you refuse to look at the past. The war against Jewry came about because an alien people on German soil arrogated the political and spiritual leadership of the country, and, believing itself triumphant, flaunted it brazenly.

Prediction of the Racial Dissolution of America

And yet, history does not stand still. The forces of life and blood exist and will be effective. The very state that today charges us with

---

[60] The King David Hotel bombing was an attack carried out on Monday July 22, 1946 by the Zionist terrorist army, the Irgun. The hotel was the British administrative headquarters for Palestine. 91 people of various nationalities were killed and 46 were injured. This reference by Rosenberg provides an accurate dating for his memoirs.

crimes against humanity, the United States of America, ought to listen with particular attentiveness to the theories of race and heredity if it wishes to preserve its power.

Fourteen million Negroes and mulattoes, four to five million Jews, the Japanese in the west, and the rest, are more than America can carry without endangering the heritage of her pioneers. But if the present generation fails to do something to elude the fate of someday having twenty-five million Negroes and mulattoes, ten million Jews and half-Jews in America, then a later generation will certainly be harsh in its judgment. The Americans will have to decide whether they want a white America or whether they want to make the choice of their President ever more a question of additional concessions toward mulattoisation.

In the latter case, the United States of America, in a few centuries, will go the way of Greece and Rome; and the Catholic Church, which even today has black bishops, will be the pacemaker. The day will come when the grandchildren of the present generation will be ashamed of the fact that we have been accused as criminals for having harbored a most noble thought, simply because of its deterioration in times of war through unworthy orders.

Study of Ancient India

India came first, Schröder, Böthlingk, Schlaginweit, Schack,[61] and so on. Everything concerning its philosophy and literature was dug up. Only then did I begin to comprehend the whole wealth of this culture, once so great: the aristocracy of its thoughts and the beauty of its poetry. I excerpted many volumes and kept the excerpts through all the years.

In 1943, when my house was bombed, I found a last half-torn page in the rubble. I picked it up and stuck it into my pocket. Now that, too, is gone.

Whenever I dreamed about a place of work for my declining years, I invariably considered the utilization of India's wisdom, and actually founded in Munich a research office for Indo-Germanic history.

A prominent historian had laid out an ambitious plan, and a four-volume edition of *Indien und der deutsche Geist* ("India and the

---

[61] Nikolaus Wilhelm Schröder (1721–1798), Otto von Böhtlingk (1815–1904), Emil Schlagintweit (1835–1904), and Adolf Friedrich, Graf von Schack (1815–1894), all famous German Orientalists, Sanskrit scholars, philologists and students of Far Eastern cultures.

Germanic spirit") was in preparation. Much had been started; but now everything has collapsed.

The basic theme upon which we built all our plans, however, was a philosophy of art. In Reval, I had finished an article begun at Shednya, on *Form und Formung* ("Form and Forming"), to prove a certain polarity between Greek and German styles. Here, a tangible, restrained greatness; there, a constant inner readiness, activity, and motion. These thoughts had been born out of the rejection of the current classic philosophy of aesthetic contemplation, a mere passive contemplation or conception of ideas. To me a certain willful mobility seemed the very core of all art and thus also its goal and purpose. Now I had to devote myself in all seriousness to a study of aesthetics.

Kant's *Kritik der Urteilskraft* ("Critique of the power of judgment"), Schiller's philosophical works, and Schopenhauer's dissertations, all had to be studied exhaustively. The latter was particularly important inasmuch as it was he who had introduced an entirely new concept of the will, almost diametrically opposed to what, until then, had been understood by that word. This led to the writing of a lengthy essay which, in a somewhat changed form, was later incorporated into the *Mythus*.

The Aesthetics of Art

I had come to regard our entire aesthetics of art in such a light that I explained their falseness by the fact that the majority of people were not artists themselves, and simply accepted the perfection of a completed Greek work of art as their criterion. But anyone who creates a work of art and, in doing so, feels within himself the glow, the excitement, the reality of his will, cannot possibly desire the spectator to experience nothing more than passive contemplation.

This one central idea led to all my studies on art and, beyond that, to the investigation of many other more general phenomena of life. That this particular field of my activities was least appreciated by the general public disappointed me a great deal. It was almost exclusively the polemic-historical part of my work that was read.

The fact that I had also evolved an entirely new philosophy of art opposed to classic aestheticism, as well as to some contemporary theories, was rarely discussed. All the public wanted to listen to was a polemic politician—never a man who looked upon life from the vantage point of art—the art of the eye. Since Europe adapted itself only gradually to a religion that came from abroad, art became the road to European piety. Without art, neither the chronicles of the Bible nor the passion of Jesus of Nazareth nor, particularly, any of that welter of dogma would have survived. If all the confessors were taken on face value, and everything contributed to Christianity by the souls of the European peoples were eliminated, little would be left but the story of a noble man who, once upon a time, had been crushed by the might of Palestinian hatred.

Christianity Aids and Abets Miscegenation

In their whining against nationalistic and racial prejudices, even the zealots live on the artistic soul of these peoples, on the symbolic force of their five senses that appeared simultaneously with the appearance of their blood; and they would perish if the mulattoization of the world, aided and abetted by Christianity, were to become a fact.

Never will a Hottentot, believer though he may be, build cathedrals; never will a Negro write a Fifth Symphony, nor even understand it. And it is actually unfair to expect it of them.

Is religion self-assertion or self-negation? Gottschalk and Eckehart, Goethe and Lagarde believed the first to be true, while Paul and Ignatius, Gregor VII and Pius IX taught the second.

Once upon a time it was possible to house the Royal Rider in the Cathedral at Bamberg; but the spiritual flagellantism rampant since the Council of Trent has ostracized him.

Luther was still able to call God a fortress; but the confessors of today have fallen back on the sentimental revelations of the Eastern Mediterranean. Whether to see our inner self (the precise translation of India's Ãtman) as an image of God or as a sinful depravity is a question that cannot be answered by Christian dogma.

Race and Racial History

It would have been sentimental to have expected quick recognition abroad of the National Socialist revolution and its social aims. On the contrary, we were prepared for bitter criticism, but all this whipped-up enmity was anything but natural. Primarily, it was directed against something that serious historians had exhaustively studied for decades—racial questions and racial history.

At this point I should like to make a sharp differentiation between scientific conclusions and their practical application to political life, since these two aspects of the problem must, needs be, measured by entirely different yardsticks.

Few deny that different races do exist. But this in itself means that something constant exists, something characteristic which indicates that a certain individual belongs to a certain race; otherwise it would be altogether impossible to speak of racial unity or of races as such. This, in turn, presupposes the existence of certain laws of inheritance, regardless of how these laws may be formulated in detail.

However, under close scrutiny, the division into races according to the color of skin turns out to be quite the crudest and most obvious method, since there are noticeably inheritable characteristic racial differences among people of identically colored skins.

Basically, the recognition of the existence of a race—meaning a type of man who has inherited and preserved certain definite characteristics—is no more than the recognition of a law of nature, a law not made by man and, at first only dimly perceived, but later positively recognized, and finally scientifically proven during the 19th century.

Today the acknowledged existence of this law is just as completely independent of the fact that it is rejected by some circles as was once the general acceptance of the theory that the earth turns around the sun, discomforting though that great truth may have been to some institutions at the time.

The final recognition of lawful occurrences in nature, however, is in itself awe-inspiring.

In some of my speeches I have put it like this: The recognition of race as a fact demands not racial contempt but racial respect. Unfortunately, the close proximity of two races at a time when the basic truth of that law had just been accepted, made for comparisons and disputes. And it was because of this that certain sections of the people rejected not only comparisons but also the truth itself.

Even though the study of the problem is by no means finished, it is an established fact that all the peoples of Europe belong to one or the other of the five or six basic racial types indigenous to the European continent. These basic types are represented in varying strength, and the preponderance of one or the other lends a given nation the characteristics of its temperament, ideals of beauty, and style of life. Thus the Mediterranean type is dominant in Spain, the Dinaric type among the Serbs, the Nordic type among the Germans and the English.

Races have basic traits and possibilities; peoples, on the other hand, are realities resulting from political fate, language, and nature. This means that nowhere in our historical life is a race identical with a people. The act of becoming a people is a long, rather mysterious process in which inner attitude, outward pressure and spiritual desire gradually begin to form the picture of a unified culture. That, too, is a law of nature, and as such worthy of our respect.

Few have expressed this as beautifully as Herder;[62] but it was Lagarde[63] who coined this immortal phrase: *Peoples are the thoughts of God.* It was fated, no doubt, that peoples should always be welded together by competition and battle.

There is no exception to that rule in this world. In the midst of battle each one of these peoples became conscious of itself, and was confronted with that basic question of fate, the metaphysics of religion. It is not particularly surprising that, as far as the peoples of Europe are concerned, many individual or collective intermediary stages can be established.

Since European peoples are related to each other, they have often been assimilated, like the Huguenots in Prussia, many Alsatians in France, and others on the eastern borders of the Reich. Nevertheless it is the desire of all nations to preserve whatever they have made their own—their mode of life, the forms of their art and their conception of fate—to preserve these by means of conscious training, education, and living example.

However, these remarks have led me further afield than I had intended to go. What impressed me most, conditioned as I was by a trained eye and the teachings of many thinkers, was the shape, or rather the shapes, of life. Two things helped open my eyes, my drawing and the study of Indian philosophy.

In India I was certain I could see shape from within. The hymns

[62] Johann Gottfried von Herder (1744–1803), a philosopher, poet, and literary critic. He is associated with the periods of Enlightenment, Sturm und Drang, and Weimar Classicism.
[63] Claude François Chauveau-Lagarde (1756–1841), a famous French lawyer who won renown for his skillful legal representations during and after the period of the French Revolution.

of the Rig-Veda—the times of Aryan emigration, the Ãtman cult—the great spiritual pause for breath after the many battles with the outside world. The multiplicity of systems—our being made uncertain by the intermingling of races. Then many important details—thinkers, poets.

But diminishing size automatically causes a shrinking of inner shape. In other words, the people participating in this process were not always complementary to each other, or at least capable of living harmoniously side by side, but were completely antagonistic. The organic life circle of both the Aryan Hindus and the natives had been broken.

Since the former were in the minority, their shape, their blood with a very few exceptions—was absorbed; but since they had ruled for a long time, their thoughts and their creations were frequently taken over, though not understood, and, therefore, distorted to the point where now they often represent the very opposite of what they originally stood for.

Racial Theory and Science

When I took up this chain of thought, I knew little about modern biology. My starting point was my own artistic experience. I didn't read Günther's[64] books until years later.

It was he, however, who gave me, and all of us, new, sharper eyes. Even in the multiplicity, that was the European norm, we could now conscientiously study people in their various interrelations.

This was a discovery that couldn't be ignored any longer, irrespective of what conclusions we might arrive at. If opponents of these truths were confronted with similar biological facts paralleled in animal breeding, they would invariably counter with the disgusted claim that, after all, human beings certainly could not be pure-bred like dogs or horses, an answer which is a combination of truth and falsehood.

To begin with, nobody will deny that among dogs and horses certain races are fit only for certain tasks, that some crossbreeds turn out well while others are unfit for any kind of work.

---

[64] Hans Friedrich Karl Günther (1891–1968), one of Germany's foremost racial scientists who taught at the universities of Jena, Berlin, and Freiburg, writing numerous books and essays on racial theory. His most famous work in English is *The Racial Elements of European History.*

But this means that outside of the purely physical elements, something else plays a part which may sometimes intensify or complement a certain characteristic trait, and at other times mar or even destroy it. The contempt for animals is based on a purely religious limitation; the same great laws of nature govern the animals as well as plants and man. It is permissible, however, to claim that the animal has something a plant does not have, while man has certain faculties that reach far beyond those of the animal. And here lies the justification for the above rejection. It is, indeed, impossible for psychological reasons to breed human beings artificially for the purpose of long-term observation.

But, and this is decisive, the history of the peoples known to us must be looked upon as the great experiment of life itself, and to interpret that requires not only the services of philologists but of men who have an eye for the symptomatic, that is, for the totality of the outward and inward shapes of art, religion and life itself.

These were approximately the points of departure from which *The Myth of the Twentieth Century* was written, although I had not planned it so. In 1917, I began to put ideas down on paper simply to clarify this or that in my own mind. I continued my studies in Munich for the benefit of my own education; but all the basic thoughts in what I later said or wrote go back to these years.

Only gradually did the book grow around a focal point; its contents as well as its arrangement were the result of detailed study. That focal point around which it grew, however, was my preoccupation with the shapes in art. What I attempted to do was to sketch these shapes and values in bold, simple outlines, and to lead on from there to the interrelationship between the world of Europe and its total inheritance. In the third volume I came to some conclusions and made some suggestions by analyzing a necessarily time-conditioned cross-section of the actual political situation, fully aware of the fact, however, that all this could be of only temporary value.

The fact that certain maladies can be inherited is not denied by anybody, nor does any serious scholar question the inheritability of racial attributes. Since Mendel's discoveries have been made twice over again, quite independently of his findings, only conscious mendacity could possibly deny the above facts.

But just as with Copernicus and his discovery, Christianity and other teachings need a long time to immunize their adherents.

First the significance of racial ideas as a unity of body, soul, and spirit is denied; then its application to thinking and acting is attacked as running counter to Christian revelation, while zealous Jesuit biologists are busily trying to find a way to remove the poison from this new danger.

Then unproven claims are discovered, a certain plausibility in its purely physiological aspects is admitted, while other conclusions are rejected as being the same old materialistic arguments.

Finally fanaticism—yes, among Jesuits!—and even a dissolution of national unity is feared. In the long run, it is hoped, this mutation will destroy the entire scientific structure—and a great discovery is talked to death, so that after a hundred years or so, all danger to the broad masses of adherents (confessional church, Catholic believers, citizens of the world, and the rest) seems eliminated and, thanks to the deterioration of character, the hypnotizing of spirit, and the paralyzing of instinct, truth no longer is recognizable.

But a scientific discovery simply cannot be cancelled out. Just as the great figures of national cultures were able to preserve Protestant freedom of conscience through research, while the Renaissance and humanism removed it from the influence of rigid confessional dogma, so the 19th century led to million-fold dissension and a basic atheism. I had come to the conclusion that a reunification of these millions was more than desirable.

The discovery of the strength of blood in world history, that is, the recognition of fate as predestined by body and soul, seemed to me a most appropriate approach to the conquest of purely materialistic, pseudo-Darwinistic Marxism.

Encouraged by Houston Stewart Chamberlain, I found in the old Hindu philosophers, as well as in Greek sculpture, a parallelism between outer decay and inner distortion. This was the real inspiration for the *Mythus.*

The cultural tragedy of Hellenism (and Romanism) has been described often enough. Many causes have been noted. But outside of the acknowledged causes (tribal strife, wars among cities, migration to the colonies), there were still others: deforestation and its consequences, the diminishing of arable land, the drift to the cities and, most important of all, the intermingling of the Greeks with alien peoples from Asia Minor.

This law of life governs all ages. The half-breeds of Marseilles and Toulon spread the same seeds of disease as those of Corinth and Salonika in days gone by. The port quarters of London and the slums of New York both harbor the same sinister forces. Mulattoisation is on the cards for the United States of America; the colonies are a jumble of whites, Malayans, Hindus, Chinese, and South Sea tribes.

Part Eight:
Policy Considerations

Euthanasia Program: Justified but Badly Implemented

Petric Christianity ruled Rome; Paul's was Dominant in Luther; and John's, truly representative of charity, led a third-rate existence, usually only as a means of assuring the continued rule of the other two; and this despite the very real devotion of those in subordinate positions who nursed the sick and wounded (but also the insane, the alcoholics, and the paralytics).

Here philosophies collided in the most ominous fashion. The Reich had to raise about one billion marks per year for the care of incurables. Ten thousand healthy women gave their lives to the service of such incurables, either under Roman Catholic discipline, because of threatening unemployment, or in a spirit of self-sacrifice. Was it humane to keep these wrecks alive?

The tendency of the entire modern world was to answer No, while the Christian churches replied with a very emphatic Yes. The human spirit, they maintained, was alive even in the insane, and the will of God must never be interfered with. The power of Christian charity found its truest expression in caring for the sick.

During the war, as has been found out recently, the Führer took such radical steps that the outside world disregarded all existing psychological justification and characterized the entire procedure as murder. Like so many other unfortunate things that happened, these actions had been kept a carefully guarded secret. I and, no doubt, many others had heard of an order given to Bouhler[65] to introduce euthanasia,

---

[65] Philipp Bouhler (1899–1945) Chief of the Reichschancellery, charged by Hitler with setting up the Aktion T4 euthanasia program after a German father had appealed directly to Hitler to grant his legless, armless, blind and retarded daughter a mercy death. The program was extended across Germany in specially-convened Eugenic courts. After the war, it was incorrectly claimed that a quarter of a million handicapped people had been granted mercy

but only under the supervision of medical organizations. Whether it was to be carried out at the direct order of the Führer and with the consent of the families involved, and to what extent it would go—all this was exceedingly vague. Then we heard about clerical protests being made in sermons and ecclesiastical letters. At that time rumor had it that after the insane would come the aged and the wounded. But I, and those who told me, considered this merely malevolent gossip. Then again it was rumored that the Führer had canceled these orders.

Before the outbreak of the war this problem was openly discussed in the film *Ich Klage An!* ("I accuse!") Both sides were represented. If a government had come to the conclusion that it was in the interest of humaneness and the nation's future that euthanasia be resorted to in some cases, this should have been openly discussed with all its pros and cons.

After listening to all arguments, and after frank discussions with the families concerned, a law passed over the objections of those who opposed it as a matter of principle need not have caused that miserable awareness of having been lied to which apparently resulted from the manner in which the measure actually was carried out.

In my *Mythus* I openly demanded that medical steps be taken for the protection of public health. Now this sound, humane idea has been falsified and polluted to such an extent that any discussion of it is put simply beyond the pale by the one word "murder." However, the problem is there just the same; when the clouds have passed, life itself will once again confront the people and demand an answer.

And then I shall take the same stand as before, namely, that it is humane to consign the soulless husk of man to the earth, and to prevent the congenitally sick from passing on their illness to hapless children. This, however, requires absolute frankness, open discussion, and the spiritual participation of the entire people, as well as precise legal provisions to prevent any possible abuse.

And, most of all, the voluntary consent of the family involved. If the family should fail to agree, it should be compelled to provide the necessary nursing personnel from among its own members.

Otherwise refusal would be entirely too easy, and would simply burden others with painful obligations.

---

deaths under the program, but the official records showed that only a few thousand were involved. Bouhler committed suicide while in a U.S. internment camp.

Any measure of this sort would bring about heated discussion, but would, by being open and aboveboard, prevent the onset of that bad odor which now prevails. This is yet another instance of a law of life being distorted and falsified by the method of its execution.

Democracy and Form of Government

The necessary criticism by a new order of discarded political forms similar to those yet prevailing among other peoples, is invariably considered by the latter as a personal attack.

Since it was impossible to make the mental reservation that whenever the parliamentary system was mentioned, it meant Germany's own parliamentary system, many people abroad were under the impression that we were attacking their institutions. I tried repeatedly to prevent this but, it must be confessed, not even I always remembered to make the above reservation. Before foreign audiences, however, I made every effort to clarify the situation.

Prompted by similar considerations, Hitler said at one time that his goal was really a Germanic democracy in contrast to the spineless international one that, in 1918, had taken over the helm in Germany.

Speaking to representatives of the Scandinavian countries and Finland at a meeting of the Nordic Society in Lübeck, I specifically pointed out the differences in the meaning of identical words, and cited Hitler's own statement as an example. Before diplomats and representatives of the foreign press I also tried to prove that mere philosophical differences must never be permitted to lead to open conflict in the field of foreign policy. I declared myself opposed to the use of the term National Socialist by political parties in foreign countries, even though they might have similar objectives. It was impossible, I declared, to change the name of a whole historical complex suddenly and unilaterally. This might result in national tension. Who, in that case, would decide which National Socialism was the right one and which the wrong?

Oswald Mosley's Mistake in Choosing the Word "Fascist"

For the same reason I also considered it a grave mistake for Sir Oswald Mosley to call his party British Fascist. In a country as justifiably proud of her own tradition as England, it was a grave psychological error to use a nomenclature of foreign origin for a party which, incidentally, was certainly not cut to the measure of British life (for example, in its hierarchic-theatrical aspects).

At the same time, such a movement thus deprived itself of all moral elbow room in case of a conflict with Italy. This had already become apparent during the Italian Ethiopian war, when Great Britain took a pronouncedly anti-Italian stand, probably with the support of the majority of her people.

In this event Mosley's party, even though it stood for British interests exclusively—something that can be taken for granted—could scarcely go into opposition without becoming suspect of some sort of connection with Mussolini's Fascism. This in itself discredited the party from the very first, and certainly limited its political freedom of action.

For similar reasons, any active attempt on Mosley's part to aid in bringing about a German-British rapprochement, still keeping only British interests in mind, would have been burdened by the same political mortgage.

That's why I avoided any contact with Mosley and his crowd during my two visits to London in 1931 and 1933, and why I never got to know him personally.

Nevertheless, the foundation of parties similar to the National Socialists was oil on the fire of the existing propaganda against us, since it was considered an indication that the National Socialists proposed to gain a foothold in all foreign countries, and thus to influence their development from the outside. In the course of time this caused one misunderstanding after another, although these misunderstandings were most often due to the mental attitude of non-Germans. The various democracies considered themselves justified in propagating their principles throughout the world, and for this reason came consciously or unconsciously to the conclusion that National Socialism, like Marxism, proposed to organize branches among foreign peoples.

This misconception could not be eradicated, and was nursed with special care by those who were opposed to a friendship with the German Reich anyway.

That all nations should defend themselves against new, unproved ideas, and refuse in particular to take over institutions already existing in other states, is not only their right but their duty. If such technical or social institutions eventually prove their value, they may still, after thorough examination, be taken over in whatever form seems most fitting for other nations.

Foreign Translations of *Myth of the Twentieth Century*

In this connection I should like to mention that I received many proposals for the translation of my book into foreign languages. I turned them all down.

Only a Japanese translation was published without—so far as I remember—my permission. However, for Japan the contents of my *Mythus* were no more than a scientific curiosity anyway.

In 1942, I was sent a French translation. Though I had it thoroughly checked, I was still hesitant to agree to its publication. An Italian translation would no doubt have been subject to sharp attacks by the Church; and no prominent personality would have dared come to my defense.

Its publication could only have inspired scientific, and possibly even political, controversies in alien cultural circles which, if they themselves had produced a similar critique, would have done so for entirely different reasons.

I have always considered this attitude of mine as both spiritually and politically correct as well as rather decent, especially since it was at variance with a literary vanity that would like to see a book translated into as many languages as possible. Permission was given only for the translation of some of my speeches on more general subjects, but I never bothered to find out whether they actually were translated or not.

The Nordic Society

In later years Heinrich Löhse,[66] the son of Holstein peasants, told me repeatedly that it was from me that he had first heard details about Hitler, his speeches, the Feldherrnhalle and our program. The

---

[66] Hinrich Lohse (1896–1964), later president of the state of Schleswig-Holstein, served as "Reichskommissar for the Ostland" (the Baltic states was a Nazi German politician, best known for his rule of the Baltic states during World War II.

decision he made that day at Weimar was final. So he went to call on his hard-headed, mistrustful peasants who, like those in Oldenburg, were constantly up in arms against any name that contained the world Socialist. It took a long time to break down their resistance, but he did finally succeed. Löhse was a man of natural shrewdness and of unusually sound instincts. Unfortunately, he was often stubborn about completely unimportant things. And since stubbornness can so easily turn into bitter enmity, it was frequently difficult to guide him by mail. Just an average man, with all his good qualities, but also his drawbacks.

During our battle I was frequently up there. When the *Nordische Gesellschaft*[67] held its yearly meetings in Lübeck, and this city was assigned to Löhse's Gau, closer cooperation was inevitable. Our joint labours were made easier by our mutual enthusiasm for a better understanding between the Reich and Scandinavia (including Finland).

It gave me a great deal of satisfaction to foster cultural understanding between the Reich and Scandinavia (with Finland). Later on we invited Scandinavian scientists and artists to Germany. The magazine *Der Norden*[68] (The North) gave the German public reports on occurrences in the northern states, and a press syndicate contributed its share to the improvement of economic relations. All of this has now been held against me as some sort of conspiracy!

Martin Mutschmann and Saxony

Martin Mutschmann, the *Gauleiter* of Saxony, I had already met in 1923, on our first Party day. After listening to my speech, he told me that he had immediately said to himself: *This is my man!* When he moved to Dresden after the *Machtübernahme*,[69] his long-drawn-out war against Berlin, against such hydrocephalic characters as Schacht, began in all seriousness.

Unfortunately his rough manner of speaking, his blustering criticisms voiced at *Gauleiter* meetings, caused the Führer to rule out all public discussion on such occasions. Devoted to the Muses only as

---

[67] The *Nordische Gesellschaft* ("Nordic Society") was an association formed in 1921, with the objective of strengthening German-Nordic cultural and political cooperation. After 1933, Rosenberg became its leader and Heinrich Himmler became a member of the board.

[68] "The North"—of one the official publications of the *Nordische Gesellschaft*.

[69] The "Taking of Power"—a reference to the January 1933 appointment of Hitler as Chancellor of Germany.

a matter of duty, Mutschmann preferred to hunt in his woods. In the homes of Saxony's huntsmen he really could relax after a strenuous week of work. He installed trout hatcheries, practiced pistol shooting, and entertained frequently.

I always got along with this roughneck, and our comradeship lasted to the end. Of course, if we had been in constant close contact, clashes no doubt would have occurred. His ministers certainly didn't have an easy time of it. He hated petty intrigue so much that he never made long-winded attempts at conciliation; he simply threw the intrigants out of his office. His Kreisleiter[70] were as much in awe of him as officials had once been in awe of the late lamented King August the Strong. But like all these husky men he had a soft heart, and could be a good-natured, devoted friend. During the last few years he found an educational field very much to his own taste. He discovered that in humorous magazines, operettas, and comedies, Saxonians always came off second best.

In view of their great accomplishments he was honestly enraged by that. He considered it inadmissible to depict an entire tribe as dim-witted and idiotic just to amuse the public. Thus, he forbade any performances of the *Raub der Sabinerinnen*[71] in the Kingdom of Saxony. The dialect, frequently the target of both good and bad jokes, wasn't Saxonian at all, he claimed, but merely a bad habit of Leipzig. In the Vogtland, another district of Saxony, for example, they talked quiet differently. I thought his *pronunciamento* sounded rather like that bad Leipzig habit, but held my tongue. There are things, after all, that can hurt even though they may be funny.

Later on Mutschmann actually started a series of courses in diction to help his fellow Saxonians to get rid of their dialect. Whether he was successful or not, I am unable to say. Mutschmann was one of the most embittered enemies of Himmler's police system and carried on a sustained feud with all of the higher S.S. and police officials. His sound instinct warned him that there was great danger for both party and state in this direction. I counted on him as a partner in the future battle for party reforms.

I was Mutschmann's guest at the Grillenburg (Cricket Castle), the hunter's home near Dresden, on three different occasions, the last

---

[70] Regional district leaders.

[71] A comical-farce named after the classic Roman era tale of the "Rape of the Sabine Women" by Franz and Paul of Schönthan, which premiered in 1884.

being when the Red troops were already in Silesia. And it was then that we met for the last time in our lives. When we were taken from all corners of Germany to Mondorf, we kept asking each other about the fate of the others. Of Mutschmann I heard that he had stayed in hiding after the Soviets had marched in, but was later betrayed. When he was captured they tore off his clothes and stood him up naked on the base of a monument, where he was forced to remain all night, surrounded by the howls of the Communists. Then Mutschmann (who had a severe heart condition) suffered a stroke and died.[72]

---

[72] Rosenberg had been misinformed about Mutschmann's fate. In fact, he had been arrested by the Soviets on May 7, 1945. Taken to Moscow and put on trial in a Soviet court, Mutschman was sentenced to death and executed by firing squad in 1947.

Part Nine:
Internal Party Conflicts

Alfred Meyer and Westphalia-North

Doctor Alfred Meyer[73] liked good manners and ceremonies. Whenever an official visitor came to Münster, the heads of the party, state, and city council forgathered in the venerable great hall of the *Rathaus*.[74] There, after appropriate speeches of welcome, a huge old goblet was handed around for a drink of welcome.

Later, when in answer to a personal declaration of war against me by Bishop Galen, I was made an honorary citizen of Münster, this was turned into a particularly solemn affair. The official certificate itself was of the finest parchment, encased in a magnificent leather folder with beautifully wrought metal clasps. Meyer esteemed me very highly, always addressed me as *Reichsleiter*, and considered himself as holding no more than an intermediary position.

His absolute loyalty gained him innumerable friends. For this reason he was not considered among the power grabbers of the party to be a great *Gauleiter*, and for this same reason he was certainly one of the best. I believe that he was particularly well esteemed in his own Westphalia. In the evening, after a speech, we would sit around in the Ratskeller,[75] and the lanky Oberbürgermeister[76] would invariably assure me that Münster had only two honorary citizens: the Führer and myself.

Or else we went to some inn. To Pinkus Müller's,[77] for example, where we imbibed mightily at the massive oaken tables in his smoke-

---

[73] *Gauleiter* of Westphalia-North.

[74] "City Hall."

[75] Cellar restaurant.

[76] Lord Mayor.

[77] Pinkus Müller, one of the only original remaining breweries and beer halls in the town of Münster. First opened in 1816, and still operational to the present day.

filled rooms. Sometimes Pinkus[78] himself would give us a rousing song befitting the occasion. Drinkers and card players can enjoy themselves like children, listening to the same old jokes. Meyer used to praise his national drink, Steinhäger, to the blue skies. Not liquor, he claimed, but medicine.

And occasionally the old story was told again, about the sermon of the pastor of Steinhagen who announced the death of a fellow citizen with these words: It has pleased the Lord to take unto himself yet another Steinhidger.

The Strasser Brothers and Conflict within the Party

Gregor Strasser was a huge and powerful man, forthright, gifted with a keen mind, anxious to gain prestige, and a very popular speaker. Intellectually, his younger brother, Otto Strasser, has not been without influence on him.

The latter also joined the party. Together they founded the *Kampf Verlag,* and published a number of weeklies in Berlin. That is where the trouble started. Goebbels, the local *Gauleiter*, demanded political control over all publications appearing in his district; Strasser underscored his superior position as *Reichsorganizationsleiter.*[79]

Rumors made the rounds that Goebbels had told some people that Strasser's mother was Jewish. I wrote Hitler, who happened to be in Berlin at the time, that such underhanded methods were insufferable, and that Goebbels ought to be dismissed. Hitler told me later that the various gentlemen would simply have to cooperate, and that he, personally, would straighten things out.

In due time a formal reconciliation came about, but the feud kept on smoldering. Outwardly, Strasser's power seemed to grow greater and greater. He had built up his leadership of the organizational program to the point where he took care of almost all the current business for the entire party. His office at the former Reichsadler was practically an independent unit.

Otto Strasser came over to us from the camp of the Social Democrats, after having had close contacts with its leaders. I felt that he was less interested in following the party line of the National Socialist German

---

[78] A descendant of the original founder of the brewery, Johannes Müller (1792–1870).
[79] Organizational Leader of the Reich.

Workers' Party than in propagating certain undigested ideas of his own. When he told me that he considered an entirely new economic structure of paramount importance, I replied that it wasn't sufficient to write a number of articles; what he should do was write a well-rounded, carefully thought-out book to give people a chance to study his ideas. This he did not do.

The conflict came in spite of the fact that Hitler did his utmost to hold Strasser. Together with some of his followers, he seceded from the party. His brother Gregor remained. I still remember a discussion I had with Hitler a little later. Thank God, he said, that Gregor Strasser has remained true, a great thing for all of us. He was genuinely fond of him, even as Gregor Strasser proved his own brotherly love for Hitler by consoling him when his niece died and the Führer was considering giving up his entire political career.[80]

Strasser had been joined by another rather outstanding personality, the former First Lieutenant Schulz, who had a great number of contacts among officers and officials. In Berlin, Cologne, and so on, he introduced Strasser to them.

These people flattered Strasser in the hope of eventually making him the leader of a more acceptable party in case of a change in the form of government. And that was where Strasser's tragedy began. He felt that he wasn't consulted often enough, that Göring and Goebbels were pushed to the fore, and he was by no means convinced of the latter's ability—quite the contrary. Thus he took steps behind the Leader's back that were simply criminally stupid. Rumors about Strasser's betrayal began to make the rounds. But when I heard them, I frankly doubted them.

I ran into Strasser that forenoon when I arrived in Hitler's anteroom at the Hotel Kaiserhof.[81] I started to greet him, but he merely made a hopeless gesture with his hand and left the room. I heard that he had just resigned from all of his posts. That was a heavy blow. I remembered the many speeches which he had always brought to a close with these

---

[80] Angela Maria "Geli" Raubal (1908–1931) was Adolf Hitler's half-niece. When she enrolled at college in Munich in 1930, she stayed at Hitler's apartment in the city. After breaking up with a boyfriend, she committed suicide in her room at Hitler's residence. Hitler, in the middle of a major election campaign, was devastated and nearly quit politics. Many utterly false legends have grown up around Geli's death, with the most common lie being that Hitler had a romantic or sexual relationship with her.

[81] The hotel in Berlin which served as Hitler's headquarters during the period of intense political negotiations which led to his appointment as Chancellor.

words: *I fought as one of Hitler's men, and as one of Hitler's men I want some day to go to my grave.*

That was all over now. He probably lacked the clear vision necessary for a clean-cut rebellion, quite aside from the fact that he undoubtedly was deeply attached to our movement. He left. Hitler didn't take any disciplinary measures against him. After the *Machtübernahme*, Strasser, by Hitler's direct order, was never molested. On the contrary he was assigned to a leading position in the pharmaceutical organization.

During the Röhm-Putsch Strasser and Schleicher were killed. We all thought they had been involved in some way, but the police remained silent. The Führer made arrangements for the financial security of Strasser's widow, an extremely pleasant woman. During the war, both of Strasser's sons fell as officers at the front.

This is the sort of tragedy that is inevitable in the course of a revolution. Whenever I think of Strasser as he was in those days, I see before my eyes his tall figure and his light, kind eyes. I remember his generosity, and, occasionally, also that apparent uncertainty which eventually led him to his doom. As the Führer told me later, he had intended to make Strasser his Secretary of the Interior. In that case, many things might have taken a different turn.

Clashes with Doctor Robert Ley

A permanent latent tension existed between myself and Doctor Robert Ley, the leader of the Reich organization, and later the chief of the German Labour Front. Not because of any feeling of enmity, but in spite of attempts on both sides to bring about a more comradely relationship. There was something between us which I shall refrain from examining more closely, but something that time and again led to explosions and harsh words.

Such tension can be rather desirable, theoretically, as a sort of test and inducement to self-examination. Ley came from the Rhineland, had been shot down as an aviator during World War I, and had spent two years in French captivity. Captivated by Hitler, he had become active in Cologne. At first *Gauleiter*, then transferred to serve under Strasser, later his successor. Ley had a strongly creative talent, and his suggestions, innovations and undertakings were numerous. In looking back on what he accomplished, what he started, what he promised, it is a pity, indeed, that all this was later taken over by less skilful hands, added to, modified, and finally torn to pieces in order to make room for an old, outmoded welter of ideas and organizations.

Everything that was concerned with paid vacations, the office of *Reisen and Wandern,*[82] the modernization of industrial buildings, the providing of cultural goods, and so on, represented the beginning of social theory being translated into practice.

But Ley placed two obstacles in his own path: organizational schematization and gigantomania.[83] One of the first entries in my notebook for 1917 reads: *Moderation is one of the most important rules in art; any theory carried out to the bitter end must lead to absurdity.*

This thought, inspired by Goethe, seems to me a basic law of life. I cannot claim that I myself have always obeyed it; but subconsciously this dictum certainly has had an effect on all of my activities. Ley, on the other hand, schematically carried the admittedly necessary discipline of the movement to extremes.

His speeches on the glory of the entire organization, from the leader of a mere cell up to the Führer himself, were frequently boring in their fatuity; but it was obvious that such generalizations were inevitable at this point and would gradually be eliminated.

The political guidance of people and Reich has been examined during the current legal process[84] on the basis of Ley's ledgers. It is in such intricate detail that neither I nor any of the others, I am sure, ever heard the like of it.

If Ley had been taken seriously, all future political leaders of the Reich would have had to run the entire gamut of his organization. This was a schematic abstraction that would have been impossible to put into practice, and in due time a sufficient number of people from within the party itself would have protested against it.

In the educational field I had more than one clash with him. At first he had asked me to take over the direction of the spiritual education of the party members, and the Führer had thereupon made me his delegate in such matters, but unfortunately I had neglected to ask for precise directives.

---

[82] "Traveling and Hiking."

[83] Gigantomania is the creation of abnormally large works.

[84] The Nuremberg Trials.

The National Socialist "Training Castles"— *Ordensburgen*

However, after Ley considered himself quite safe in his office, clashes between his chief training center and my own office were frequent. I accepted the Gau instructors as my own Gau delegates, but when they adapted their activities to my ideas, Ley began to protest forthwith against this breach of discipline.

A basic controversy, recorded in our exchange of letters, arose in connection with his *Ordensburgen*.[85]

It was a completely sound idea to prepare future leaders of the movement most thoroughly, to teach them history, politics, and culture, as well as to train them physically and morally.

All this, however, was to be done in a strictly military fashion, and the number of boys to be trained was so large that individual success seemed out of the question. I wrote Ley and warned him not to build *Ordensburgen* for as many as a thousand *Ordensjunker*.[86] He was offended. I wrote him that, according to experience, such large numbers did not assure success, but on the contrary, frequently the very opposite.

He was displeased by this criticism of his plans, and declared the party needed trained youngsters in exact proportion to the capacity of four large *Ordensburgen*.[87] Besides, the Führer had already concurred. What with ever new additions, these castles grew quite out of bounds. Professor Klotz built Krössinsee and Vogelsang.

The Pomeranian Burg was a cluster of low houses beautifully grouped around a large open campus, but the dining hall as well as the lecture hall lacked architectural grace. A memorial for the martyrs of the movement had a colonnade with a straw roof; it was open on two

[85] The *NS-Ordensburgen* ("National Socialist Order Castles") were schools developed for the elite of the NSDAP and its members. The most famous surviving center is the Ordensburg Vogelsang in North Rhine-Westphalia.

[86] The *Ordensjunker* ("Junker" derived from Middle High German Juncherre, meaning "young nobleman") were young candidates aged between 25 and 30 years old, and members of the NSDAP.

[87] The four institutions were: Ordensburg Vogelsang in North Rhine-Westphalia (focus: racial philosophy of the new order); Ordensburg Sonthofen in Bavaria (focus: administrative and military tasks and diplomacy); Ordensburg Krössinsee in Pomerania (focus: development of character); and Ordensburg Marienburg, in West Prussia, which was never completed. To complete the training, course, each candidate would have had to spend a year at each center, effectively qualifying with a four-year degree at the end.

sides, and enclosed a lawn. This was utterly impossible; a straw roof might be put on living quarters, but certainly not on a monumental building! Ley was quite heartbroken when Hitler made a remark about an Ashanti village. Thereupon: reconstruction. Somehow the four massive corner towers of castles built by the knightly orders in medieval days had captivated Professor Klotz's fancy. So Krössinsee was torn down and rebuilt.

Among other architectural oddities which resulted, in the enlarged dining hall it appeared that one wing had a different roof from the others.

Strength through Joy Vacation Ships

Similar energy was devoted by Ley to the construction of his *Kraft durch Freude*[88] vacation flotilla. An excellent idea to show German workers at a minimum of expense what other countries were like, and thus to strengthen their love for their homeland; to acquaint them with different social conditions, and to impress them with the fact that more was done for them at home than for workers elsewhere; to give them a feeling for the open sea and the beauty of the world in Norway's fjords.

This Ley did accomplish. He could really be proud of his ships. It was the social idea behind them that aroused the ire of certain circles—the fact that National Socialism fulfilled certain dreams which abroad had for decades remained no more than empty promises, and which had to be opposed because they might cut into dividends.

The Volkswagen

In Germany there was frequent criticism of the Volkswagen,[89] and the building of a gigantic factory, near Fallersleben, for its construction.

[88] "Strength through Joy." Part of the German Labor Front's program for workers during the Third Reich's peace years was the building of a number of cruise ships which gave ordinary people inexpensive—but lavish—holidays abroad for the first time. These ships were so successful that the British government eventually barred them from visiting the United Kingdom, out of a concern that British workers would see how well-off their German working colleagues were in comparison.

[89] The world-famous characteristic shape of the Volkswagen "beetle" was sketched by Hitler personally, on a napkin given to Dr. Ferdinand Porsche who was having lunch with the German leader.

Theoretically, declared the Führer, the automobile, which was frequently considered a barrier between the various classes, was to become instead a bridge between them; in other words, it was to cost no more than a motorcycle, and was to be large enough for four or five persons.

The Volkswagen turned out to be fast, solid, and convenient. It was criticized by biologists and statisticians who claimed that each Volkswagen meant one child less. This seemed plausible enough. The Volkswagen definitely did stand in the way of attempts to assure a large and healthy new generation. The Führer himself probably realized this. But I shall leave the question open as to whether he may not have considered too rapid a growth in population dangerous in view of the limited available living space.

The Spa at Rügen

Then Ley began to build spas for his office, Reisen and Wandern. Sound enough, if the idea of relaxation and solitude would have been kept in mind. But Ley went completely haywire when he began constructing—on the island of Rügen, of all places!—a spa for twenty thousand.

Giesler[90] complained bitterly when, in my consternation, I questioned him. I told him that in attempting to give workers and employees a short respite from the pressure of the city, Ley was now driving them into a still worse crush of people. On Rügen, no less, where this noisy horde of twenty thousand would spill over into all the other spas.

Giesler pointed out the technical impossibilities. The new spa, he said, would actually have to put up its own slaughterhouse. Since water wasn't available in sufficient quantities on the island itself, a huge pipe line to the mainland would also have to be laid, and so on. But Ley kept on proudly publishing pictures of the vast halls, the dance pavilion, and so on. Here a sound social idea became utter nonsense in reality. Something was begun which had to turn into the very opposite of what might have resulted from sound planning.

---

[90] Paul Giesler (1895–1945), from 1941 Gauleiter of Westphalia-South, and from 1942 also acting Gauleiter of the Gau Munich-Upper Bavaria. From November 1942 to the surrender of Germany in 1945, he served as the Premier (Ministerpräsident) of Bavaria. He committed suicide on the day Germany surrendered.

Cultural Community Competition

Similar insanity governed Ley's activities as an intermediary for the arts. Originally I had incorporated into our National Socialist Cultural Community subgroups for concert and theatre attendance. Those interested in the theatre were thus enabled to attend performances of carefully selected plays at low cost. In many cities this, in itself, actually improved the quality of the plays performed, and helped improve public taste also. In the beginning Ley admired this plan and turned some of his funds over to us to make it available to his *Kraft durch Freude* movement.

Then, he suddenly demanded the incorporation of all these groups into his own organization. After many arguments, the Führer finally arrived at the Solomonic decision that, since Ley had always supervised organizational plans, whereas I was in full charge of all directives, it would be no more than fair for Ley to take over the organization of all theatregoers.

And suddenly, a rather smoothly running machine, in the service of education and improvement, turned into one that was merely out to break records. At every annual meeting of the *Kraft durch Freude,* Ley appeared with new record-breaking figures on performances and attendance. No doubt, much beauty was thus made available to many who had previously not been able to enjoy it, but at the same time artistic values were bandied about like so much mass-produced confectionery.

I remember *Kraft durch Freude* week-ends, when the Ninth Symphony was played in the morning, a museum was visited during the afternoon, and Tristan was performed at night. At the same time *Kraft durch Freude* took over a number of musical comedy and even vaudeville theatres, quite without rhyme or reason. Instead of assisting enterprising, gifted individuals, *Kraft durch Freude* turned into a cultural trust with paid officials, and soon began to exhibit all those unpleasant side traits that accompany the assignment of posts and parts—all this going on in the office of an organization that called itself National Socialistic and was headed by a *Reichsleiter*!

The chief of the division for serious art (Holzapfel[91]) had been

---

[91] Carl Maria Holzapfel (1890–1945), executive officer of the Reich Association of German Stagecraft and from 1937 onwards, deputy head of the NS Cultural Community in the Strength through Joy organization. He was arrested by the Soviet occupying forces in June 1945 and

taken over from our original National Socialist Cultural Community. He frequently came to me in utter desperation. But instead of listening to me, Ley sided with Goebbels, who was only too glad to have him on his side.

These are a few incidents that characterize Doctor Ley. Let us add to all this some samples from his speeches that frequently made him appear absolutely ridiculous. He didn't mind proclaiming, in one and the same speech, the very opposite of what he had just said, and all of it in ringing tones of conviction and at the top of his lungs. At such moments, he completely lost control over himself and went merrily sailing on along the irrepressible stream of his own oratory.

Those who knew him well realized that he must have just heard the Führer make some remarks on the theme under discussion, which Ley now proceeded to enlarge upon and distort to the point of complete absurdity.

At the end of May, 1945, Ley joined us in Mondorf.[92] He had been arrested in the Alpine region of the Wilder Kaiser.[93] He was as vacillating in his moods as ever. Now, however, this was rather understandable. As all of us did at Nuremberg, he, too, got caught in the mill-race of cross-examination. His recorded ecstatic speeches were considered obviously criminal. At the beginning of November, 1945, we learned through a communiqué that Doctor Ley had died under circumstances that made suicide probable. He had hanged himself!

---

executed without trial.

[92] Mondorf-les-Bains, a town in south-eastern Luxembourg where all the major surviving NSDAP leaders were held prior to their transfer to Nuremberg in 1945.

[93] The Wilder Kaiser is a rural area located in the present day state of Tyrol in Austria.

Part Ten:
Clash with Dr Joseph Goebbels

Troubled Relationship with Dr. Joseph Goebbels

My comradeship with Karl Kaufmann, the *Gauleiter* of Hamburg, was more or less a question of distance. He had studied my books thoroughly and had repeatedly invited me to come to Hamburg. At night, within the circle of his closest coworkers, the state of the party was frequently discussed. Invariably, one man stood at the very center of the general disapproval, to avoid using a stronger term: Doctor Goebbels.

Karl Kaufmann was as much an enemy of this vain and theatrical varlet[94] as myself; and he knew many details which strengthened me in my attitude but which, unfortunately, made no impression on Hitler.

During the Party Day of 1937, I, as the first among the living, received the new National Prize for Arts and Sciences. Inwardly seething but outwardly completely master of himself, Goebbels had to make the announcement that brought about a prolonged stamping of feet in approval.

When I think over the human relationship among those who gathered in Berlin after 1933, it seems rather strange that I was really familiar, or had personal contacts, with so few of them, even though many of them lived close by in Dahlem. Those who eventually offered their services—albeit with somewhat sour miens—to the National Socialist revolution, did not take the pains, at least as far as I was concerned, to try to establish a personal relationship.

It is not easy for me to talk about Doctor Joseph Goebbels. From

---

[94] A varlet: an attendant or servant, also a rascal. An interesting word which well decribes Rosenberg's opinion of Goebbels.

a purely human point of view, his dying in Berlin, together with his wife and five children,[95] takes the sting out of much that is past. Nevertheless, his activities from 1925 until the collapse remain something in the development of the National Socialist revolution that must be studied from a historical point of view. And that, whether open or secret, they were of tremendous importance, I know very well without being cognizant of details. He was the Mephisto[96] of our once so straightforward movement.

After the reorganization of the *Völkischer Beobachter* in 1925, a party member from the Rhineland called on me. He told me that he knew of an intelligent, modest writer who certainly would like to become a contributor. I wrote to the address he gave me.

Soon thereafter I got an article by Doctor Joseph Goebbels in the form of an open letter addressed to Count Reventlow (or someone else). I thought it rather vivid and published it. Then a second, and similar, contribution arrived. A little theatrical, I told myself; but it, too, was published. Additional articles (with possibly one exception) I did not print. They seemed to me too artificial and lacking in spontaneity.

Some time later Goebbels came to Munich and spoke at the Bürgerbräu. Hitler and I were present. Goebbels's appearance is too well-known to require my description. At the time I accepted him without reserve. He spoke impressively, with a consciously pointed theatricality, elaborating on some of Hitler's ideas, particularly the always effective theory that when a people was divided, with 50 percent on the side of the middle classes and the other 50 percent on the side of the proletariat, it was no longer capable of another great joint effort because of this division of strength. To change this state of affairs and create a unified front was the task of the new movement.

Hitler and I looked at each other and nodded. I was quite willing to forget any instinctive aversion I might have felt. The revolution set him afire. Stürtz and others told me how they all wanted to re-enact, so to speak, certain parallel roles that had once been played in the French Revolution. To become important by joining the opposition was in Goebbels's mind, too, when he came to the fore with articles and speeches.

Considering his character and the depth of his social thinking, I came

---

[95] On 1 May 1945, the day after Hitler had committed suicide, Goebbels and his wife Magda killed their six young children with cyanide, and then committed suicide themselves.
[96] Mephistopheles, the devil in Goethe's *Faust.*

to the conclusion that there was no obstacle that would have prevented Goebbels from joining the Communists. But somehow and somewhere within himself—this much I am willing to admit unreservedly—he, too, loved Germany. That's why he turned to Hitler. This was the good that existed even in Goebbels, and that gave to all his activities the magnetic power of the genuine.

After a long period of speechmaking, Goebbels was finally appointed *Gauleiter* of Berlin. But he had hardly assumed his new post when something showed itself which really was the quintessence of all his speeches and acts: the continuous pushing of his own person into the limelight by whatever means he had at his disposal. To begin with, his publicity office announced that Hitler had sent his best man to the Reich capital.

Then it sent out an account of Goebbels's visit to Sans Souci, and of how he, a man small of figure, had walked up the steps to the castle where once upon a time another man who also had been small of figure (Frederick the Great) had lived.

This already seemed to suggest the presence of that sickly egocentric trait which I, completely unprejudiced though I was at first, could not help but notice, and which I later tried again and again to fathom. The sum total of everything Goebbels said and wrote is drastically condensed in a quip which Wilhelm Kubes used in his review of Goebbels's book, *Vom Kaiserhof zur Reichskanzlei:*[97] "I About Myself!"

After Goebbels had been active in Berlin for some time, I suddenly received a complaint from him about the *Völkischer Beobachter*. It had printed, he claimed, the announcement of a dance to be given at some restaurant by the Munich section of the party.

Berlin's Storm Trooper men, Goebbels wrote, were horrified by such frippery in these serious times. I asked him to keep his childish remarks to himself.

As I learned later, Goebbels was at that time playing the role of an ascetic. He didn't smoke, wore a dark blouse in the Russian manner, and spoke in character. His propaganda against the system probably impressed the worldly inhabitants of the Reich capital.

The acidity of his speeches no doubt went halfway to meet Berlin's acid wit. In Goebbels's newspaper, *Der Angriff* ("The Attack"), a

---

[97] "From the Kaiserhof to the Reichschancellery." Goebbel's account, via diary entries, of the weeks leading up to the assumption of power by Hitler in Berlin in 1933.

gifted caricaturist (Mjölnir[98]), by constant and impressive repetition, established the prototype of our Jewish and Marxist adversaries. As far as pure energy was concerned, Goebbels did prove himself extraordinarily active and enterprising. Nor did he lack courage, and would probably have acted bravely enough during the constant attacks the Storm Troopers had to fight off.

During a controversy with Strasser he had described Strasser's mother in a way that was highly insulting. Disgusted, I wrote Hitler, who happened to be in Berlin, that such underhanded methods were simply insufferable. Schwarz, too, was of the opinion that such a man ought to be recalled from his post in Berlin. Upon his return, Hitler told me that the gentlemen simply would have to learn to get along!

Goebbels then published a revocation. In the end it was not he, but Strasser, who fell. In the meantime the Stennes-Putsch[99] occurred in Berlin.

According to all I learned later, Goebbels was not completely innocent in this attempt to wrest the leadership from Hitler. Some things he was supposed to have said, such as his remark that he wouldn't think of always playing second fiddle, were no doubt authentic.

For a while the only entirely reliable party group in Berlin was the office of the *Völkischer Beobachter* under Schickedanz. There Hitler held several conferences and very quickly regained the heart of the Berlin party which, after all, had merely been taken by surprise.

Goebbels's oath of allegiance at the Circus Krone in Munich made a dubious impression, in spite of its smoothness. When Hitler, at the occasion of the Röhm revolt, took Goebbels along with him to Wiessee,

[98] Hans Schweitzer (1901–1980), known as Mjölnir, was an artist who produced many posters for the NSDAP. In Teutonic mythology, Mjölnir is the name of Thor's hammer. Schweitzer was named a professor in 1937, "Reich Commissioner for Artistic Design" and chairman of the Reich Committee of Press Illustrators. After the war, he was fined 500 Deutschemarks for his work as a propagandist but managed to work once again as a graphic artist for the West German federal press and information office.

[99] The Stennes Revolt was a revolt within the NSDAP in 1930–1931, led by Walter Stennes (1895–1989), the Berlin commandant of the SA. The revolt arose from the left-leaning socialist part of the party—particularly strongly represented in the Berlin SA, many of whom were former members of the Communist Party recruited in to the NSDAP by Goebbels. At one stage, members of the SA came into physical conflict with SS men when the party headquarters became the scene of an internal clash. Stennes was expelled in 1931, and left Germany in 1933, moving to China where he worked as a military adviser to Chiang Kai-shek until 1949. He returned to Germany in that year, and lived in the west, where it was alleged that he also served as a Soviet agent.

the party understood this to mean that Hitler had wanted to show him ad *oculos*[100] how he proposed to handle recalcitrants. (At that time Stennes was already a military instructor for Chiang Kai-shek.)

In 1933, it appeared that the others had prepared themselves well for eventual jobs in case of a *Machtübernahme*. Goebbels then married the beautiful and sympathetic Magda Quandt, and set up an attractive home in her apartment. Hitler was a witness at the wedding. He loved to visit Goebbels's home on the Reichskanzleiplatz, something quite understandable for a bachelor.

This purely personal relationship, later intensified by the many children who were constantly being photographed with Hitler, constituted the tie that caused Hitler to stick to him, in spite of the fact that Goebbels had been on his political deathbed no less than three times.

The sort of a person Goebbels really was must have been known to the Führer. But he remembered former days, and pitied the cripple whom he felt he had to protect. Hitler knew very well, of course, that I understood art and culture much more deeply than Goebbels, who could hardly look beyond the mere surface. In spite of this he left the leadership in a field that he loved passionately in the hands of this man because, as I realized at many future occasions, Goebbels was able to give Hitler the kind of setting I should never have been able to contrive.

Goebbels took beautiful and gifted artists and great actresses to the Führer. He told him stories about life among artists. He fed the theatrical element in his nature with gorgeously mounted products of the lighter Muses, thus providing that relaxation which the Führer, under the constant pressure of foreign policy and economic problems, simply had to have.

Whenever the Führer happened to be in Berlin, Goebbels always had lunch with him. When I ate with the Führer, once every three or four weeks, he usually sat around with us, too. He invariably had a new story to tell, or made some little malevolent remark about this or that person. This was his approved method of entertaining the Führer, and of slowly building up in him an aversion toward certain people.

Occasionally he was actually quite amusing. He also played the role of an art enthusiast rather effectively whenever Hitler spoke about something outstandingly beautiful in the field of the new sculpture,

---

[100] Visually.

and shrewdly enlarged upon whatever sarcastic remarks the Führer might make in connection with some event.

At night Hitler frequently invited one or another person for a long talk before the fireplace. Goebbels, Ley, and a few others were favorites, outside of the usual group at table. I can't speak with authority because I was never invited. This was no doubt the time when emotion held sway, and most of the passionate decisions made must have been born during these hours.

Goebbels kept a diary on his talks with the Führer, intending, no doubt, to capitalize on them some day by publishing some filtered extracts from it. Since he had proved in *Vom Kaiserhof zur Reichskanzlei* his complete inability to either understand or describe the essential and the concrete, how these diary entries of the Leader's opinions must have looked, along with the constantly underscored intimate relationship between our Doctor and Hitler! Goebbels managed to see to it fairly soon that Darré[101] had to give up his apartment in the garden of his ministry on Wilhelmstrasse under direct orders from the Führer. The house was torn down and a new one built for Goebbels. It probably was nicely fitted out. I was never inside.

Thus Goebbels had his office opposite the Reichskanzlei, his service quarters on Wilhelmstrasse, and his home on Schwanenwerder where, I heard, the Führer himself had a private room. The children congratulated the Führer in his name, and every day Goebbels was a guest at lunch. With a thousand tentacles did he thus attach himself to the strong one who was no longer able to free himself without self-incrimination.

The tendency of the National Socialist movement to put an ever more emphatic accent on health, on racial-hygienic considerations, and racial questions as a whole, must have made Goebbels's position ever more difficult. I believe, however, that everyone was ready to make concessions in this particular case and to acknowledge Goebbels's accomplishments, the more so since he enjoyed Hitler's permanent protection.

---

[101] Richard Walther Darré (1895–1953), Reichsminister of Food and Agriculture from 1933 to 1942. He was an SS-Obergruppenführer and the seventh most senior officer of the SS. He resigned from his office on health grounds. After the war he was sentenced to seven years imprisonment, but released in 1950 and died three years later of cancer. He was the undisputed founder of the modern "green" and ecological movement, a fact often overlooked by contemporary ecological activists.

Far from appreciating this, Goebbels countered with the increasingly more emphatic utilization of his personal power over the film industry, the radio, and the press, the use of which he granted or denied others, entirely according to his own sympathy or antipathy for them.

At the Leader's table I never heard Goebbels say a single decent word about anyone; but he was invariably voluble in support of criticism whenever it might be expressed. Goebbels had been given every assurance that an entirely new ministry would be created for him at some future date. And he got it too, eventually, in a form that was upsetting not only to me but to many others seriously interested in culture and art: a combination of political propaganda and art!

I understood well enough that art in the hands of the average schoolteacher could easily descend into mediocrity. But essentially art was and is, in all its finer manifestations, a personal confession of faith, and never something tactical or political.

The enabling document signed by Hitler made Goebbels the executive head of the entire German news service and of public enlightenment. I never concealed the fact that I considered this innovation wrong, and considered it doubly wrong to place this most important instrument in the hands of a man like Goebbels. I never bothered to attend the yearly conferences of his so-called Chamber of Culture.

In the course of these years, Doctor Goebbels had not one original or creative word to say about art, but mouthed innumerable trite phrases about laurel wreaths on artists' heads, and smoothly delivered, though only half-understood, rehashes of what the Führer had said. Neither in this nor in any other field was Goebbels able to see any problem concretely or to present it plastically.

When Baldur von Schirach[102] protested against this characterization of mine by claiming that Goebbels was nevertheless a writer, I answered: *No, merely a scribbler.* Whom did this man support as artists in the Reich capital? Hanns Heinz Ewers and Arnold Bronnen, both pronouncedly morbid personalities. When, between 1932 and 1933, Ewers started work on a novel about Horst Wessel, I protested against it to the Führer, who hardly knew Ewers. In reply to my demand that a half-rotted person like Ewers should keep his hands off Horst Wessel, he said that such a book might make new friends for the party.

---

[102] Baldur Benedikt von Schirach (1907–1974), leader of the Hitler-Jugend (Hitler Youth), and later Gauleiter and Reichsstatthalter ("Reich Governor") of Vienna. Sentenced and served twenty years in prison, he was released in 1966.

Goebbels had probably told him some nonsense about Ewers' great influence in artistic circles.

Later, when Goebbels was welcomed by the new Chamber of Culture, Ewers was present to celebrate the event in the name of the creative artists. Then he disappeared from view.

Bronnen is the author of some evil sodomitic scenes, is half-Jewish, and a most dubious character. (See H. Hartner's *Erotik und Rasse*[103]). For a while Goebbels kept him on as the manager of television,[104] but even there he proved to be impossible, and finally he disappeared also.

Once Goebbels had become propaganda chief, the public was regularly provided with pictures of him at carefully measured intervals: Goebbels with the Führer in front of the fireplace on Obersalzberg, at the Christmas market accompanied by his daughter, at his desk holding important conferences, making speeches in Berlin, Cologne, Hamburg, and so on. His speeches always had to be reported at great length and had to be commented on in accordance with cues which he provided. Every unimportant measure of the sort that is part of the routine of any department was presented to the public as an outstanding statesman-like action.

The great works of the N.S.V. (W.H.W.),[105] exclusively the creation of von Hilgenfeldt, were discussed by Goebbels at the Sportspalast. Hilgenfeldt was merely permitted to propose the *Heil* to the Führer. *In fine,*[106] it was a painful spectacle, and completely lacking in dignity.

I had feared these developments, though I hadn't foreseen that they would be quite so disgusting as all this. In my *Mythus* I had symbolically called the party a German Order, and had stated that, even though in the beginning of a new creation Lutheran figures would necessarily

---

[103] "Eroticism and Race," First published in 1925.

[104] The first regular electronic television service in Germany began in Berlin on March 22, 1935, as *Deutscher Fernseh Rundfunk.* Very few receivers were ever privately owned, and viewers went instead to *Fernsehstuben* (television parlors). During the 1936 Summer Olympics, broadcasts, up to eight hours a day, took place in Berlin and Hamburg. By the start of the Second World War, plans for an expansion of television programming were soon changed in favor of radio. The Berlin station, along with one in occupied Paris (*Fernsehsender Paris*), remained on the air until later in 1944.

[105] The *Nationalsozialistische Volkswohlfahrt* (NSV), or the National Socialist People's Welfare, and the Winter Support Program (*Winterhilfswerk*, W.H.W.). Both under the control of Georg Paul Erich Hilgenfeldt (1897, presumed dead in 1945), who served as head at the NSDAP Office for People's Welfare and as Reich Commissioner for W.H.W., which provided the needy with welfare during the winter months.

[106] Latin: ultimately, in the end.

be in the majority, Bismarck's system would eventually have to be replaced in the interest of our future by the Moltke system.

In other words, the concentration of all functions in the hands of one man and the accompanying unavoidable suppression of all others would have to be replaced by a system encouraging the principle of dutiful opposition, as in the days of Moltke, when even the Chief of the General Staff was requested to set down in writing whatever objections he might have to his supreme commander.

I said further—and this was directed against Goebbels as even the only half-informed National Socialist must have known—that at the center of the Order there must be absolute integrity, a demand before which everything else, including propagandistic considerations, would have to give way.

Unfortunately this wasn't the case. Formerly nobody knew anything about propaganda: now it was overdone and credited with entirely too great a power in shaping public opinion. Perhaps it would have accomplished many things in the National Socialist state if it had been clever and good.

In spite of all apparent support given Goebbels by the Führer, a growing, healthy attitude of protest was alive in the party, and found expression in two demonstrations that were not only uncommonly clear in their meaning but, in view of the usually excellent party discipline, almost unheard of. They occurred during meetings of the approximately 700 Kreisleiter, who were in more constant and immediate contact with the population than the *Gauleiter*.

On one occasion Goebbels wanted to play the role of the all-knowing and didn't make a speech, but suggested that questions be asked instead. In giving answers he was either superficial or, when he was unable to give the desired information, he tried to get away with arrogance. The meeting responded with interruptions, shuffling of feet, and whistling. Goebbels finally had to give up. One party member wrote him suggesting that, since he must necessarily know what the party thought of him, he should resign. Mutschmann told me that throughout the entire country it was constantly necessary to repair the damage Goebbels had caused. Bürckel[107] declared that no propaganda ministry at all would be preferable to the existing one.

---

[107] Joseph Bürckel (1895–1944), Gauleiter of Vienna in 1939 and 1940, and from 1941, governor of the Gau Westmark, in south western Germany.

After quite an interval, another meeting of the Kreisleiter was held at Sonthofen, and all expressions of disapproval were forbidden by an order from on high. Goebbels tried to regain lost ground by making a lengthy speech. About ten hands applauded. This time he left the hall bathed in cold sweat, but all this merely spurred him on to ever new attempts at keeping himself in the limelight.

A particularly shocking example of this sickly desire, and the failure to understand the almost universal aversion toward such misuse of public funds, was a family film produced during the war.

I didn't see it, but my personal assistant, Doctor Köppen,[108] actually blushed when he made his report on it. The family Goebbels at Schwanenwerder;[109] heel-clicking servants; the royal children surrounded by innumerable silk cushions and toys; rides on charming little donkeys, and so on.

The old social envy had largely disappeared in Germany, and nobody begrudged a leading personality appropriate service and living quarters. But this attempt to foist such arrogance upon the public proved that the man had gradually lost all sense of tact and decency. Köppen told me that the showing of the film had actually brought forth loud protests. He himself had left the theatre enraged and ashamed. After a while the film was supposedly withdrawn.

Hitler's Willingness to Forgive his Enemies

Any just evaluation of historical developments must needs make a differentiation between words spoken and acts performed during times of strife and war, and governmental measures carried out later by a victorious regime.

Human passion being what it is, such an evaluation will also take into consideration certain inevitable revolutionary after-effects. Thus, it was indubitably a sign of statesmanship when Hitler did not cry for revenge and resort to the guillotine, but instead tried to steer his revolution into the course of a new, stable government.

---

[108] Werner Köppen (1910–1994). Köppen retained his loyalty to Rosenberg, writing an essay in 1977 titled "Thoughts on Alfred Rosenberg's Eastern Politics," in which he complained that in the postwar period, "the nonsensical claims and rumors about the person of the former Reich leader and Reich Minister Alfred Rosenberg."

[109] An island in the Havel river in Berlin, Germany, where Goebbels had his residence. A well-to-do suburb.

A really comprehensive account, that only the more or less distant future will be able to provide, will establish how much the activities of the emigrants who found support everywhere abroad had to do with a change in this attitude of the Leader's.

It will also establish the part played by certain disappointed elements in the country itself, and by others who exerted constant emotional pressure which frequently crossed up cautious and shrewd concepts.

According to everything I have been able to find out, it was always Goebbels who urged Hitler on to radical actions by claiming they were genuinely revolutionary, possibly because he wanted to prevent National Socialism from becoming middle class.

Thus Goebbels stood behind all those painful excesses like the burning of the books, the day of boycott, and particularly the anti-Jewish action of November 9 and 10, 1938.

Incapable of any sound judgment in connection with the general cultural decay, he simply went out in search of some theatrical effect, and staged this book burning under pressure of florid speeches and films.

On November 10, 1938, when I drove through the streets of Berlin, I saw many broken windows and a burned-out synagogue. At my office I aired my feelings about such unworthy excesses, and learned that Goebbels had initiated them.

Göring had been against them. At first I thought this action had been limited to the *Gau* Berlin, but then I learned that similar incidents had taken place elsewhere, too. Their total extent I learned only here at Nuremberg.

It was always Goebbels, plus a few lesser lights, who threw his weight on the side of emotional eruptions.[110] Yet, he wasn't at all genuinely emotional himself. He treated his assistants quite coldly, and I suppose he considered that particularly statesmanlike. He was very changeable. I have heard many say that they considered him intelligent, but have never met one who revered, or even esteemed him.

---

110 This paragraph reveals Rosenberg's unrelenting hatred for Goebbels. In reality, Goebbels was not behind the *Kristalnacht*, but instead was the one who publicly ordered it halted, as reported in *The New York Times* of November 11, 1938. Also, the one day boycott to which Rosenberg refers, was a counter to the far larger and longer lasting boycott of German goods organized by international Jewry. See Goebbels' *From the Kaiserhof to the Reich Chancellery*, ISBN 978-1491274187

Complaints to Hitler about Goebbels

Time and again I felt an inner revulsion against Goebbels's course, since I recognized in it no sensible approach to what was necessary and good. Once, I frankly expressed this opinion to the Führer, and told him that others felt as I did. This resulted in no more than an embarrassed silence around the table and Hitler's redoubled interest in his vegetarian meal.

For a long time, for instance, even during the war, the false displays that crowded show windows in department stores were defended. Among proprietors and employees alike this caused a deplorable unwillingness to give service, since all these beautiful items existed only in the display windows. Or else propaganda insisted upon calling skimmed milk not by the name that indicated its actual consistency, but by some name especially invented for the purpose—a subject for ridicule in every dairy store.

These were excrescences of a brain which woefully underestimated the sound and decent instincts of the German people. I could not help calling them Levantine. During the war, Goebbels always wrote the leading article for the big weekly *Das Reich* (at 4,000 marks per article!) which was also read twice over all broadcasting stations. Obviously, an accomplishment that cannot always be measured by strict criticism.

But whenever I overcame my aversion and read one of these articles out of a sense of duty, I invariably found the polemic against our enemies so formless and cheap that twice I sent Göring letters of protest. I told him that, after all, it was his duty as chairman of the ministerial council to see to it that the German minister of propaganda did not picture himself as a cur who intended to cling to Churchill's coat-tails, as he chose to express it.

Göring told me later that he had shown the Führer my letter, and that Hitler had replied, Rosenberg is absolutely right; what Goebbels wrote was mostly twaddle. But nothing was done about it.

I have tried hard to do Goebbels justice. He was born with a clubfoot, and thus automatically eliminated from all boys' games, from all their youthful joys. He was forced to witness, at first with pain and later with envy, how they all grew into healthy manhood.

As a student in Heidelberg he had to see how the others went on their rides, how they flirted with the girls. And all his energies had to come into focus on one ambition: to prove to these healthy, gay, straight ones that he, too, could accomplish things!

In his war propaganda he had insisted that he would remain in his Gau. By the end of April his position had become untenable in every respect. Deep down below, and despite all attempts at self-deception, he knew full well that he owed that position entirely to the Führer, and that without him he didn't dare venture anywhere in the country. Thus, he eventually drew the inevitable consequence.

It is a human tragedy, just the same, to go to one's death together with one's own children. But this is one thing for which I, too, had prepared when I was ordered late on the night of April 20, 1945, to go north.

It is also a tragedy to be forced to face your accusers day after day for a full year and to be accused, instead of Goebbels and others, of things for which they were primarily responsible.

I hadn't intended to offend Mephistopheles when I called Goebbels Hitler's Mephisto, for he never grew to that size. Actually, he was only one of many. After a while there were three: Joseph Goebbels, Heinrich Himmler, and Martin Bormann.

Part Eleven:
Heinrich Himmler and the Danger of Political Control over the Police

Dislike of and Clashes with Heinrich Himmler

Mutschmann was one of the most embittered enemies of Himmler's police regime, which even then was beginning to appear. He carried on a sustained feud with all of the higher S.S. and police officials. His sound instinct warned him that there was a great danger for both party and state in this direction.

On November 9, 1923, Heinrich Himmler appeared in Strasser's retinue, and was later remembered as the standard bearer of the so-called *Reichskriegsflagge*[111] at the Munich War Ministry. Then he became Goebbels's propaganda representative, and later took over the S.S.

This required the services of brave and cautious men, for the task of guarding and protecting our speakers. Accompanying them wherever they might go was certainly not a post for milksops in those days. For this reason nobody could possibly consider Himmler's connection with the S.S. dangerous, not even when he strengthened the discipline, nor even when he took over the police forces of the various provinces, and then of the Reich itself.

Himmler came from an extremely religious teacher's family. He escaped this influence and became an opponent of all political Catholicism and of Roman priests in general. He was a peasant; we met on the various Peasant Days at Goslar.

Ours were parallel ideas; in fact, Himmler always underscored his

---

[111] Reich War Flag.

anticlerical attitude as being very similar to my own. We also shared our interest in historical research. Even in my early days I had among my coworkers Professor Reinerth Tübingen who, in 1932, in the N.S.M.[112] I suggested the founding of a Reich Institute for Early Germanic History.

Himmler Founds *Ahenerbe*

From 1933 on, he worked together with Kossina,[113] whose pupil he was, for the realization of this plan. Later Himmler founded his so-called *Ahnenerbe*,[114] an institute for research, subsidized by him. I would have had no objection to these scientific interests as such; but how he went about it, in the course of the years, very soon gave me an insight into the depths of his character.

A certain Doctor Teudt had done some important work in connection with the history of the so-called Externsteine[115] and had founded an organization for this purpose. Himmler was interested. Through direct pressure, by-passing the *Gauleiter*, Teudt was induced to incorporate his organization into the *Ahnenerbe*. Thus, he was eliminated. He turned over his material and became honorary president of his former organization, but was no longer permitted to supervise the investigations, since Himmler's own historians held different opinions than he. I heard of this affair in installments. It proved that Himmler used the S.S., originally founded for entirely different purposes, the police force now behind the S.S., and the transformed scientific research organization, for purely personal ends. This was accompanied by the nomination of a very large number of so-called *Ehrenführer* (Honorary Leaders).

---

[112] National Sozialistische Mitteilungen, National Socialist Information.

[113] Gustaf Kossinna (1858–1931), professor of German archaeology at the University of Berlin. One of the most influential German prehistorians, and was creator of the techniques of *Siedlungsarchaeologie,* or "settlement archaeology.

[114] The *Studiengesellschaft für Geistesurgeschichte, Deutsches Ahnenerbe* (Study Society for Primordial Intellectual history, German Ancestral Heritage) was founded in 1935 by Himmler, Herman Wirth, and Richard Walther Darré, with the express purpose of launching archeological and historical research on the racial history of the Germanic peoples. It was renamed in 937 as the *Forschungs- und Lehrgemeinschaft das Ahnenerbe* (Research and Teaching Community of the Ancestral Heritage).

[115] The Externsteine are a distinctive rock formation located in the district of Lippe within the German state of North Rhine-Westphalia. The Externsteine may or may not have been a centre of religious activity for the Teutonic peoples and their predecessors prior to the arrival of Christianity in northern Europe.

Röhm had started this custom in the Storm Troopers, Himmler continued it in the S.S., in order to tie up officials, scientists, writers, and so on, who had nothing to do with the party nor even with National Socialism as such, to make them dependent on him, and to force them eventually into the service of the S.S. in connection with matters that actually had nothing to do with the real tasks of the S.S.

Repeatedly I called Himmler to account. He replied that since, as I must know, the police was primarily concerned with the darker side of life, he was trying to awaken the interest of his subordinates in scientific matters. He didn't want to interfere with my work, but begged me to understand his side of the problem, too. I answered that I was glad to hear of his scientific interest, but considered it unseemly for him to use his organization for purposes alien to the tasks for which it had been created, and that his S.S. was simply not scientifically competent.

During those years Himmler came twice to my house to discuss these things. The Research Organization had, in the meantime, become a subdivision of the S.S., and its chief, ambitious Professor Wüst,[116] was particularly active in S.S. matters. Himmler told me he would ask Wüst to call on me to clear up any possible misunderstanding. However, these conferences led precisely nowhere. Doctor Wüst never called on me, nor did Himmler give up his attempts to bring scientists under his discipline by putting them into uniforms.

After the Anschluss of Austria, the *Ahnenerbe* took over a great number of magazines of the most divergent content. They were taken over exactly as Doctor Teudt's organization had been. During the war, and more especially after Heydrich went to Prague, plans for the founding of an S.S. university were announced. Prague was to become the seat of that university. For Stuttgart I had planned a School of Biology and Racial History as a branch of the future great National University. Its task at first was to be the compilation of a textbook for these studies, and later to keep it up to date.

Debate over Use of "Nordic"

For this purpose I had intentionally selected a southern German city because the word Nordic, as used by some speakers, had acquired

---

[116] Walther Wüst (1901–1993), a prominent scholar who became Rector of the University of Munich from 1941 to 1945.

a certain geographical connotation. And this had occasionally led to what Nietzsche once called *Rassentiments,*[117] though such sentiment was completely unjustified and unjustifiable.

In the first place, although many decisive virtues are in the keeping of the Nordic race, quite as many others are characteristic of other racial groups who, together, make up the family of European peoples. Besides that, the Nordic race extends deep down south into Lombardy, and is a unifying agent for all Germanic tribes.

And finally, national history simply must not be projected from the vantage point of individual habit. Thus, one of the chief objectives of the planned Stuttgart institute was to counteract such dangers.

Himmler was very well aware of the fact that Hitler had designated this future high school to be the headquarters for teaching and research, and that it was not so much a matter of comradely loyalty, as it was his duty, to communicate with me. He did the exact opposite. I could not interpret this attitude in any other way than as indicating Himmler's intention of subjugating the respective scientists to the will of the S.S. even before the national university was actually established, and thus, indirectly, bringing even me under his control by making our high school, in a manner of speaking, an S.S. institute.

In further pursuance of his plans Himmler then founded the *Nordland Verlag*[118] which issued novels, books on the Jewish question, and so on. He would not permit scientists not under his influence to work in the libraries he controlled, and once again put the police to work on research. This obviously constituted a great spiritual menace, and my relationship with Himmler became ever more precarious. In due course I became quite outspoken about this and said more than once: It is possible to leave the Catholic Church ten times over and yet remain a Jesuit.

Officially I was concerned only with the Educational Office of the S.S. This office edited the so-called S.S. booklets, against which little could be said. They were quite decently done, giving examples of the dutiful performance of assigned tasks taken from both the past and the present. The sayings of great men rounded out their contents most effectively. The same opinion holds good for many other publications of the *Nordland Verlag*. In the beginning many excellent men joined

---

[117] Racentment—strong feelings pro or con on racial grounds. A reference to the debate between "Nordicists" and pan-Europeanists.
[118] Northland Publishing House.

the S.S., undoubtedly animated by their will to serve the people and the Reich.

Mistake to Let Police Fall under Political Control

As a new organization, the police realised the necessity of handling the public with politeness and decency. The Protective Police was to be a friend and helper to the people. The rubber truncheon, an instrument we all had come to hate since our days of battle, was done away with. And this, together with many other things, was certainly indicative of a positive will and of psychological understanding.

Lutze,[119] staff chief of the Storm Troopers, was also watching Heinrich Himmler expand his influence, not so much by means of positive accomplishments as by sly pressure made possible by executive power entrusted to him by the state.

It may be that Lutze lacked the gift of finding new tasks for the slighted Storm Troopers that really would have given it a new lease on life; but, historically speaking, it is also possible that the Storm Troopers was so exclusively identified with our battle for power that it would have taken a long time before such new tasks could have been found for it.

Many Obergruppenführer (Chief Group Leaders) complained to Lutze. The sports insignia of the Storm Troopers seemed inadequate, nor did the plans for a large German sports competition to be held during the Party Day at Nuremberg satisfy them. Thus the Storm Troopers lost a number of its old leaders to the foreign diplomatic service, and others to the S.S.

Himmler countered Lutze's aversion, which he considered a purely personal prejudice, by stating that it was he who had suggested Lutze as chief of staff to succeed Röhm.

The Führer, he claimed, had also offered him the leadership of the Storm Troopers, but he hadn't wanted to fall heir to the leadership of an organization that others had led during battle. Now Lutze showed his gratitude by making these unjust accusations.

Later on, secure in his personal victory, Himmler declined even to see Lutze. However, this antagonism was by no means personal but, rather, a matter of principle. How justified it was, now becomes apparent at

[119] Viktor Lutze (1890–1943), commander of the Sturmabteilung ("SA") who succeeded Ernst Röhm in 1934. He died from injuries received in an automobile accident.

Nuremberg. When we discussed this matter, Lutze told me that every young state needed a harsh police executive which occasionally had to use methods running counter to accepted morality, quite without regard to party affiliations.

Thus, it was bad for the National Socialist movement that a party organization should be so intimately tied through a personal union with the secret service, the state police, and the rest, and that a man like Himmler should draw these ties even tighter.

This was necessarily harmful to the party's reputation among the people, who began to identify certain necessary steps taken by the state with the party and its political identity. In addition, Lutze said, instances of vile corruption in S.S. leadership as well as indefensible chicanery on the part of the police had occurred.

Just then—and this was already during the war—he couldn't bother the Führer with such things. But later on he would submit all his material to the Führer together with an either-or. But even noble Viktor Lutze couldn't possibly guess at that time what Himmler and Heydrich were really up to.

Over 300 NSDAP Members Murdered by Communists During *Kampfzeit*

That the police kept habitual criminals in jail and saw to it that some of our worst enemies landed in concentration camps was no more than natural. The records of the National Socialist German Workers' Party showed that over 300 individuals had been murdered and more than 40,000 wounded by Communist acts of terror, while hundreds of thousands had been driven out of their jobs and homes.

Any revolution is accompanied by explosive actions. That a few paltry thousands were imprisoned was considered no more than right, and occasional excesses were looked upon as unavoidable isolated incidents.

It was announced that among the 800 Communist Party functionaries taken into custody, the average of previous prison sentences amounted to four years. Besides that, on January 30 and 31, a Storm Trooper leader (Maikowski) and a policeman had been murdered in Berlin. In other cities, too, murders occurred throughout the entire year.

Taking decisive steps seemed no more than a dictate of self-preservation, and necessary to prevent acts of personal revenge. Listening to a *Reichstag* speech concerning these matters, I learned that among those shot were quite a number of S.S. men who had maltreated prisoners. This could only be considered proof of the fact that the entire security personnel was expected to maintain an attitude of absolute justice.

Atrocity stories in the foreign press, telling about supposed mass murders committed by us, were fully reported to our people, since we knew full well with what self-control our adversaries in the fourteen-year-old battle had actually been treated.

In the Ministry of the East I was continuously aware of Himmler's and Heydrich's political opposition. Over my protests the Gestapo was made an independent unit. All ties with my office were completely severed, and orders were executed of which I learned only here at Nuremberg.

That this was part of a systematic campaign to undermine the theoretician Rosenberg became ever more apparent, even though I, being still caught up in my old notions about comradeship, did not begin to realise to what extent this unscrupulous scheming had gone.

For whenever I spoke to Himmler he was amiability personified, and acted as if he esteemed my opinions most highly. Even his liaison officer, S.S. Gruppenführer Berger, not only protested his personal admiration for me (even today I believe that it was genuine), but also his willingness to come to an understanding, expressing quite freely his aversion to Heydrich's methods.

Once, however, what might almost be called a vision, had a definitely eerie effect on me. Berger had invited me and Schickedanz[120] to have a glass of wine at his service quarters. From where I sat I saw an enlarged photograph of Himmler hanging on the wall of the adjoining room. I couldn't keep my eyes off it. And then it occurred to me that I had never had the opportunity to look Himmler straight in the eyes.

His were always concealed by his pince-nez. Now, from the photograph, they stared at me unblinkingly, and what I thought I saw in them was malice. Next day I talked to Schickedanz about it. And then, in making a mental check on his known activities, we suddenly

[120] Gustav Abraham Schickedanz (1895–1977), a German entrepreneur who in 1927 registered the mail order company Quelle, which later Europe's largest mail-order house. A member of the NSDAP, he was later "rehabilitated" and allowed to carry on his business after the war.

knew what his real objective was: by means of his police power, by terror and promise, he wanted to secure position after position and, anchored in all branches of the service, by hook or by crook, become Hitler's successor.

Whether it might be publishing houses, art institutes, medical journals, popular quizzes, the manufacture of porcelain, concentration camps, the planting of Kog-Sagys rubber roots, or the strengthening of the S.S.—all this was merely, as I later put it, a collecting of points to prevent others from doing their duty, and eventually to take over their posts. No longer was the S.S. a group of the fittest; it had long since become a collection of the ambitious, attracted from all professions by their hope to gain through power, positions otherwise unavailable to them. Whether a man like Harmjanz ,in the field of folklore, received the title of professor, or Professor Wüst was given a free hand in the elimination of undesirable scientists, served only one purpose, just as did the future enmity displayed toward Lutze, toward me, and toward many generals who did their best to prevent Himmler from gaining undue influence over the army.

Unable to Foresee the Future

Without knowing precise details, I began to feel quite uneasy about these developments. When, in 1942, I had an opportunity to speak to the Führer alone—it was the last time!—I told him Himmler had so many tasks that it was quite impossible for him to do them all justice; something that could cause bad blood, as was proven in the resettlement of the Wartheland (Polish territory along the Warthe River).

The Führer understood me all right, but he merely answered briefly that, so far, Himmler had always managed to take care of things. Under the pretext of fighting for Germanic values, Himmler had introduced a completely un-Germanic trait into the S.S., and had defiled its noble name. He had been given the task of securing the interior of the Reich.

But his activities couldn't help but give rise to disgust with the government and its leaders; at first, among our enemies abroad, something that was to be expected anyway; then among those only half won over to our cause; and finally, among us who hated to see a great cause dishonored. Unfortunately, the coming of the war prevented the making of any change and, in fact, increased the might of this man to an extent that, even in 1939, nobody could possibly have foreseen. At the same time Hitler, the Chief of State, was completely surrounded by a news service that drove his will, already misdirected, off in the direction of world historical demonicism, the result of which was the loss of a thousand-year-old battle for the German Reich. What he built up with the one hand and the aid of millions of the most faithful men, he tore down with the other!

In attempting to visualize the typical in Himmler, to find something that was constant in the frequently contradictory expression of his activities, I recognize in him the sectarian come into power. That Himmler was just that in the field of science, I had known for a long time; for it was in this field that I collided with him most often. But that it was part of his very self, I must confess, did not occur to me until here in Nuremberg where I read his speeches about the Slavs, the asocials, and the rest. I had found his scientific sectarianism sometimes uncomfortable, occasionally disturbing, but I was convinced that its effects would soon be a thing of the past.

When I saw what strange people were among Himmler's protégés, I remembered the crackpots who, between 1920 and 1923, had appeared on the scene in Munich, only to disappear again; I recalled the strange spirit-rapping Christianity of Dinter's that is completely forgotten by now, and the rest. Strange figures do, indeed, come and go in the great experimental hall of history. I considered it one of my tasks to see to it that the face of the movement remained unblemished by such excrescences. That Himmler's sectarianism was a trait of character that made him overdo everything and, combined with his limitless egotism, made him forget all regard for comrades, honor, Germany, is it punishable negligence not to have realised this in 1933?

The converse question is obvious: How could anyone believe Himmler capable of these proven cruelties? What right had any one of us to accuse him of such things? Didn't we all have our weaknesses? Wasn't I forced to tell myself that we, too, were often biased, though once our bias was recognized we did our best to eliminate it?

Could the participants in the French National Assembly possibly foresee that one man among them, Robespierre, would someday behead them and immerse them in a tremendous bath of blood? No! Historical developments cannot be prejudged; and much will remain forever indecipherable. Eventually, discontent over Himmler's police regime had manifested itself in almost all districts.

The party itself always took a firm stand against the S.S. as an Order, irrespective of a certain comradely reluctance to trespass, which was inevitable among the services and which, incidentally, was largely due to some understanding S.S. leaders who did their level best to keep up the old warm personal relationships. It was too late. The sectarian had gained victory over the idea.

Time Needed to Resurrect the Ideal from the Rubble of the Reich

It will take a long time before the idea can rise again, purged, from the rubble of the Reich. The palace of Philip II of Spain, with its luxurious halls, contained also a small octagonal room. There, once a week, the king's private secretary reported everything of importance to his monarch—or at any rate, everything that seemed important to him. Then Philip made the decisions that were issued to the nation in the form of royal edicts.

So influential was the private secretary that this sort of political control has been known ever since as a camarilla, the Spanish word for a little room. That was the point the government of the Reich had reached. An open-hearted man had turned into a misanthropic supreme commander, sulking in the bunker of his headquarters, and had begun to rely more and more on the advice of a very few intimates. It was precisely these advisers who were least qualified to give advice and counsel during those fateful years.

Part Twelve:
Martin Bormann, Arthur Axmann, and the Alpine Redoubt

Martin Bormann's Career

Not even the wildest fantast could have foretold Martin Bormann's career. In Munich I had hardly ever heard his name. Married to the daughter of Walter Buch, the so-called Supreme Court Judge of the party, he was in charge of welfare funds at the Brown House. This was a most unimportant job. In 1933, we all read with astonishment: Martin Bormann appointed Staff Leader to the Representative of the Führer, and *Reichsleiter*. That is how I came in contact with him.

Whenever I visited Hess, he usually was present; later on, always. Once in a while he wrote me concerning party matters. I heard that he was vulgar in his dealings with his subordinates and the public. When I had dinner with the Führer, Bormann and Goebbels were usually there. Hess had obviously got on the Leader's nerves, and so Bormann took care of requests and assignments.

Here is where he began to make himself indispensable. If, during our dinner conversation, some incident was mentioned, Bormann would pull out his notebook and make an entry. Or else, if the Führer expressed displeasure over some remark, some measure, some film, Bormann would make a note.

If something seemed unclear, Bormann would get up, leave the room, but return almost immediately—after having given orders to his office staff to investigate forthwith, and to telephone, wire, or write.

Then it might happen that before dinner was over Bormann had an explanation at hand. These were certainly qualifications any leading personality needs, and nothing can be said against such prompt reporting, provided it is objective and personally disinterested.

But that, of course, is the ideal, and everyone would have been willing to allow Bormann that all-too-human measure of ambition. Nor were things really bad as long as Hess was still around. But when Hess flew to England, the Führer did not appoint a new personal representative, but assigned Bormann as heretofore to the new Reich Office.

Theoretically, Bormann was no more than before, but since he now took orders directly from Hitler, whose instructions he passed on to the party, he was in effect more influential than Hess had ever been. For each of Bormann's letters had to be accepted as having been written at least with the Leader's knowledge. Under the pretext that the Führer was again going to take the leadership of the party into his own hands, Bormann got one power of attorney after the other.

He alone was to handle church problems for the party. He took over from Doctor Ley the procurement of personnel for the high party leaders. From then on *Gauleiter* and their assistants were selected by Bormann, a hint to all to maintain friendly relations with him. Whenever there were differences of opinion among the *Reichsleiter*, he was the arbiter.

The Supreme Court of the party was instructed to submit all of its decisions to Hitler, that is, to Bormann. This, in reverse, also meant that any steps that seemed important to Bormann had to be taken. Meetings of the *Reichsleiter* as well as the *Gauleiter* were called by Bormann, who also presided over them. On these occasions he had to say a few words of thanks to the speakers, always hesitant stammerings indicating that he was in no way the equal of his position.

Whenever I talked to him personally, no coherent statement ever passed his lips. When I told him that his *Open letter on Christianity* lacked the proper form and shouldn't have been issued as a party statement in any case, he was very embarrassed.

This didn't deter him from sending out other formless documents into the world. He preferred to evade making clear-cut decisions, and usually wrote entirely different opinions from those accepted without protest in conversation.

Everybody agreed that he was an unbelievably energetic and tireless worker. He was always with the Führer, made notes of everything, dictated, kept voluminous records—always in a much vulgarised form—carried on constant telephone conversations with the various *Gauleiter*, and often hauled his coworkers in Berlin and Munich out of their beds in the middle of the night to check something in the files.

It happened ever more frequently that Bormann issued political orders that should have come from the Chief of the Reich Office. Thus a new title was found for him: Secretary to the Führer. On letterheads with this imprint he now could issue orders in every direction and to any office.

Alliance between Bormann and Himmler

With Himmler, Bormann made a close alliance. Bormann was vitally interested in having Himmler's reports jibe with his own and, of course, so was Himmler. Both were equally determined not to let anyone break into the closed circle around Hitler, to frustrate the ambition of all other *Reichsleiter* and ministers, and to let the future take care of the rest.

Slowly I got wise to their game, a game against which I instinctively rebelled. People I had engaged were attacked in reports. On Bormann such *Sicherheitsdienst* reports had the effect of sublime revelations. He requested me to dismiss some of my employees. But he had little luck with me, even though he indicated that official orders for these dismissals would certainly be forthcoming if he showed the reports to Hitler.

I told him that I wouldn't dream of dismissing people without an investigation. And the result of these investigations were often so devastating for his spies that even Bormann deemed it wise to wait for better opportunities in the future.

Once I received a document that gave evidence of the cheapest kind of collusion. In preparation for the possible installation of a civilian administration in the districts east of White Ruthenia, steps had been taken by a sub-organization named *Aufbaustab R*[121] (Reconstruction Staff Russia).

Certain men were being considered for key positions. One of these had received a letter containing general directives that somehow fell into the hands of the S.S. In connection with this an S.S. leader then

---

[121] Literally, "Establishment Team R"—or Reconstruction Staff Russia.

wrote a letter to S.S.-Obergruppenführer Berger, who showed it to me for my personal information.

The letter deplored the incident as indicating a dangerously neglectful attitude toward state secrets, and concluded with the admonition that Berger report it in detail to Bormann who, in turn, would report to Hitler, seeing to it that I was kept in the dark about the whole matter to prevent my squaring the incident with the Führer.

In other words, we had already sunk into such foul depths, and were caught among such repulsive creatures, that it seemed almost impossible to extricate one's self. When the war necessitated the consolidation of various offices, newspapers, and magazines, Bormann was given the necessary powers to do the job. I declared my willingness to economize as much as possible, provided that the same was done elsewhere, and that my work wasn't taken over by others.

I realized that Bormann now saw an opportunity to effect his long-hoped-for party reform. His aim was obviously to gain recognition for only one single *Reichsleiter*—himself—and to subordinate all the others as mere department chiefs under his orders. Naturally, this could not be done overnight. Even Bormann could hardly expect silent agreement on my part, nor on the part of Goebbels and others. But it could be arranged so that, in case one of the *Reichsleiter* died or resigned, his successor would no longer have the same rank.

Thus after Lutze's death his successor did not become *Reichsleiter*, nor did the new *Reichsjugendführer*[122] Axmann.[123] This was the direction in which the party was to be reorganized, in other words, the very opposite to what we had fought for.

Bormann never formulated or defended an idea of his own. He was no leader of men. He was an office leader. No one in the party or among the people knew him.

Nobody could identify his name with a concept, an idea, an accomplishment, a personality. Of course, such men are also necessary as cogs in the machinery of a great movement. In spite of my disgust over the whole general trend, I always insisted that it was really tragic. Bormann, too, could have been useful; he had common sense, and no doubt also an instinct for practical measures. In the proper spot he could even have done some real good.

[122] Reich Youth Leader.
[123] Artur Axmann (1913–1996), Reich Youth Leader and head of the Hitler Youth (*Hitlerjugend*) from 1940 to the war's end in 1945.

If the head of the state is at one and the same time Chief of the Party, of the Reich Office, and also commander in chief of the Wehrmacht, he simply can't listen to as many different people as he might have before. He's got to have a few assistants, quick-thinking office workers. If Bormann had accepted this post as an intermediary, he would have been rewarded with willing helpers and general esteem. His name would later have been spoken with reverence.

As it was, many *Gauleiter* were under obligation to him for his help, but his ultimate goal had to turn them into opponents, exactly as it had me. I spoke quite openly about all this to Bormann's chief of staff when he called on me. Actually Bormann retreated slightly, but I was still worried about the future development of our idea and of the Reich itself.

At that time my old comrade, Arno Schickedanz,[124] dropped in quite regularly. Occasionally he saw things much more clearly than I myself really wanted to see them. Since 1943, he had only one epithet for Bormann and his crowd: Megalomaniacal *Posemuckel*.[125]

At party meetings I had frequently spoken about similar things; about narrow-mindedness and provincialism, an unfortunate inheritance of the Thirty Years' War which we simply had to outgrow.

Then, as a more specific criticism, I wrote an editorial for the *Völkischer Beobachter* directed against practitioners without ideas, and suggesting that we think problems through, something which would necessitate a great deal of educational work.

At the party central, the article was quite correctly interpreted. But all it accomplished was that it clarified the situation without anyone being able to do anything about it. Not during the war, anyway. The situation simply cried out for reform, but in exactly the opposite direction from that advocated by Goebbels, Bormann, and Himmler.

The Hitler Youth

The recognition of this demand of the future brought me into closer contact with the leaders of the Reich's youth. The *Hitler Jugend*, too, had been guilty of certain excesses: the idolatry of youth, the

---

[124] Arno Schickedanz (1892–1945), who served as diplomat in the Foreign Affairs Office of the NSDAP (APA) and in the Reich Ministry for the Occupied Eastern Territories (RMfdbO).
[125] German expression for "provincialism."

exaggerated pride in their courageous actions, and so on, had begotten many grandiose hopes, even on the part of Schirach.[126]

But the youngest ones were no doubt justified in their conviction that the strict discipline essential during revolutionary times should now be somewhat relaxed. It was impossible to stand constantly at attention. These problems, and particularly the quite apparent transformation of the party into a dictatorship of the anteroom, were widely discussed.

My coworkers, most of whom had come from the Hitler Youth, thus conspired, so to speak, for future reforms. I declared that I, too, would once again become a revolutionary in my waning years if that would help preserve what we had fought for. If I had still been young, I undoubtedly would have left the party. My inner voice had given me sufficient warning, just as it had warned me in the past.

Axmann and the Alpine Redoubt

Around the middle of April, 1945, *Reichsjugendführer* Axmann called on me at my home. He still spoke hopefully about a possible last stand in the mountains. I remained silent. Then he asked me whether I thought that the idea itself had been wrong, or whether its translation into reality had somehow gone awry—the same questions millions were asking.

I told him that a great idea had been misused by small men. Himmler was the evil symbol of that. Axmann replied that, after all, the youth of today would have to shoulder the burden of the entire future. Youth acknowledged the great things accomplished by the generation of World War I, but could really believe in only a few of them.

They hoped I'd stand by and give them counsel. I was deeply moved, understanding full well the sorrow of a generation that certainly hadn't known a gay childhood, that had stared death in the eye a thousand times, and that now faced a dark fate.

I have thought often of that hour I spent with Axmann.

In the spring of 1946, we read that he and a few of his assistants had been arrested because, under cover of their supposed scientific research, they had attempted to build up a new organization.

---

[126] Baldur Benedikt von Schirach (1907–1974), head of the Hitler-Jugend until his appointment as *Gauleiter* and *Reichsstatthalter* ("Reich Governor") of Vienna.

Bormann's Death in Berlin

It had become completely impossible to see the Führer. Every attempt to do so was thwarted by Bormann, under the pretext that Hitler was too busy with war problems. The *Gauleiter* received the order: Victory or Death.

The night after the Führer had taken his own life, witness Kemka, told this court, Bormann was seen at Friedrichstraße Station. German armoured cars drove by, Bormann walking beside one, Kemka about four meters farther back. Suddenly there was an explosion.

The armoured cars blew up, flames shot up to the sky and, as he fell, Kemka saw Bormann's body sail through the air. That was all he knew. The riddle of Bormann's death has still not been definitely solved.[127]

---

[127] At the time of writing (1946) almost none of the Third Reich's enemies believed that Bormann had died in the manner here described. Only in 1972 was his body finally identified and Rosenberg's account confirmed.

Part Thirteen:
Adolf Hitler, Man and Myth

Cannot Judge Adolf Hitler Yet

What Hitler did, what Hitler ordered, how he burdened the most honorable men, how he dragged into the dust the ideals of a movement created by himself, all this is of such ghastly magnitude that no everyday adjective is adequate to describe it. Nor do I have the right to pass historical judgment. All I propose to do is to put down on paper some part of what I thought about him in these many years, and to mention a few characteristic details that have clung to my memory.

I must say that it was absolutely uncanny how similar our opinions frequently were. Once, after I had written an article on the problems of alcohol for the *Völkischer Beobachter,* and was just reading the galley proofs, Hitler called on me at the editorial office. He had with him an article on the problems of alcohol which he wanted me to publish in the near future. With a laugh I showed him mine.

Then we read each other's articles and found that, starting from different premises, we had reached identical conclusions.

When I told him that I naturally would kill my own article, Hitler said, under no circumstances; it was excellent, and it would be a good thing if both of them were published. Thus the *Völkischer Beobachter* published the two articles in the same issue.

Hitler insisted that most of the important speeches to be made at party conventions be submitted to him. Once, when I personally handed him one of mine, he read it immediately and said: This is as much like mine as if we had compared notes beforehand.

I might describe the gradually developing personal relationship somewhat like this: he esteemed me highly, but he did not love me.

That *per se* was not particularly surprising. For one who came from the Gulf of Bothnia brought along an entirely different temperament than one from Braunau on the Inn.

What was surprising, on the contrary, was our miraculously similar judgment regarding the basic traits of so many problems. On many southern Germans I simply had the effect of a wet blanket, and behind many completely irrelevant remarks of mine they frequently sensed irony.

Hitler felt more at home in the company of Esser, Amann, Goebbels, Hoffmann, and so on, and had the disconcerting feeling that I was there more or less as an observer.

Later on this was definitely the case, after I had recognized the pettiness of the crowd surrounding him, and their constant anxiety to adapt every one of their remarks to his moods. Sometimes Goebbels actually flirted with an occasional contradiction, only to be persuaded after a while to express his enthusiastic agreement.

Since 1920, I had attended most of Hitler's meetings. From the very first I knew there was a very firm spiritual foundation, but I also saw a growing maturity in the treatment of the many problems, for the discussion of which he called the people to the large circus building on the Marsfeld[128] in Munich, or for debates to one of the halls of the Café Neumayr.[129]

I noticed that Hitler definitely kept *au courant*[130] with contemporary political literature, with everything that had to do with the Treaty of Versailles, with the outbreak of World War I, or with rearmament in the various countries.

Strangely enough, he never studied the various Marxist theories, though he talked often about some of their basic principles, depicting their effects on political events.

In his battle against this world of Marxism, he certainly utilized all the tools of passion, propaganda and irony, but never permitted himself to be side-tracked, particularly in meetings intended to attract the working classes. When the Social Democrats and the Communists were looking for new problems to solve, they stumbled over what they

[128] Marsfeld, located in Maxvorstadt, Munich. A former military area with a large barracks.
[129] The Café Neumayr at Petersplatz 8, just south of St. Peter's Church in Munich, was where Hitler went every Monday night to sound out his associates on various new political ideas in the early 1920s.
[130] Figuratively, "fully informed."

chose to call *Fürstenenteignung*.[131] Most of the German provinces and principalities had already arrived at some agreement with their deposed princely houses, but in view of its domestic and foreign political dilemmas, Marxism was constantly on the lookout for new ways to prove its social tendencies.

In contrast to men like Hermann Esser, Hitler never permitted himself to be caught up in such demagoguery. He declared that as long as private property was recognized as one of the foundations of national life, he would not yield, irrespective of how good or how bad the rulers of the various states had been.

The National Socialist German Workers' Party adopted this point of view, not without pointing out at the same time that, strange as it might seem, Marxism intended to leave unmolested the millions of war profiteers and exchange bandits. In due time a popular referendum finally rejected the Marxist catchword.

Hitler a Principled Politician

Later, when Hitler ran against Hindenburg for Reichspräsident,[132] it was definitely decided not to attack Hindenburg personally. So much of the great German history is identified with him, Hitler said to me, that we must not under any circumstances damage his reputation. The election propaganda was to be based on the claim that the times called for a man of the younger generation who was still in the midst of the fight, and had attracted followers by means of his political activities.

In other words, even in this case which concerned him personally, Hitler adhered strictly to his principles, and shunned all tactical temptations.

This decent attitude, which he displayed time after time, was what imbued me with ever new respect for Hitler, even though I might take exception to other tendencies of his, or at least consider them odd. Especially when they occurred in the field of foreign policy.

Hitler very soberly conceded that a lost World War had certain harsh but inevitable consequences. He emphatically repudiated the

---

[131] The *Fürstenenteignung* was the proposed expropriation of the dynastic properties of the former ruling houses of the German Empire during the period of the Weimar Republic. These princes had been deposed in the German Revolution of 1918–19.

[132] March and April 1932.

demands for the old frontiers of 1914, claiming that a changed world presupposed changed methods. In connection with the rejection by the Allies of all claims for treaty revision, he declared that demands could be made only by a strong unified German government, something the November State definitely was not.

Hitler Sought Alliance with England

But even then these demands would have to be based on the sober question of which countries, in their own interests, would be against the destruction of the heart of Europe. His answer: Italy and England. If this answer were right, he concluded, it was necessary to give up certain things which might prevent these countries from arriving at an understanding with Germany.

On the one hand, this meant giving up all claims to southern Tyrol, on the other, the abandonment of the colonial policy, and placing the demand for the return of one or the other of Germany's former colonies on the basis of a friendly agreement with Great Britain.

Hitler had the courage to proclaim this in the face of strong middle-class, nationalistic opposition. In spite of our love for the Tyrolians, their fate had to be subordinated to the interests of the other seventy million Germans.

Thus Hitler by no means chose the way of least resistance but, on the contrary, deliberately courted all sorts of opposition to his activities on behalf of principles he had recognized as correct. On the other hand, however, his other self, hampered him considerably. His best intentions were frequently thwarted by the injection of purely personal things—matters of emotion.

But since Hitler invariably managed to overcome with redoubled energy whatever crisis had been conjured up by this element, I finally began to doubt my own judgment, and came to the conclusion that he was, after all, the wiser in permitting the existing forces to run their course.

Today, however, I am inclined to believe that it was this side of his multifaceted personality that made possible the advent of people like Goebbels, Himmler, and Bormann, and all the dire consequences of their coming to power.

Hitler Should Have Taken Control of Weaker Party Leaders

All those in whom I recognized the tell-tale symptoms of the great illness of National Socialism could have been useful in subordinate posts. Somewhere in the middle, under the unequivocal orders of a far-seeing leader who would instantly stamp out disloyalty at the first sign, they would either have been prevented from giving free reign to their base instincts, or they would have been broken.

It would seem that, considering Adolf Hitler's authority, this could easily have been done. But it was he who permitted this misuse of power and saw in every criticism of his functionaries a criticism of his own person. They could not withstand the temptations of power. Hitler lost his steady hand. And for this reason all questions asked must always and invariably lead back to him.

Hitler Supported *the* Wehrmacht When Others Did Not

German officers found themselves in a rather tragic position: formerly unpolitical, though naturally pro-Kaiser; then, after the first eddies of the November revolution, safely established on the supra-political island of the *Reichswehr*;[133] and since 1933, living in a new state.

Many others, outside the small Wehrmacht, took up all kinds of bourgeois professions, their hearts full of old traditions, hating the November republic, but at the same time filled with distrust for National Socialism and the non-bourgeois methods used in its political battles.

We Balts certainly all revered the old Prussian state, though our way of life was completely un-Prussian. The Scandinavian admixture had given us less rigid forms and a more generous way of thinking than those produced by war-hardened Prussian state ethics. But I, as well as many others, saw Prussia as the heir to the old knightly orders, and followed its history from Fehrbellin[134] to Sedan[135] with genuine concern

---

[133] The German army.

[134] The Battle of Fehrbellin (June 18, 1675) was fought between Swedish and Brandenburg-Prussian troops. The Swedes were defeated by the forces of Frederick William, the Great Elector, and the battle went down in history as Prussia's baptism of fire.

[135] The Battle of Sedan (September 1, 1870), was the decisive battle of the Franco–Prussian

and prejudice against all of Brandenburg's enemies. From my earliest youth Frederick II had always seemed to me a half-legendary figure, and I read and reread the history of the Wars of Liberation.

The crisis that came after 1871 was something I understood well, since I had studied its literature during my student days. Almost the entire old corps of officers died on the battlefields of the First World War, but a new one grew up during the latter part of that war.

The comradeship transcending all classes and parties certainly was a great experience. It gave birth to Front Socialism. And to change this into National Socialism was the task the soldier, orderly, and corporal, Adolf Hitler, had set for himself.

Historical truth requires the admission that at a time when epaulets were being ripped off the shoulders of German officers, when one Captain Berthold[136] was literally torn to pieces by a mob, and when the press poured waves of hatred down upon their heads, it was Hitler who in public meetings always stood up for those officers and their honor. I attended these meetings and the lectures at the Munich Hofbräu where he spoke in defense of historical justice, just as he did without fail in Red cities.

Thus Free Corps officers who had fought in Silesia and the Baltic states, as well as Bavarian officers disgusted with the new republic and hoping for a new turn of fate, got in touch with Hitler. Around them grew up various nationalist organizations like *Oberland, Reichsflagge,* and the rest.

Thus, until 1933, I had very little contact with officers, and could observe the various undercurrents in the *Reichswehr* only from a distance.

Hitler followed an absolutely straight course by refraining from interlarding the *Reichswehr* with National Socialist cells, and by keeping it away from political strife. He meticulously kept the oath

---

War which resulted in the capture of Emperor Napoleon III and large numbers of his troops.
[136] Hauptmann Oskar Gustav Rudolf Berthold (1891–1920), commonly known as Rudolf Berthold, was a German flying ace of World War I. After the war, he organized a *Freikorps* to fight against the Bolsheviks in the Baltic states, and in March 1920 returned to Hamburg to help suppress a socialist purring in that city. After a firefight with Communist trade unionists, a truce was agreed and Berthold and his men were assured of safe passage if they withdrew. Taking advantage of the ceasefire, a mob of Communists attacked Berthold, and after a struggle, seized his handgun and shot him dead. His medals and rank badges—including his *Pour le Merite*—were ripped from his clothes by the mob, and later recovered in a trash dump.

sworn at Leipzig,[137] something that later led to a violent dispute with the Chief of Staff of the Storm Troopers, Captain von Pfeffer[138] (who resigned after the Stennes revolt). As a former soldier, Hitler knew that an army is worthless if opposing political groups within it wrestle daily for the soul of every man. Hitler told me the Commander in Chief of the Army, General Freiherr von Hammerstein, once said to him: *Herr Hitler, if you come to power legally, I'm satisfied. If not, I'll shoot.*

The epilogue went like this: After his resignation in 1931, Pfeffer, much to Hitler's satisfaction, had behaved very loyally. In 1933 he was given a post in Hess's office, and also returned to the Reich Office. It happened that Hitler was conferring with a few generals, and that Pfeffer was present.

Suddenly Pfeffer remarked that he had had quite a few previous conferences with *Reichswehr* officers. Hitler got red in the face. Before the Leipzig trial he had asked Pfeffer several times whether he had lived up to his orders, a question Pfeffer had always answered with a categorical yes. When Hitler asked him in disgust why he hadn't told him the truth before, Pfeffer replied that he hadn't wanted to make him feel uneasy. This incident enraged Hitler so much that first he forbade Pfeffer ever to enter his house again, and later expelled him from the party. He felt himself disavowed in front of those officers, and betrayed in a matter that had involved his oath and the entire fate of the movement. He wondered what would have happened if one of the officers with whom Pfeffer dealt had spoken up.

Whenever I think back to Hitler's later talks to generals on his policy and his public speeches, I am confronted with a psychological riddle. I can explain things to myself only by assuming that, up to the end of 1937, he worked for an understanding with the Western powers, always with the hope that his grandiose plans for an alliance might yet come to pass.

Then, apparently, he lost hope and, despite the conclusion of the Munich Pact, passion overruled common sense. Fate ran its inexorable and terrible course.

---

[137] September 1930, when Hitler appeared as a witness in a trial of three army officers charged with "inciting treason" among troops. At that trial, Hitler declared that he would only seek power through legal means.

[138] Franz Pfeffer von Salomon (1888-1968), also known as Franz von Pfeffer, was the first commander of the SA upon its re-establishment in 1925, following its temporary abolition in 1923 after the abortive Beer Hall Putsch.

Ernst Röhm, Homosexuality, and the SA

An entirely different type was Captain Ernst Röhm, young, revolutionary, aggressive, active, who had joined Hitler very early and participated in our action of November 9, 1923. He always treated me with the utmost amiability, though he was somewhat reserved toward me, a civilian, who was still a stranger in Bavaria.

He is said to have been very musical, and to have been very close to his mother. After the Hitler Putsch he went to Bolivia to reorganize the army, and upon his return took over the leadership of the Storm Troopers.

There were the well-known stories about his perversion.[139] It was said that he had acquired the habit in South America. Captain Röhm was a changed man. Odd friends appeared on the scene, people like Hanns Heinz Ewers,[140] who felt obliged to call on me, too. Later on, in Berlin, Ewers told everybody that he had been well received in Munich by everyone but me. To me he was as unacceptable as were his works.

In 1932, before my trip to Rome, I called on Hitler to ask him whether he did not wish to eliminate Röhm, since it seemed impossible to hold him. Hitler himself was very unhappy about the whole thing, but couldn't bring himself to dismiss Röhm. In Berlin I tried to avoid Röhm whenever I could, even though our offices were close together. I noticed that the Storm Trooper leaders under his influence frequently behaved rather arrogantly. The way they rushed around in their automobiles seemed particularly obnoxious.

This reckless attitude in a large city proved that it was contempt for others, rather than mere thoughtlessness, that was at the root of their behaviour. I talked to Hess about this, hoping that he would ask the entire party to be a little more careful in this respect. It was about a fortnight before the fateful June 30, 1934.[141]

---

[139] Röhm, leader of the SA, was well-known to be a homosexual.

[140] Hanns Heinz Ewers (1871–1943) was an actor, poet, philosopher, and writer of short stories and novels. While he wrote on a wide range of subjects, he is now known mainly for his works of horror. In 1934 most of his works were banned in Germany, and his assets and property seized, even though he had joined the NSDAP in 1931. Ewers died from tuberculosis.

[141] The infamous "Night of the Long Knives" when the (economically) far left wing of the NSDAP was suppressed in the face of an imminent *Zweite Revolution* ("Second Revolution") which was aimed at overthrowing Hitler and replacing his government with one under SA leadership which would place the emphasis on implementing radical economic socialist policies.

I was still living on Tiergartenstraße, and was accustomed to walk to my office on Margaretenstraße by way of the Standartenstraße. I noticed from the corner of my eye that Röhm had just pulled up, but I did not stop. He called: *Herr Rosenberg, why are you avoiding me? Why don't you join me in a cup of coffee?* So I walked over to his building. He took me into the stable where he kept his riding horses, patted one of them on the neck and said sadly: *Animals are better than men.*

His office was very elegant; the breakfast prepared with all the niceties of a gourmet. The office of the Chief of Staff of our Storm Troopers! We discussed various aspects of the foreign situation. Later on, it became obvious that Röhm wanted to pump me to find out whether I knew anything about his activities. After Röhm's death the Führer told me that he (Röhm) had hated me particularly.

Naturally I accepted as inevitable much of what the revolution brought in its wake, but never did I fail to give voice to my fears and critical opinions whenever I conferred with Hitler. Still unaware of one of the traits of his character, I saw him as a man who needed to be told such things. In 1932, the attacks on Röhm became ever more ominous, and Hitler himself spoke with distaste of Röhm's notorious perversion.

While discussing a speech I planned to make before the European Congress to be held in Rome, I took advantage of the opportunity to tell Hitler that such a man could not possibly remain at the head of the Storm Troopers.

Hitler reminded me of Röhm's former accomplishments and asked whether I knew of someone who, under the circumstances, could take over the leadership of the Storm Troopers. Now, just as it was understandable that Hitler did not want to force anyone into the camp of the opposition before he himself had captured the executive power of the state, so it was completely non-understandable to me that Hitler not only left Röhm in his immeasurably strengthened position after the *Machtübernahme*,[142] but even had Hindenburg appoint him Reichsminister; and that he himself issued a proclamation stating that the Chief of Staff of the Storm Trooper would automatically be Reichsminister (like Hess, as the personal representative of the Führer).

Thus Hitler silenced the opposition to Röhm—except for Röver who warned Röhm that if he ever dared come to Oldenburg he would

---

[142] The "take over of power" which occurred on January 30, 1933.

have him arrested by the police—and permitted him to strut around in the most obnoxious fashion, posing as one of the great men of the revolution, and surrounded by the similarly inclined sycophants who always collected around him.

Nor did Hitler eradicate the pestilence of these homosexuals later on. In seeming to do so, he merely suppressed a political revolt by men who wanted to take over the leadership of the *Reichswehr*. Fully conscious of Röhm's unnatural inclinations, he had nevertheless given him his appointment. In his *Reichstag* speech against the sect, he really dodged the issue, since it was he who had placed members of this sect at the head of the Storm Troopers, the members of which gnashed their teeth but had to obey Hitler's orders.

Later on Hitler told me that Röhm hated me fervently, and added that he had never invited Röhm to a private dinner. He seemed offended when I remained silent; he realized that to me this just didn't seem enough. The whole affair gave evidence of a psychological problem, an attitude which in its end results and its effect on other persons decisively influenced Germany's fate.

Did Hitler, by increasing Röhm's power, intend to tempt him into taking illegal steps so that he could then completely eliminate him? Was it a debt of gratitude he was paying the old Captain Röhm of 1923? Or was it merely a matter of letting things slide, that tendency to avoid making personal decisions which was becoming ever more apparent?

To answer these questions, one would have to be cognizant of the entire development of this Röhm complex. Hitler's *Reichstag* speech doesn't give enough information, since it is obviously a reconstruction in retrospect to show things in the light in which Hitler wanted them to be seen. But when I compare Hitler's attitude in the Röhm case to that he maintained in other, similar ones before and after the *Machtübernahme,* I become more and more convinced that it was some fatal shyness that made him incapable of differentiating clearly between guilt and innocence, right and wrong, to rectify the situation once and for all and go on from there.

In 1924, when the really despicable attacks were made on me by Esser and his ilk, Hitler avoided making any investigation and refused to pass judgment. *Both of you,* he said, *put yourselves at my disposal at a time when this no longer required the making of sacrifices, and for this reason you must now bury your personal feuds and start afresh.*

Hitler Tried to Get Party Factions to Compromise

When the conflict between Strasser and Goebbels came, Hitler again insisted upon a compromise and a reconciliation. He shunned investigations that would have clarified matters, so that in effect the dishonorable attacker remained the equal of the attacked, as did Esser with me, and Goebbels with Strasser.

Thus it was always the one attacked who had to be generous enough to refrain from causing Hitler further trouble, and who had to make sacrifices. I was to be made aware of this fact once more, and in its most bitter consequences, by the case of Koch. Only in this instance, the controversy, distorted by the Führer into another personal conflict, actually had a bearing on the fate of the entire Reich.

By temperament I have always been in favor of taking preventive measures. But in all justice, I must admit that there were weighty reasons for retaining even completely undesirable elements in the party, at least until the *Machtübernahme,* instead of provoking, by their expulsion, the formation of a new nationalist opposition.

The Otto Strasser incident[143] was warning enough, and undoubtedly had an increasingly strong influence on the tactician, Hitler. If in the beginning he was understandably cautious, if later he realised that even rather undesirable forces could not be forever neglected, there is no doubt that in after years Hitler deliberately allowed antagonistic groups to exist within the party, so that he could play umpire and Führer. I thought I had observed that tendency even on a much earlier occasion.

As already reported, I had been given the task of reassembling the scattered members of the party after the failure of November, 1923. And even though Hitler later agreed with my methods, he still received loudmouthed wiseacres like Esser and Streicher who prated about the betrayal of the Hitler spirit, and who were pathologically incapable of understanding or judging the situation.

That is why I wrote Hitler at Landsberg that my honor would not permit me to take these things lying down, and asked him to relieve me of my mission. At that time I had the uncanny feeling that Hitler rather <u>liked the idea</u> of intra-party bickering.

[143] Otto Johann Maximilian Strasser (1897–1974), together with his brother Gregor Strasser, was a leading member of the NSDAP's left-wing faction, and broke from that party in a 1930 split. He went into exile and only returned to Germany in 1955.

He considered himself the real leader of our national awakening, and probably thought his position would be easier to maintain if he encountered, upon his return, not a closely knit organization, but a lot of antagonistic groups. For in the first case he might have had to face a struggle to regain his old influence; while in the second, he would appear on the scene as a savior to the squabbling, disintegrating party.

At the time these ideas seemed almost blasphemous to me, but subconsciously I knew even then they were correct. In any case, I did not wish to remain a cause of such bickering, and stepped out. And for this reason I also stayed away from the theatrical reconciliation festivities of February 24, 1925.

When the war came he wanted to be an officer, as he had been in World War I, but was rejected. Something else, however, provided an absolute tragic sequel to the Röhm Putsch.

Although Lutze was on the best of terms with the leadership of the army, the reactivated old colonels and generals often were political opponents, ultra-reactionary, and frequently identified with the former *Stahlhelm*[144] organization. Thus it came about that Storm Trooper leaders who during the First World War had been only captains, but who now led tens of thousands of men, were taken over by the army without promotion in rank. In such inferior positions they fell, the victims of a new Reich for which they, too, had struggled ardently.

Hitler and the Wehrmacht

As Reich Chancellor, Hitler treated the Wehrmacht with the utmost consideration. Not only because it was directly under Hindenburg, but primarily because he realized that here were all technical prerequisites for possible future reinforcements.

The Storm Troopers was not an armed force but an instrument of political protection, and it was to remain just that. This was a great disappointment to many Storm Trooper leaders, a disappointment that previously had led to the Röhm revolt.

Their subjugation, together with the resultant changed attitude of the Storm Troopers, was meant to reassure the old army officers, many of whom, in due time, gave allegiance to their new commander in chief, Adolf Hitler.

[144] "Steel Helmet" organization of ex-soldiers.

First of all Hitler set out to capture the hearts of Blomberg and Hindenburg. He often invited Blomberg to the Obersalzberg; Blomberg in turn displayed an honest veneration, something that was not disproven even by later developments.

Hitler and Hindenburg

As for the aged Field Marshal, the solemn act of state at the tomb of Frederick the Great, in the Potsdam garrison church, deeply moved him. Then and there he must have found in the young revolution a confirmation of the values he himself had unselfishly upheld all his life. The relationship between Hitler and Hindenburg improved considerably.

Hitler visited the Field Marshal on his Neudeck estate in East Prussia. There the two of them went riding in a dog-cart. The offensive stipulation that the new Reich Chancellor must not make his official reports unless von Papen, the Vice Chancellor, were present, was revoked by Hindenburg himself. I was under the impression that Hitler had a feeling of true reverence for Hindenburg. Whatever promises he gave him he kept: Doctor Meissner[145] remained Chief of the Presidial Office, and Franz Seldte, Minister for Labour.

When Hindenburg died I wrote the memorial article for the *Völkischer Beobachter*, and dined with Hitler. He spoke most solemnly about the deceased and added: *Your memorial article is very good, the best of all of them.*

Interment took place in the Tannenberg Monument. I remember it vividly. Everybody of any importance at all in Germany was present. Old tradition and the young revolution sat side by side, meditating on the career of the dead Field Marshal which had led from Königgrätz to the crowning of the Emperor at Versailles, which had carried him to the very pinnacle of fame, but had also made him a witness to the collapse of the Reich. This was the man who had been recalled from retirement, when the founders of the Weimar Republic were no longer

---

[145] Otto Lebrecht Eduard Meissner (1880–1953) was head of the Office of the President of Germany during the entire period of the Weimar Republic under Friedrich Ebert and Paul von Hindenburg. Meissner submitted his resignation in 1933, but this was turned down, whereupon he assumed responsibility primarily for delegational duties. In 1937, he was raised to the rank of Federal Minister, with the title, "Chief of the Presidential Chancellery of the Führer and the Chancellor."

able to control their own creation, to help make a success, in a strictly legal way, of the German revolution.

The Protestant army bishop spoke first. Seeing before him that huge gathering, he should have been inspired to speak with all his spiritual strength in memory of a great past. But his speech was dull and without life, practically nothing but a succession of quotations from the Old Testament, so that in the end the whole thing was less a German address than a wretched stammering. The Lutheran Church lost a great deal of respect that day.

Hitler spoke simply, formally, obviously with reverence. And when he finished with the words: Dead Field Marshal, enter now into Valhalla! these words lacked completely the mustiness that can make such phrases positively unbearable.

Hindenburg was decently buried, not by the representatives of his own tradition but by the maker of a revolution once so alien to him. The relationship between Hitler and Hindenburg undoubtedly was proof of great tactfulness on the part of Hitler rather than anything else. It showed up a side of Hitler's character that could be extremely delicate whenever he felt true respect for someone. But this receded more and more into the background during the years of disappointment. This disappointment had its origin not only in the rejection of his foreign policies, but more often than not in the former corps of officers. The bloody suppression of the Röhm revolt had shown the Wehrmacht that the new chancellor recognized it as the only legitimate armed force, and rejected unconditionally any usurpation of its functions by the non-military.

National Socialism and the Military

There was also something else that I remember most vividly from a conversation I had with Admiral Wagner[146] at Mondorf in Luxembourg. The admiral had suffered a hemorrhage in his ankle and had to stay in bed for some time. Thus we lay side by side on our field cots, when he said that May 1, 1933 was one of his most moving memories. Up to then vicious attacks had been made on officers whenever they allowed <u>themselves to</u> be seen by the Red marchers on May 1.

[146] Gerhard Wagner (1898–1987), a leading German naval officer of the war, who took part in the surrender negotiations of 1945. Remarkably, he ended his career as a Rear Admiral of the German Navy of West Germany.

Then suddenly: marching workers' columns again, but from all sides, friendly words, comradely hails. This to him had been proof supreme that the general attitude had been changed from within, and that the class war had been brought to an end.

But there were others too. There were the ones who, to be sure, had been bitter toward the Weimar Republic: ex-officers who worked as travelling salesmen, bank clerks who still insisted upon sullenly looking back rather than ahead. All they saw was the past, when rank and uniform commanded respect, and firmly established traditions had an answer to every question.

Many of these were staff members of the *Reichswehr*, a very large number of them were in the *Stahlhelm,* or had retired to their estates. After the *Wehrhoheit*[147] of Germany had been re-established, these former officers were again called in for periodical training. Many of them were reactivated and quickly advanced in rank.

And during this process of filling out the officer corps, many of these always-yesterday people landed in important positions. Thus the National Socialist Reich took thousands from humdrum offices and stores and put them back into their old profession, and the German officer, cursed and spat upon for fourteen long years, was once again up front and honored.

Certainly there were many among them who were aware of this and were honestly appreciative, but only very few of them seemed to come to what should have been the obvious conclusion. They gladly accepted gifts, but they failed to see that these gifts were bought and paid for by courage and by a new form of state.

Instead, they tried to reintroduce the same old spiritual and disciplinary methods that had been abandoned in 1918, condescending to accept from National Socialism whatever conformed to these old traditions, but fighting bitterly against everything belonging to the changed new world. No party politics for them! This formerly justifiable phrase became a convenient excuse. Blomberg, who honestly tried to bridge the abyss, was frequently the object of such sarcastic remarks as *Hitlerjunge Quex!*[148]

---

[147] "Right to bear arms"—the rearmament of Germany.

[148] "Hitler Youth Quex," a 1932 novel based on the life of Herbert "Quex" Norkus (1916–1932), a Hitler Youth member murdered by German Communists. The 1933 film *Hitlerjunge Quex: Ein Film vom Opfergeist der deutschen Jugend* was based on it and was described by Joseph Goebbels as the "first large-scale" transmission of National Socialist ideology using the medium of cinema.

At a meeting of high officers in Berlin, Blomberg suggested that some National Socialists address them on party activities. I made several such addresses, but always refrained from any mention of religious matters.

After one of these meetings Blomberg said: Herr *Reichsleiter*, you said the other day that Christianity was ennobled by the very fact that so many Germans believed in it. Thank you very much for this thought. I think it is most felicitous.

In 1943, when I was at the *Führerhauptquartier*,[149] I ate alone with Hitler, though Bormann dropped in later. Great bitterness toward the officer corps was quite apparent. It was difficult to discuss anything with the officers except military affairs, and they thought only of their own advancement, and so on. I was unable to check the veracity of these claims, but in my estimation it was sufficient if these gentlemen understood their trade. In all justice one could not expect them to have the all-embracing understanding of a Moltke!

Important to Keep Army out of Politics

Once upon a time, the motto was, *With God for King and Fatherland,*—a motto for which soldiers had long fought and died. *For Kaiser and Reich* said the same thing in a new and prouder form. But nobody had dared invent the slogan, *For Reich President and Republic.*

Nor could even the towering figure of Hindenburg make anyone forget the fact that the republic had not been born as the result of a national movement, but had merely been the outcome of November 9, 1918.[150]

In 1933, another motto, *For Führer and Reich,* became somewhat more popular. But it would have taken many long years to give it real inner strength. And here, I think, a grave psychological mistake was made. Even though Hitler had to be addressed by party members as *Mein Führer*—something that I had not accepted without reluctance, the introduction of this formula into the parlance of the Wehrmacht was, to say the least, precipitous.

In its early use this address indicated an extremely personal and intimate relationship which was to be expected among fellow fighters,

---

[149] Führer headquarters.
[150] The German surrender at the end of the First World War.

but certainly did not exist between Hitler and high-ranking officers of the army.

Such a form of address would have presupposed a ripe old age for the Führer, and could have become universally accepted only after future generations, divested of psychological reservations toward the guardian of the state's highest office, had become accustomed to it by long usage.

Hitler wanted something quickly that could, by its very nature, ripen only slowly. On top of this came the German greeting. At first it was required by the Führer only when official reports were made; but after four and one-half years of war its use became general and mandatory. A foolish mistake, indeed, since the jerking up of one's right arm on a crowded street had a simply ridiculous effect. The customary military salute would have been much more appropriate.

And finally, the universal use of *Heil Hitler!* At one time it had been the battle cry of a revolution. For party rallies and large demonstrations it might have been retained. But the order to make it exclusive and universal cheapened its intrinsic value.

Neglecting to use it gave fanatics a chance to make sarcastic remarks; and it certainly failed to create that feeling of being a part of a whole which the Ministry of the Interior no doubt had expected when it issued the order for its use. Within the officer corps this form of salute involving the name of a still living young chancellor most certainly met with violent antagonism.

One of the many examples of what allowances must be made for psychological considerations, even in times of radical change. Withal, Hitler had not really intended to issue such an order. On that fateful January 30, 1933, when he returned to the Hotel Kaiserhof after his official installation as chancellor, a number of his old collaborators were assembled in his room, I among them.

Hitler greeted us very solemnly and said: *Gentlemen, now I think I have been justified,* and added that he did not want us to address him henceforth by his title but, as before, by his name. In the long run this was impossible, of course, just as all that followed was so completely superfluous.

During our days of battle Hitler once said to me: *To build up a real army requires at least a century.* What he meant was that military slogans can turn into deep-rooted traditions only in the course of several generations; that military rules, commands, intra-service relationships, and military forms, must become part of the flesh and blood to guarantee the smooth functioning of a large military body under all conditions and in its most minute details. But this very man later came to believe he could overtake fate in only a few years.

Artistic Side of Hitler Led to his Downfall in Foreign Affairs

In Jakob Burckhardt's[151] works I found a quotation from Plato according to which its ultimate downfall is already apparent in the rise of any *Theatrokratie.*[152] This is precisely what is duplicated in the misuse of National Socialist philosophy. It was the prerequisite for its degeneration at a time when that theatrocratic element, together with the secret police, began to constitute the retinue of that man who planned so wisely and widely, who spoke and designed so clearly, only finally to permit the artistic side of his character to overwhelm him in a paroxysm of self-intoxication. In domestic politics this could be overcome; but in the field of foreign politics it led to the end of the Reich.

Adolf Hitler was often careful enough about weighing political chances and, when politics demanded it, frequently forbade expression of the most justifiable emotions. But he also learned that a movement must be strongly emotional if it is to survive prolonged battles, and that it is the heart and faith of the people that help them survive persecution and defeat even at a time when common sense tells them to give up.

He got his strength from poles so wide apart that, figuratively speaking, he frequently seemed to be torn in two. Those speeches of his that have become known only recently are the explosions of a man who no longer seriously bothers to seek counsel from anyone, but still believes he is listening to his inner voice; they are soliloquies, in part still logical, in part merely extravagant. And—again this terrible thing— even in the field of foreign politics, that theatrical, that propagandistic element.

Besides music and the theatre, Hitler devoted himself from his very first days in office to the entire field of art. In Munich I had seen some

[151] Carl Jacob Christoph Burckhardt (1818–1897), a leading and influential art and culture historian, known as one of the major progenitors of cultural history.
[152] Literally, a "theatrocracy." In Ancient Greece, this meant a government by an assembly of citizens, or, as was the more probable usage intent here, rule by spectators in a theater.

Memoirs

architectonic designs done by him. As was to be expected, they were less skilled in the treatment of form than the drawings and aquarelles dating back to the First World War which I saw either in the original or in later reproduction. They showed a natural gift, a feeling for the essential, and a pronounced pictorial talent.

Hitler, Art, and Architecture

As soon as the Führer was in Munich, he sat down with Professor Troost[153] who, in 1932, had rebuilt and furnished the Brown House.

To replace the burned-down Glaspalast,[154] Hitler wanted to give Munich a new House of Art, and for this purpose he started an endowment fund; and so they planned and dreamed, while the work on party buildings continued apace.

During a visit with Troost we discussed a subject that was somewhat embarrassing to both of us. Along with his great understanding for the requirements of modern architecture, Hitler had, as far as painting was concerned, strictly lower middle class taste that frequently did not go beyond genre. He was disgusted with the trend that tried to hide a lack of artistic ability under a plethora of paint and arrogant brush strokes or, worse, succeeded in palming off a complete lack of ability as a new style by means of expressionistic distortions.

Hitler declared that the art of painting would have to begin at the beginning again, with skillful design, studies of form, and honest artisanship, if it ever hoped to regain its health. Thus it would have to go through a period of mediocrity, would have to exclude problematical outsiders from all great national exhibitions, and permit no experimenting.

Hitler also believed that the much criticized 19th century had actually produced a great number of works of art and that, in any case, 19th-century painters were certainly more skillful than the people who in the last few decades had become destroyers of all form. For

[153] Paul Ludwig Troost (1878–1934). Famous in his own right, he is best remembered as Hitler's foremost architect whose neoclassical style became for a time the official architecture of the Third Reich.
[154] The *Glaspalast* (Glass Palace) was a glass and iron exhibition building in Munich modeled after The Crystal Palace in London. The Glaspalast opened for the *Erste Allgemeine Deutsche Industrieausstellung* (First General German Industrial Exhibition) on July 15, 1854. It was destroyed in a fire on June 6, 1931.

148

this reason he set about with an ever growing passion to acquire 19th-century paintings, which he intended to assemble some day in a gallery in the City of Linz, which was to be completely rebuilt.

Hitler's aversion to the artistic development of the 20th century as a whole undoubtedly made him one-sided and unjust. Clean artisanship soon became the one and only measuring stick for all annual art exhibitions, so that they eventually got muddled in lower middle class banality.

An intensive hunt was started for works by Spitzweg[155] and also for anything by Grützner,[156] who were placed on almost the same high level as Keller,[157] Raabe,[158] and Busch.[159] To be sure, as a *bon mot* by Raabe has it, the German spirit does draw a third of its power from Philistinism, but it isn't absolutely essential to search out the art of only this third!

That the Führer bought several large paintings by Zäper[160] is still understandable; but that a man like Ziegler[161] should become President of the Chamber of Art, and a professor to boot, is a dubious omen. Ziegler was a talented and amiable man who had been helped along with an assignment to paint frescoes in some private house. But his selection for such an important position was evidence of Hitler's limitations.

Ziegler's laborious pictures prove that he could neither draw nor paint, and was really no more than an academic beginner. To see a large painting of his hang in the *Führerhaus*[162] was positively painful. The picture disappeared, as I found out only recently, when Ziegler was arrested.

---

[155] Carl Spitzweg (1808–1885), a leading German romanticist painter and poet.

[156] Eduard Theodor Ritter von Grützner (1846–1925), a painter and professor of art especially noted for his genre paintings of monks. One of Hitler's favorites, of whom he told Albert Speer that he considered Grützner on the same level as Rembrandt.

[157] Ferdinand Keller (1842–1922), a realist who specialized in scenes from German history.

[158] Wilhelm Raabe (1831–1910), a novelist. His early works were published under the pseudonym of Jakob Corvinus.

[159] Heinrich Christian Wilhelm Busch (1832–1908), a German humorist, poet, illustrator and painter.

[160] Max Zäper (1872–unknown), best known for his landscape scenes. A contemporary of Hitler and also a personal friend.

[161] Adolf Ziegler (1892–1959), an early favorite of Hitler, who was tasked with overseeing the purging of "modern" art from German art galleries. During the war, he was arrested for expressing opposition to the war and served six weeks in Dachau.

[162] Hitler's house on the Obersalzburg in Bavaria.

However, as is the case with so many who have acquired unlimited power, Hitler's great love was for architecture.

In 1917, I had written in my notebook that it could often be observed that someone who was a revolutionary in one form of art was a conservative in another.

If what Troost told me one day was true, that Hitler had stopped in the field of painting at the year 1890, then he certainly showed a remarkable understanding for architecture. In Greek architecture he saw the embodiment of the art of the Nordic race, something that led to many critical remarks about the Gothic. He also professed to recognize certain echoes of Greek architecture in the most modern trends, without being blind to modern improvements.

The party buildings in Munich[163] were only a beginning: Correctly designed, not groping up into space, simple in their horizontal lines, effective in the two dark contrasts of eagle and balcony railing.

A mistake, on the other hand, were the two temples[164] with their sarcophagi; open above, lopsided in construction (which Schultze-Naumberg[165] could justifiably criticize as mere applied art).

Besides, as I told Hitler: at the *Feldherrnhalle*[166] sixteen men had fallen, not two times eight. The attempt at symmetry had most certainly done harm to the whole design.

But in my opinion that was not so bad as what I must call the killing of space by paving the entire Königsplatz with granite slabs. This had its origin in Hitler's mania for banning nature from architecture. He was disturbed not only by an open space before a large building, but even by the lawn in front of the Glyptothek.

And again the theatrical: to make enough room for two marching

---

[163] The still-existing *Führerbau* (Führer Buildings) in Munich, situated on the Königsplatz in that city.

[164] The *Ehrentempel* ("honor temples") were two structures in Munich which housed the sacrophagi of the sixteen members of the NSDAP who had been killed in the failed 1923 putsch. They were located right next to the *Führerbau,* but were destroyed to foundation level in 1947.

[165] Paul Schultze-Naumburg (1869–1949), an architect, painter, publicist and politician. He joined the NSDAP in 1930 and was an important advocate of National Socialist architecture and a leading critic of modern architecture.

[166] The still-existing "Field Marshall's Hall" in Munich, built between 1841 and 1844 to honor the Bavarian Army. After the Franco-Prussian war of 1870, a new set of statues were added to celebrate the German military leaders victorious in that conflict. It was at the *Feldherrnhalle* that the NSDAP's 1923 putsch ended when police opened fire on the marching crowd.

columns, the entire Königsplatz was treated like the training field of an armory. When I saw this immense desert of slabs I was disgusted. Every building surrounding the Königsplatz was practically killed off, shoved aside, deprived of its symmetry. In other words, here Hitler's passion for deploying troops had completely negated his truly great feeling for the monumental.

The Plans for Berlin and other Cities

What the Führer planned for Berlin, Nuremberg, Munich, and the rest, is fairly well known. But when I saw Speer's model of the future capital of the Reich, together with the individual designs by various architects, and the dimensions were explained to me, I was even more flabbergasted.

Naturally I took a personal interest in the building that was to house my own offices. It was agreed to put up a medium-sized building in the government quarter of Berlin, and separate buildings in the new southern section of the city for training schools and exhibitions.

There is no need to describe Hitler's plans in detail. But I might mention that in spite of the terrific sums involved, they would not have cost as much, according to Speer, as two or three months of the Second World War. Behind all this planning stood a great energy with remarkable vision and glorious ideas about the Reich and German creative power. Hitler planned truly great things for Germany, great things for himself, and even more, if greater resources were made available to the German people. These he wanted to achieve.

Side by side with these political manifestations of Hitler's character went those of his artistic nature; and in this lies much that is decisive for an understanding of his personality.

Hitler as a Disciplinarian and Bohemian

In 1925, when he asked me to take over the management of the *Völkischer Beobachter,* he also discussed Ludendorff's dabbling in politics during the past year. He claimed that Ludendorff had to fail politically because he was unmusical. He, on the other hand, as a musically sensitive person, understood men better, and also would be better able to lead them.

I never forgot these words, remembered them often, and was reminded of them quite forcefully during some of the terrible hours of 1945.

What Hitler wanted to say is that only a musical person can really feel the vibrations of a people's soul, and thus find the right words to influence it, so that he alone before all others, can take the proper steps to lead it politically.

But his political common sense, usually so clever and deliberate in the weighing of possibilities, was frequently derailed by sudden outbreaks of passion, just as the profound understanding of serious architecture often gave way to the irresponsible musical emotion of the moment. In everyday life he was a conscientious disciplinarian, but also a Bohemian without ties to family, court, convention, or whatever the decisive attachment to custom or tradition may be called.

All this, I feel, has nothing to do with pedantry or moralizing on my part, but is merely an attempt to describe a personality whose success is based not upon strength alone, but also wells from a source which carried many negative attributes to the surface of his life. For Hitler the one instrument with which to influence people was speech.

In *Mein Kampf* he relates how relieved he was when he had finally proved to himself that he could speak easily and freely before a crowd. There is no doubt that the spoken word can move people much more deeply and can spur them on to action much more readily than the written or the printed word.

On the other hand, it is equally true that the effect of a speech, always somewhat hypnotizing, is not so lasting as the impression made by a book which can be read and re-examined in any mood. That is why the public meetings could never be allowed to stop.

Origin of the Swastika Flag

But that is also why this method of shaping the will of the people was extended and improved by Hitler in every possible way apt to stir the imagination of the masses. One of these means was the new flag. Every sacrifice, every success, was implicit in this symbol. It had been present at the first great meetings; it had been soaked with the blood of the dead in front of the *Feldherrnhalle;* it flew over the graves of our murdered comrades, and rode at the head of many marching columns until, on January 30, 1933, it was triumphantly borne under the *Brandenburger Tor*[167] and into Berlin. It combined the old colors of the Reich, black-white-red,[168] with an old Germanic sign.[169] I was with Hitler when he called on the manufacturer of the first standard which he himself had designed. He was as pleased as a little boy.

At the end of January, 1923, we witnessed the first formal massing of the colors during our otherwise rather simple party rally in Munich. In the middle of the winter, a parade on the Marsfeld. The first speech of welcome in the name of other nationalist organizations delivered by Colonel von Xylander.[170] Then Hitler spoke. He reviewed the parade twice, rode back to town to watch twice more the march through the streets of Munich. Thus his own creation acted as a fortifier on himself.

As a means of influencing people, Hitler invariably used the same huge red placards that not only announced a meeting, but also aroused curiosity with some cleverly worded text. After 1924, the uniforms of the various groups were added to the display, until party rallies at Nuremberg turned into a colorful ritual that, constantly repeated, became an easily remembered tradition. This is how national customs always evolve.

Mass Rallies as a Cultural Phenomenon

Along with these came other manifestations: cultural rallies, congresses, special meetings. These years made speakers out of many of us. But Hitler's insistence that only great speakers, and never great writers, had made history, sounded dubious to me.

Great men have influenced the history of nations in many ways: as statesmen in office or leaders in the field, as revolutionary soldiers (Cromwell, Napoleon), and finally as powerful speakers. It was Luther's theses and his other writings that conceived and sustained the greatest

[167] The Brandenburg Gate.

[168] The colors of the "First Reich," established in 1872, when the German states were first united as a nation.

[169] The swastika emblem was originally a Sanskrit symbol meaning good fortune, and was based on the ancient symbolism of the sun, as an orb with rays spreading out in all directions. It had been used by all Indo-European peoples from the earliest times, and was commonly used in western architecture in Europe and North America right up to the 1930s.

[170] Oskar Ritter und Edler von Xylander (1856–1940) was a Bavarian *General der Infanterie*, the commander of the I Royal Bavarian Corps during the First World War.

revolution the German people ever experienced. In other words, the means by which great effects have been produced are extremely varied, and this speaking-writing comparison is therefore nonsense, though subjectively understandable, since, after 1918, speeches were the universally used method of approach because every kind of Putsch had proved not only impractical but idiotic.

Under these circumstances, Hitler's attitude was understandable, and his allegation merely another way of underscoring the importance of speech-making. I dwell on this because it also touches upon the artistic field.

Inevitably the speeches, the massing of the colors, the form of salute, and so on, had in them a strongly theatrical element. The temptation to dazzle the eye and intrigue the imagination instead of appealing to common sense was great, particularly when the Führer himself succumbed to the pomp of a great mass demonstration, not only during hours of justifiable exaltation, but also in hours that ought to have belonged to sober contemplation.

It was quite right, of course, to use all available means to stimulate the emotions, faith, and will, for it required a sustained state of exaltation to start from scratch—without a name, without money, and in direct opposition to all existing parties—a mass movement, destined some day to embrace all of Germany.

Only one who is utterly incapable of comprehending the great events governing the fate of entire nations will deny the existence of these forces or their importance. A man like Moltke,[171] for example, in 1919, would certainly not have chosen to face a seething people and, working tirelessly, constantly traveling the length and breadth of the land, continuously pouring his heart into impassioned speeches, try thus to capture its soul.

We all had to jettison our preconceived ideas as to what was right and proper in the political arena. Insight into facts as they were, combined with this intoxication by faith, were the secrets of success. For that, history did not need a Moltke but a Hitler. At least, until January 30, 1933. On this day the tribune ceased to exist. The test of the statesman began.

---

[171] It is unclear whether Rosenberg was here referring to Helmuth Karl Bernhard Graf von Moltke (1800–1891), a Field Marshal and chief of staff of the Prussian Army for thirty years, or his nephew Helmuth Johann Ludwig von Moltke (1848–1916), who commanded the German Army at the outbreak of the First World War.

Hitler as Chancellor

With incredible tenacity Hitler had refused all offers to appoint him vice chancellor. And eventually he did succeed in enforcing what he and millions of others considered essential. In doing so Hitler fought a difficult battle with himself. After he had been chancellor for a short while he told me with evident pride: *All week long I have managed each day to clear my desk of all current work.* I actually felt like laughing, for this, of all things, certainly was not his *forte*.

And, sure enough, he soon gave up these attempts at bureaucratic systematizing, not only because Lammers,[172] Meissner, and others quickly adapted themselves to his needs, but also because he now began to concentrate all his energies on one rather than on many problems. Once immersed in that he refused to listen to the pleas and complaints of any other department until he thought he had fully acquainted himself with all relevant details.

During the days of Munich,[173] for example, he once ordered every available book on the fleets of all nations. These he studied for weeks at a stretch, often until four in the morning. The result was that he was later able to make decisions that sent the admirals, who had very skeptically arrived for a conference, out of the office of the new chancellor shaking their heads over the expert knowledge he had displayed.

Even after Hitler's death, Admiral Raeder[174] admitted emphatically: *I often felt like one being taught, rather than like a teacher.* Admiral Dönitz[175] admitted he had felt the same way.

Or else Hitler would order fifty or a hundred bound volumes of old magazines, to study the technique of criticism applied to music and the drama. He was enraged by modern critics who commented on artists obviously giving their best, with nothing but caustic witticism

---

[172] Dr. Hans Heinrich Lammers (1879–1962), a jurist who served as head of the Reich Chancellery.

[173] The Munich Conference of 1938.

[174] Erich Johann Albert Raeder (1876–1960), a career navy man who attained the highest possible naval rank—that of *Großadmiral* (Grand Admiral)—in 1939. Raeder led the German navy for the first half of the war; he resigned in 1943 and was replaced by Karl Dönitz.

175 Karl Dönitz (1891–1980), a career Navy man who is credited with developing the "wolfpack" U-boat tactic, who replaced Raeder in January 1943. Given the rank of *Großadmiral* (Grand Admiral), Dönitz became one of Hitler's most trusted men, and was appointed by the latter as his successor in 1945. Dönitz remained as head of the German Government until his arrest by the Allies on May 23, 1945.

and arrogant condescension. Once he told me: *How clean, decent, and understanding the critics were, by and large, in 1850! They tried hard to understand and help instead of tearing down and destroying by sarcasm.* These studies were responsible for Hitler's later demand that we forgo the idea that a critic's chief is to criticize. Instead, he said, they should approach musicians and actors in a spirit of benevolence. Hitler's effectiveness had its source in this ability of his to concentrate; a corollary was the neglecting of a great many other problems.

Hitler as Military Strategist

Hitler never forgot that the generals had looked down upon him from the pinnacle of their strategic knowledge, as the corporal of World War I. That is why he spent years studying every single type of military writing, the published works of general staffs, and all the new technical improvements. Finally, and in spite of certain mental reservations, he forced them to take cognizance of his amazing knowledge, so much so, that Colonel General Jodl[176] one day frankly declared that Hitler was a great strategic thinker.

But beyond the purely strategic, Hitler also had that spark which even many generals lacked when faced with modern developments. The new tactics used in the conquest of Eben-Emael[177] were Hitler's personal triumph, just as he mapped out the campaign in France, which, in many essentials, did not follow the old Schlieffen Plan,[178] but specified a break-through and the rolling up of the enemy front toward the Channel. This was an achievement quite as great as the forcing of

[176] Alfred Josef Ferdinand Jodl (1890–1946), Chief of the Operations Staff of the Armed Forces High Command (Oberkommando der Wehrmacht, or OKW) during the war. He signed the unconditional surrender of Germany as a representative for president Karl Dönitz.
[177] Fort Eben-Emael was a large concrete emplacement located between Liège and Maastricht, on the Belgian-Dutch border, near the Albert Canal, designed to defend Belgium from a German attack across the narrow belt of Dutch territory in the region. Constructed in 1931–1935, it was reputed to be impregnable and at the time, the largest in the world. The fort was successfully neutralized by glider-borne German troops (56 men) on 10 May 1940, an action which cleared the way for German ground forces to enter Belgium, unhindered by fire from Eben-Emael.
[178] The Schlieffen Plan was a 1905 German General Staff thought-experiment which later became a deployment-plan and set of recommendations for German Commanders. It essentially entailed all of the German army being deployed on the German-Belgian border so it could launch an offensive into France, through the southern Dutch province of Limburg, Belgium, and Luxembourg.

the Maginot Line, considering all the negative memoranda on this plan which were submitted by generals who were later made field marshals. I did not hear about this until later.

From Hitler himself, he said only this much: *Now the gentlemen want their memoranda back. But I shall keep them in my safe for future study.*

Did success in military matters also produce—megalomania? I also wondered. For in the course of events it became ever more apparent that Hitler, who formerly had been so open-minded, was not only becoming stubborn in political matters, but also in the fields of art and science, an attitude that frequently resulted in tension and intolerance.

In the course of the Nuremberg trials such mediocrities as Schirach and Fritzsche[179] maintained that the Führer had cheated them, had told them untruths and outright lies. High-ranking officers whom Hitler had either kept in the dark politically, or had told only the barest essentials, now claimed this, too.

As a matter of fact, the head of the state was under no obligation whatsoever to keep his generals and ministers informed about confidential matters or the decisions he made. Gossip had to be avoided, the respective persons might be transferred and, after all, it was Hitler who made, and was responsible for, all important decisions.

What must be examined is what he did and ordered, not whether he informed certain officials accordingly.

Hitler Self-Educated

Schacht[180] once said that Hitler's book was written in the worst possible German, but neglected to explain why he constantly kept on offering his services to him. This remark touches upon something that,

[179] Hans Georg Fritzsche (1900–1953), permanent secretary to the Propaganda Ministry. A relatively minor official, it was clear that he had been charged in the place of Propaganda Minister Joseph Goebbels. He was acquitted of all charges.
[180] Hjalmar Horace Greeley Schacht (1877–1970), economist, banker, liberal politician, and co-founder in 1918 of the German Democratic Party. He served as the Currency Commissioner and President of the Reichsbank under the Weimar Republic. He was a fierce critic of his country's post-World War I reparation obligations and became a supporter of Hitler on account of the latter's opposition to the Versailles Treaty. He served as President of the Reichsbank and Minister of Economics until 1937, when his opposition to the rearmament policy caused his dismissal and retirement. He was tried at Nuremberg and acquitted.

more than anything else, enables the observer to watch Hitler's growth. In his youth he had been deprived of a thorough schooling, and no amount of self-education can possibly make up for that.

Besides, his work in Vienna took up practically all of his time, nor did four and one-half years of war among real soldiers tend to improve his style. Hitler wrote and dictated, furthermore, as a speaker, and it was often difficult to untangle his sentences and pour them into a more permanent mould.

I still remember how Stolzing-Cerny,[181] the editor of the *Völkischer Beobachter,* sweated over the galleys of *Mein Kampf* after Hitler had asked him to proof read. Naturally, certain questionable lines were discovered and corrected, but they simply couldn't be rewritten into entirely new sentences. In the meantime, however, Hitler's language and style improved so remarkably that some of the speeches he later made before cultural rallies were absolutely outstanding examples of German linguistic art.

Hitler Rejected Christianity

The Führer correctly differentiated between the religious beliefs of the individual and political reasoning. What his own beliefs were he never told me in so many words.

Once, at table, he said a high-placed Italian had asked him point-blank what his religious beliefs were. He had begged permission not to answer that question.

In his speeches, Hitler frequently referred to Providence and the Almighty. I am certain that he was inwardly convinced of a fate predestined in its general outlines, but preferred not to formulate what parts compulsion and free will played.

He became more and more convinced that Providence had entrusted him with a mission. This became noticeable upon his return from his incarceration in the Landsberg,[182] and grew ever more evident after the *Machtübernahme,* until, toward the end of the war, it assumed positively painful proportions.

---

[181] Josef Stolzing (1869-1942) writer and early editor of the *Volkischer Beobachter.* He published under several variations of his name, including Josef Stolzing-Cerny. Most famously, he edited the first version of *Mein Kampf.*

[182] Landsberg-am-Lech, where Hitler served prison time for the failed 1923 putsch.

This conviction that, as Bismarck had once been chosen to unite the northern Germans in one Reich, so he was chosen to bring the southern Germans (Austrians) into this Reich, was certainly deep-rooted in him. As for the Christian concept of God, Hitler definitely rejected it in private conversations. That I know even though in the course of the years I heard only two or three pertinent remarks. Once he told me: *Look at the head of Zeus! What nobility and exaltation there are in those features! About communion: It is primitively religious to crush one's God with one's teeth.*

He held against Gothic art that it symbolized everything dark and brain-beclouding. Later on he granted at least the impressiveness of the cathedral in Strasbourg. When, in the course of one of these conversations, I ventured the opinion that one could not destroy the churches, but could merely attempt to fill them gradually with new people, he replied: *That is a very wise thought!*

Fundamentally, as far as his attitude was concerned, Hitler had very definitely discounted churches and Christianity, although he fully acknowledged the importance of their initial appearance on earth, granted everyone the right to his own conviction, and supported the Wehrmacht in its religious and confessional demands. In fact, by setting up a Church Ministry and instituting a Protestant Bishop of the Reich, he even tried to give the strife-torn Evangelicals a chance to unite in one all-embracing social group.

For this purpose he received in audience a delegation of Protestant bishops. Afterward he spoke of this meeting with utter contempt. *You would think*, he said at dinner one day, *that these gentlemen would understand that an audience with the Reich Chancellor is in a way a rather solemn affair.*

Instead they came garbed in their clerical robes, most of which were already a bit tacky with age, and the thing that was of the greatest importance for them was—their allowance! I'll say this much for the Catholics: if they had come, they would have been more dignified.

Hitler had steadfastly refused to let himself become involved in any conspiracy. He used his appearance as a witness in a trial at Leipzig[183] to emphasize this attitude, which he maintained to the last. In utilizing his great gifts as a speaker, and in thoroughly organizing his party, he was merely exercising rights everyone has. The battle for the soul of the people was waged in broad daylight; the arguments of every single

[183] The Leipzig military trial. See footnote 137.

party were available. The attacks against us were vicious, and we answered viciously.

Admittedly, all sides committed occasional blunders. In looking over my collected articles, I admitted to myself that criticism could occasionally have been handled differently. But these articles were frequently written at seven o'clock in the morning, were based on reports that had just come in, and were thus not always considered opinions. In their attacks our opponents spared us absolutely nothing. For the middle classes we were camouflaged Bolshevists and atheists, for the Marxists, agents of Deterding,[184] capitalistic varlets, and monarchist reactionaries.

---

[184] A reference to international capitalism in the form of the Dutchman Henri Wilhelm August Deterding (1866–1939), one of the first executives of the Royal Dutch Petroleum Company and for 36 years (1900–1936) its chairman and the chairman of the combined Royal Dutch/Shell oil company.

Part Fourteen:
The Collapse of the Reich

Did Hitler Risk the Existence of the Reich by Going to War?

After 1937, when the impossibility of an alliance between Great Britain and Germany was finally accepted by him as an irrevocable fact, Hitler knew that he now had to make the most of the period during which England still was not ready for an open conflict. This conviction governed the year 1938, the year of his greatest successes.

He was so moved that he could hardly speak when, as the man who had fulfilled an old German longing, he entered the city of his youth, Linz, and when from Vienna he made his most important report to the German people. But the setting up of the Bohemian-Moravian protectorate and, particularly, the attack on Poland, were even more fateful.

Did Adolf Hitler, then, frivolously risk the existence of people and Reich? Did he, in the pride of his heart, and with the auto-suggested belief in his mission, shrink from accepting a diplomatic setback?

Did he consider too lightly Great Britain's preparedness for war?

Once more he hesitated when, after the receipt of Chamberlain's letter, he cancelled the order to attack on August 26; but later he let fate take its inexorable course.

Because of conceit? For lack of self-discipline in a decisive hour?

Or did he, as appears possible from some of his speeches that have only recently become known, foresee the following developments: an arrested economic improvement, the choking off of Germany's foreign trade by the increasing effectiveness of the boycott; a recession in agriculture, and a shortage of grain reserves in the territories under German control; the impossibility of continued large imports; unemployment and hunger?

The one great advantage Germany had—an incomparable air arm—outstripped within six to ten years?

He himself considerably older and incapacitated by a stomach ailment?

And finally, the even then threatening encirclement and crushing of the Reich, and thus the inglorious end of a great revolution?

Or did his vision encompass only the securing of subjugated borderlands, the incorporation into the Reich of the wheat-producing territories in the East, a break through the threatened encirclement, and the conquest of large spaces? Battles in the West and the East waged in succession, thus avoiding a possible war on two fronts?

But even if all these things would come true in six to ten years, did he have the right to anticipate fate? Could not many things happen in the interim, old adversaries die, and new friends be gained? All these are questions which only the future can answer.

The Cause of the Collapse of the Reich

The immediate outcome, of course, has been a complete collapse of people and Reich unparalleled in history. For a short time the flag of the Reich flew over the Pyrenees, the North Cape, the Volga, and Libya, victorious as never before.

Today this flag lies buried under rubble, torn and—this is the horrible part of it—defiled by the very ones Hitler had chosen as companions in his decisive years, people who did not favor caution, discipline, and the observance of venerable old soldierly traditions and norms, but who were all for strengthening the other side, the artistic, theatrical, passionate, egocentric side.

And the others from earlier days could no longer be counted on because they had either been eliminated or were, like Ribbentrop, without political concepts and ideas. All this did not occur suddenly. It developed over many years. The founding of a propaganda ministry, for instance, was a basic mistake; allying it with the arts, a second one.

The elevation of Himmler to the all-powerful post of chief of police, and the suspension of the accepted forms of law beyond the period of the actual revolution, were two great dangers for the National Socialist idea; the dominance of the strong men of the S.S. over arts and sciences, another.

And finally, in the war itself, there was the abandonment of all political psychology. In the beginning the Führer expected Terboven[185] to conquer the soul of Norway. But he stuck to him even after this arrogant nitwit had failed so completely. From then on Hitler relied on might alone.

Hitler Overrated Italian Fascism and Mussolini

The roots go down to an overrating of Fascism. Blind to all disillusioning experiences of the First World War, Hitler seemed convinced, at least until 1943, that the will of Mussolini had made over the Italian people, had lifted them to a new level, had made them strong enough to be able to resist Great Britain.

Did he actually believe this, or was it merely an attempt to bolster the morale of his Fascist ally when he realized that England could not be had? No, the attempt to turn Italy into a warlike nation had long since been wrecked by the individual Italian himself. And it is especially surprising that Hitler, an Austrian, persisted in his delusion when every Austrian soldier knew better.

Germany Needed Shrewd and Sober Leaders, Not Artistic Personalities

In the course of the war Göring's[186] prestige declined rapidly. He was held responsible for the inability to keep enemy bombers away. As I learned from my assistant, who had it from Hitler's secretaries, the Führer was discussing the problem of his succession.

Himmler was mentioned by Hitler; but he added immediately that Himmler was disliked by the party and was, furthermore, an inartistic man. Even in 1945, it appeared, there were no other, infinitely

---

[185] Josef Antonius Heinrich Terboven (1898–1945), an early NSDAP member, participant in the 1923 Putsch, and from 1940 onwards, *Reichskommissar* for Norway. He committed suicide in 1945.

[186] Hermann Wilhelm Göring (1893–1946), World War One air ace and head of the Luftwaffe during the Second World War.

more weighty, reasons for the candidacy of Himmler being utterly unthinkable!

At a time when it was more than obvious that the people no longer needed artistic personalities, but shrewd and sober characters! The great founders of world powers, incidentally, were certainly the most inartistic of all people—Romans and Englishmen.

But up until a short time before the end, Adolf Hitler accepted values in a field for which these very values had not only proven detrimental but fatal, while he replaced political psychology with the naked power of the sword.

Hitler Summarized

In any case, Adolf Hitler will go down in history as a demoniacal figure of tremendous size.

A great faith in his people and its mission, a tenacity that overcame all obstacles, a gift for simplification, and the creative power of a genius in many fields, a will become iron hard, overwhelming passion, sudden emotional explosions, self-intoxication by means of spectacular shows, the overestimation of domestic political possibilities in their foreign political effects, the identification of his own will and his own fate with that of the nation as a whole, and a fanatical belief in his own mission which, toward the end, actually became incomprehensible.

I need no counsellors. I go my way in somnambulistic assurance, he said in public speeches.

That is how I see the man whose life and ascent I was able to watch from the beginning of his political activities. First close by, then farther away, and in the end considered a discomfiting admonitory and living accusation against those his emotions had collected around him.

I venerated him, and I remained loyal to him to the end. And now Germany's destruction has come with his own.

Sometimes hatred rises in me when I think of the millions of Germans who have been murdered and exiled, of the unspeakable misery, the plundering of the little that remained, and the squandering of a thousand-year-old wealth.

But then again there arises in me the feeling of pity for a man who also was a victim of fate, and who loved this Germany as ardently as any one of us. A man whose fate it was to be rolled, dead, into a blanket, thrown into a hole, drenched with gasoline, and burned in the garden of the Reich Office, among the ruins of a house from which he had once hoped to rebuild, after long suppression, the honor and greatness of his nation.

To understand all this in its ultimate meaning is impossible for me.

Part Fifteen:
The Occupied Eastern Territories

Eastern Policies

I had made arrangements for the celebration of a memorial day for Niedersachsen (Lower Saxony), putting particular emphasis on the figure of Heinrich der Löwe.[187]

In spite of the fact that the Führer considered him a rebel, he still gave him a most fitting resting place in the cathedral at Brunswick, which was declared a national shrine.

Here he saw, correcting a former, somewhat one-sided, attitude, the two of them enter into history: Barbarossa[188] and the Lion. I had never gainsaid their place in history, and I venerated the Hohenstaufen;[189] but the old problem of German history, Italian campaigns or an eastern policy, never left me in peace.

Had not Germany once reached as far as Lake Peipus? Time after time, the Niedersachsen pushed ahead against that East which they had once settled in the wake of the retreating Goths, the Burgundians, Vandals and Slavs. Was it right to set the entire national power on

---

[187] Henry the Lion (1129–1195), Duke of Saxony, as Henry III, from 1142, and Duke of Bavaria, as Henry XII, from 1156. One of the most powerful German princes of his time, at the height of his reign, he ruled over a vast territory stretching from the coast of the North and Baltic Seas to the Alps, and from Westphalia to Pomerania.

[188] Frederick I (1122–1190), also known as Frederick Barbarossa, Holy Roman Emperor from 1155 until his death. He became King of Italy in 1155 and was crowned Roman Emperor by Pope Adrian IV in June 1155. He was later formally crowned King of Burgundy. The name Barbarossa comes from the northern Italian he ruled: Barbarossa means "red beard" in Italian.

[189] The House of Hohenstaufen, also known as the Swabian dynasty or the Staufer, was a dynasty of German monarchs in the High Middle Ages, reigning from 1138 to 1254. Three members of the dynasty were crowned Holy Roman Emperors.

Gero's[190] trail? I, for one, never shied away from airing my opinions on this subject, not even when the identical question came up in a different form: colonial versus eastern policy?

Hadn't the Bajuvares[191] founded the *Ostmark?*[192] Was not that the proper precedent? Was it right to permit the intrusion of the Lithuanian wedge between Prussia and Livonia that prevented all peasant migration? In any case, the power of Germandom had decreased, and the East had advanced as a result of the First World War. And today Russia reaches, temporarily at least, as far west as the Elbe and beyond Weimar.[193] That could not have happened to a German realm reaching from Aachen to Lake Peipus!

Richard Walther Darré and Himmler

Occasionally R. W. Darré called on me. In its day I had considered his first book[194] an excellent contribution to the universal nationalistic trend toward a re-routing on the land after the lopsided growth of the cities.

In his book he traced German history back to the Germanic peasantry. Thereupon Hitler called upon Darré to join the leadership as head of the so-called agrarian-political apparatus.

In Munich I had met Darré only casually. Once I accompanied him on a visit to the half-paralyzed Prince Henckel-Donnersmarck.[195] He told me then that my ideas in the *Myth*[196] concerning the formation of a new nobility had interested him particularly, since he himself was just about to finish a book on the subject. I always considered Darré a very valuable addition to the party. This he certainly was, in spite of

---

[190] Gero I (c. 900–965), a Saxon prince who expanded his territory from Merseburg into a vast territory named after him: the *marca Geronis.* During the mid-10th century, he was the leader of the Saxon *Drang nach Osten* ("Drive to the East.").

[191] The original form of the name of the Bavarian people.

[192] Austria.

[193] A reference to the Soviet Union's occupation of central Europe and eastern Germany, a situation which remained in place until the fall of the Berlin Wall in 1990.

[194] *Das Bauerntum als Lebensquell der nordischen Rasse* (1928), translated into English as "The Peasantry as Life Source of the Nordic Race."

[195] A member of the Silesian noble family, the Henckel von Donnersmarcks, from the former region of Spiš in Upper Hungary, now in Slovakia. The family lost all in 1945 when the German population was expelled.

[196] Rosenberg's book, *The Myth of the Twentieth Century.*

the way he was criticized later on. In 1933, Darré and Himmler (who had been graduated from an agricultural college) became very close. The peasant leaders usually joined the S.S., and Darré took over the management of the Race and Settlement Office,[197] which he built up to a remarkable degree of efficiency.

As Darré told me later on, this alliance was a very practical one. When I answered him that, as far as I was concerned, I could only stand by my own opinion, even if that should mean my being entirely alone, he was a trifle embarrassed. And no doubt he thought of this conversation later, when he was pushed out of office by Himmler. The peasant leaders belonged to the S.S., and any outside attempt to disentangle them from it was hopeless in view of the police powers the S.S. possessed.

Darré considered this a breach of faith on Himmler's part, and this was obviously the cause of his distrust. He felt himself constantly watched, probably because he rightly feared that Himmler would try to encircle him ever closer to prevent any possibility of independent action on his part. Here Bormann helped along, as I learned later; but even completely unbiased observers considered the later Darré to be a man who had lost his balance.

When I began to make my plans for future research within the framework of the high school as a task for my waning years, Darré, who had been sent on leave, visited me. We discussed several problems still very much in their preliminary stages.

Darré planned to write a history of agrarian law from its Germanic beginnings, and also spoke about other plans that gave evidence of his great knowledge and initiative. I received Darré, who at one time had spoken so coolly about spiritual comradeship, very amiably.

After he left Berlin to live in a small house in the Schorfheide, I did not speak to him again until he was forced to move into the Bunker Tower in the Tiergarten[198] because he had to undergo a difficult operation. We

[197] The *Rasse- und Siedlungshauptamt-SS* ("SS Race and Settlement Main Office, or RuSHA), was the organization responsible for ensuring that the SS remained racially pure. It oversaw marriages and the welfare of SS families, among other tasks.
[198] The Zoo flak tower, or in German, the *Flakturm Tiergarten,* was a thirteen-story fortified anti-aircraft tower that existed in Berlin from 1941 to 1947. It was one of several flak towers that protected Berlin from Allied bomber raids. Its primary role was as a gun platform to protect the government building district of Berlin, in addition the *Hochbunker* (blockhouse) was designed to be used as a civilian air-raid shelter. It also contained a hospital and a radio transmitter for use by the German leadership, and provided secure storage facilities for art

both deplored the conversion of the party into a spiritual dictatorship under the incompetent head of the Party Office; something that would necessarily have to provoke opposition. In other words, he also diagnosed a central illness, of which there had been certain symptoms even as early as 1939, but which only the coming of the war made dangerous for all we had fought for through twenty years.

Bormann's deplorable round-robin letters, his narrow-minded attitude in connection with the appointment of *Gauleiter* and their assistants, his invariably radical stand on questions of policy, and so on, were considered by both of us to be fatal for the future. As for his own elimination from active duty, Darré stated quite calmly that, just as he had formerly accepted the positive side of the system, he would now have to accept the negative side, too, even though it hurt him personally. That he was hurt was obvious.

Reich Commissioner for the Occupied Eastern Territories

When I was appointed Minister for the East, I suggested Sauckel,[199] the *Gauleiter* of Thuringia, as Reich Commissioner for the Ukraine. Unfortunately, this proposal was rejected, to the disadvantage of the Reich. Instead the Führer accepted Koch,[200] who had been suggested by Göring. The Führer esteemed Sauckel particularly highly, and wanted to keep him available for a better appointment.

When I began to prepare the eastern territories ministry for a possible war, Doctor Todt[201] begged me to institute a special office for

---

treasures. The Zoo tower in particular stored the Kaiser Willhelm coin collection, Nefertiti's head, the disassembled Altar of Zeus from Pergamon, and other major treasures of the Berlin museums, and provided shelter for up to 20,000 civilians during the Battle for Berlin. It took the Allies two years to demolish the *Flakturm Tiergarten* after its surrender.

[199] Ernst Friedrich Christoph "Fritz" Sauckel (1894–1946), *Gauleiter* of Thuringia and later the General Plenipotentiary for Labor Deployment from 1942 until the end of the war.

[200] Erich Koch (1896–1986), *Gauleiter* in East Prussia from 1928 until 1945. Between 1941 and 1945 he was the Chief of Civil Administration (*Chef der Zivilverwaltung*) of Bezirk Bialystok. During this period, he was also the *Reichskommissar* in *Reichskommissariat* Ukraine from 1941 until 1943.

[201] Fritz Todt (1891–1942), senior NSDAP member, engineer and founder of *Organisation Todt,* initially created to build the "West Wall", later renamed the "Siegfried Line" in 1938. In March 1940, he was appointed *Reichsminister für Bewaffnung und Munition* ("Reich Minister for Armaments and Munitions") and after the invasion of the Soviet Union in June 1941, he was appointed to manage the restoration of the infrastructure there. He died in a plane crash, and was replaced by Albert Speer.

technical problems. Nor did he, in doing so, think of prerogatives. He simply wanted to have really competent technicians working in the East.

Early in July, 1941, he spent an afternoon at my office where all pertinent problems were satisfactorily solved. He admitted without question the desirability of a central administrative office. I, in turn, asked him to assign some capable men to my central office in Berlin, where they could handle his technical problems in accord with his special wishes.

Todt figured that men who, for years, would be active in the East, would be valuable for work in the Reich itself later on.

Speer,[202] however, wanted a more rigid organization and, adorned with all the laurels of advance publicity, managed to coax the Führer into removing the technical department from the jurisdiction of the eastern administration. This would not let the others—middle-class minds gone berserk—rest until they had been given their own little authority over other subdivisions of the eastern administration, which should, by right, have been strictly unified.

When I became Minister for the East, I asked Doctor Meyer[203] to act as my permanent representative. He accepted the post immediately, and worked hard to get an insight into the new problems. That he could not forever maintain this position as the vice-leader of a supreme Reich authority, since he remained at the same time a subordinate, made his work difficult at times. But he remained just as loyal and decent throughout the years as he had been in the beginning. I wish we had had similar little *Gauleiter* everywhere!

When the last few days of the war were upon us, we took leave of each other. He went out to help defend his Gau. In Mondorf I heard that he was dead. Killed? A suicide? That man was a genuine National Socialist—not Bormann—not Himmler!

---

[202] Berthold Konrad Hermann Albert Speer (1905 1981), Hitler's chief architects and NSDAP member who replaced Frtiz Todt as Minister of Armaments and War Production.

[203] Alfred Meyer (1891–1945), an early NSDAP member, elected to the Reichstag in 1930. He also served as Gauleiter in north Westphalia, and in 1933 was appointed *Reichsstatthalter* (deputy governor) of Lippe und Schaumburg-Lippe in May 1933 and he was made *Staatsminister* (governor) of the federal government for Lippe und Schaumburg-Lippe in August 1936. In 1939, Meyer was made *Chef der Zivilverwaltung* and in 1941 he became deputy to Rosenberg in the Reich Ministry for the Occupied Eastern Territories. He was found dead by the River Weser on April 11, 1945, and it was claimed he had committed suicide, although this has never been verified, as Rosenberg says.

The fact that the Führer had assigned me to the leadership of our eastern policy displeased Himmler and Bormann considerably. And since nothing could be done about it directly, they tried indirectly. The Führer, who up to then had accepted my ideas without reservation, suddenly assumed a much changed attitude when he referred to a memorandum which, according to him, gave to the entire eastern problem a wholly different aspect than the opinions held by some of our gentlemen, meaning me.

The mysterious memorandum, which was mentioned again later, I never saw. This, then, is how my difficult fight for a more generous treatment of the fateful problem of the East began. Step by step the most urgent matters were taken care of, but much that was important was neglected. Precious, irreplaceable time was lost.

But Martin Bormann harshly upheld the interests of the Reich against the soft Rosenberg who might have had more sympathy for the Slavic people than would be advantageous to eastern policies in war times, and Himmler reinforced this attitude by insisting upon exclusive authority in combating the partisans.

The demands I made in my speech of June 20, 1941, on our eastern policies, were turned down. Himmler, Koch, and Bormann swaggered all over the place. And when volunteer battalions were recruited from among the eastern people, Himmler moved heaven and earth to get them under his command.

This was easy with the Estonians and the Letts, since they were considered Germanic peoples. But when it came to the others, particularly those formerly described as Asiatics,[204] there was a great to-do at the Leader's Headquarters about deposing the general of these volunteers with whom I was on very friendly terms.

As for the Cossacks, they were acceptable, at least as far as their use in the Balkans went. The Russian General Vlassov,[205] maligned

---

[204] Particularly the hundreds of thousands of Turkomans, Azeris, Tatars, and Azerbaijanis who flocked to aid the German military effort against the Soviet Union. In addition, up to 1,000,000 ethnic Russians also volunteered, many of them former Red Army soldiers captured as Prisoners-of-War.

[205] Andrey Andreyevich Vlassov (1901–1946), a Red Army general who took part in the defense of Moscow and who was captured by the Germans in 1942 after his army was destroyed while trying to lift the siege of Leningrad. He switched sides and began broadcasting anti-Soviet propaganda, and ultimately raising a "Russian Liberation Army" consisting of tens of thousands of former Red Army soldiers to fight on the German side against the Soviet Union. Captured by the Americans at the end of the war, Vlassov and most of his men were handed

and spat upon for two years, whose appointment I had endorsed since 1942, suddenly became popular toward the end of 1944, when Himmler, without informing me, began to influence Hitler in his favor. This was bound to offend all the other brave non-Russian combatants in the East.

Himmler knew nothing about the East; what he gradually learned from me about Berger was superficial, and even when he realized that my ideas were right, he still wanted to be the one to translate them into actuality, no matter how. Sometimes without, sometimes with, the aid of Vlassov, depending upon how it suited his sickly mania for power. Not as a strong personality, not as a brilliant thinker, but always as an insidious traducer and Jesuitic trickster.

In June, 1943, I invited two *Gauleiters* to accompany me on a trip to the Ukraine. They were wide-eyed when, from my special train, they saw the vast spaces of the East. Everything there simply burst out of the accustomed dimensions: the wheat fields, the Tauric steppe, the cherry orchards.

They heard the reports of the district commissioners on the immense improvements made in the fields of agriculture and handicraft, and the worries and wishes of the local population. They listened to the blustering of Reich Commissioner Koch, who more than once displayed his peacock-like vanity.

Then we visited Ascania Kova, the tree and bird sanctuary in the steppe, the work of the German colonist Falz-Fein. Shortly thereafter we were in the Crimea, in its magnificent Botanical Gardens, and in the peaceful mood of the evening drank some of the sweet wine of the country. We visited Livadia, and slept where it had once been Schinkel's artistic dream to build a castle above the Black Sea. We passed through Simeis where, twenty-six years ago, I had spent a summer, and looked down on the Black Sea from the Baider Gate.

In 1944, when the Army Group Middle anticipated a backward shift of the front, and the population in this space seemed in danger, General Kluge asked the Ministry for the East to remove the children of ten to fourteen in time to guarantee their safety. I, he said, was the one who would handle this task loyally. But when the same proposal reached me from other sources, I declined because I did not wish to lay myself open to the charge of having deported helpless children.

---

over to the Soviets who executed them all.

However, when I was pressed still more urgently, and realized that at least a partial evacuation was inevitable, I agreed to do the work, provided that the children were properly cared for by a number of White Ruthenian women, and that it was made possible for them to communicate with their parents, and so on. Five thousand children came to Dessau, where I assured myself they were given adequate care.

The older ones decently clothed, the younger ones either in schools under Russian teachers, or in outdoor kindergartens. A White Ruthenian woman thanked me with tears in her eyes. For the older boys the Junkers Aeroplane Works had prepared drawings with Russian texts, giving the German names, in transliteration, of all the tools in use.

The relationship between these boys and the German workers was excellent, in contrast to that with the Italians who had been there before. When I returned to Berlin, I told the head of the youth department of the Ministry for the East, who had taken over the supervision of this work: It would be nice if our own boys could be trained like this; but they must practice shooting instead!

I had never considered it possible that *Gauleiter* Koch would some day play a role in more than a very limited territory, certainly not a role that would actually reach over into the field of world politics. Koch had become a National Socialist at the time of the French invasion of the Ruhr. He came from Barmen-Elberfeld, the twin cities with the 150 sects, became a railroad official, and participated in the passive resistance against the Poincaré French.

Around 1928, Hitler appointed Koch *Gauleiter* for East Prussia. What he did there I do not really know. After the *Machtübernahme* there were rumors about the harsh methods he employed, but also favorable reports about his display of initiative in the economic field.

In any case, it was East Prussia that was the first *Gau* to report the complete elimination of unemployment. The few times I talked to Koch he impressed me as being a carefree old Nazi, given to a bit of bragging and somewhat loudmouthed, but rather kind. But later I had a few experiences that made me distrustful of Koch's judgment and character.

In 1933 and thereafter, Bolshevik polemics against the National Socialists were, understandably, extraordinarily vicious and were countered by us in kind. Koch, however, assumed a markedly different attitude, probably because he wanted to call attention to himself. His spiritual mentor at that time was a writer by the name of Weber-Krohse, a so-called landscape-politician. That is, he wanted to handle all politics in relationship to the great plain in the East, of which Poland as well as Eastern Germany is a part. A contributing factor was the influence of Möller van den Bruck,[206] an admirer of the so-called eastern spirit.

Koch published a few articles on the subject, and Weber called on me a few times at my office. In the most comradely way I pointed out to him that these theories were completely untenable, that very little was generally known about the East, and I requested him to inform Koch accordingly.

For a long time after that I paid no more attention to these things, but Koch published his collected articles in a book entitled *Aufbau des Ostens.*[207] In it he preached the unity of great spaces, expressed his trust in the youth of Dostoyevsky and Johann Huss, and called the youth of Soviet Russia, the Orient of German youth.

Koch became more and more a conceited braggart. But he was a favorite of Göring, who had a high regard for Koch's economic talents. When the problem of administering the eastern territories became acute, Koch's name popped up.

He was backed by Göring, who considered him an expert, and recommended by Bormann. I realized even then that Koch was dangerous because he was erratic, and because he was resolved not to let Berlin interfere. In the beginning I was anxious to keep Koch out of the Balticum, and succeeded in doing so; then I intended to use him in Russia proper, and to get somebody else for the important Ukraine.

I had counted on Sauckel or Backe.[208] As I learned later, Koch had not only worked on Göring, but had also begged Backe and Funk for their support. He pointed out how successful he had been in East Prussia with the raising of pigs, and promised to extend this plan on a large scale over all of Russia, and thus make it a vast source of meat supplies

---

[206] Arthur Moeller van den Bruck (1876–1925), a German cultural historian and writer, best known for his 1923 book *Das Dritte Reich* ("The Third Reich"), which promoted German nationalism and was a strong influence on the Conservative Revolutionary movement and later the NSDAP, although he was never a member of that party.

[207] "Development of the East," published in 1941 in the periodical *Der Deutsche Baumesiter.*

[208] Herbert Friedrich Wilhelm Backe (1896–1947), senior SS Officer who was nominated by Rosenberg, as the Secretary of State (*Staatssekretär*) of the *Reichskommissariat* Ukraine. From April to May 1945, Backe continued as Minister of Food in the short-lived post-Hitler government led by Karl Dönitz.

for the Reich. So Göring won the argument in our conference of July 16, 1941, and Koch became Reich Commissioner for the Ukraine. He was told about my opposition, a fact which considerably embittered the little would-be great man. I still do not know definitely whether the memorandum concerning the Ukraine had a decisive influence on Hitler, or whether it merely caused my opponents, accustomed to pay heed to Hitler's moods, to redouble their efforts against me; and probably I will never know.

In any case Koch, who had only recently called the Soviet youth the Orient of our own youth, was now the most rabid advocate of necessary harshness on the part of the Reich, and the rejection of a centralized government and economic-cultural autonomy for the Ukraine.

Attempts to Stem Anti-Slavic Attitude

I tried no fewer than eight times to induce Hitler to change this course. Twice he gave me an argument that was also bandied about by Koch: Once before, in 1918, he said, Germany had met the Ukraine half-way. The result had been the murder of the German General, Field Marshal von Eichhorn, by Ukrainian nationalists. He maintained that it would be dangerous in the midst of a war to permit political centralization.

I answered briefly that I considered the report about von Eichhorn's murder false. The State Archives at Potsdam had enabled me to find out what had really happened. The documents available showed beyond doubt that von Eichhorn had been murdered by a Russian social revolutionary named Donskoi, aided by two Jews who escaped arrest. Donskoi was executed in August, 1918.

Through Bormann I informed the Führer accordingly, but never knew whether Bormann passed on the report to him. Nor could the entire matter have been considered a political argument, anyway. Koch and a small circle surrounding him constantly sneered at the backwardness of the Slavs, and so on.

This provoked me into issuing an order to the effect that all boastful talk about superior lordliness was to be stopped, and that a decent and just attitude toward the Ukrainians was to be observed.

I also issued comprehensive instructions on the reorganization of the local school system. But to each one of these Koch managed to add a twist of his own to establish his independence. Upon the occasion of my first visit, in 1942, he started a row with some of my assistants. In 1943, he constantly horned in on conversations with Field Marshals Kleist and Manstein, and insisted upon coming along when I inspected factories and offices, and so on, always because of the fear bordering on mania that he might be looked upon as one of the inspected rather than as one of the inspectors. A little man, he would pace up and down, hands in pockets, strides as long as possible, and gabble about the things he had done, how Riecke had interfered with his grandiose pig-raising plans, and so on, and so forth. He barked at a general commissioner, and refused to shake hands with a mere district commissioner when he was promoted.

Koch was a foil for Bormann, who twice refused to answer when I asked him whether the Reich Commissioners had behind my back submitted memoranda on my activities. Himmler also opposed me constantly. Accomplishments of the usually extremely capable territorial commissioners and agricultural leaders were credited to Koch's energy when they were really due to the common sense of the lesser officials who were in constant touch with the people.

As I heard in 1945, Hitler once spoke about Koch's trustworthy eyes. In other words, Koch's cheap performances at the Führer Headquarters had always been effective. I wonder whether the Führer eventually recognized the fallacy of his attitude?

The very capable District Commissioner, Schmerbeck, later got, again through Bormann, a large construction job in connection with the defense of Holland. He executed the task well, but Bormann took the credit.

My last chance to speak to Hitler was in November, 1943, but Schmerbeck was ushered into his presence, for Bormann's glorification, as late as the end of 1944. Telling me about his conversation, he said that the Führer expressed his great appreciation and, pointing to the *Ritterkreuz*[209] and to the *Kriegsverdienstkreuz*,[210] said he noticed that Schmerbeck already had been decorated.

Schmerbeck: I received this decoration from Reich Minister Rosenberg. Only because he had followed my instructions, he added, had he been able to achieve success in the Ukraine. If he had listened to Koch, he would probably have been slain by the people.

---

[209] Knight's Cross.
[210] War Merit Cross.

The Führer was silent for a while, obviously a trifle embarrassed, and then spoke about something else. It was really a rather painful tragedy that I was forced to tangle with this person who had been pushed into the foreground, while others in the background, themselves irresponsible, secured the protection of the Chief of State for this puffed-up mannequin.

Mine was a fight for a large-scale conception of the eastern problem; my goal, the incorporation of the peoples of Eastern Europe into the fate of the whole continent, a constant fight against the primitivity of others.

I note in passing that as late as the end of 1944, the Führer replaced Löhse, who suffered from an ailment that was partly real, partly political, by Koch. Lammers told me about it, hinting that I was not to interfere.

Then Koch assembled all administrative leaders in Riga and, leaning his heavy jowls on his hand, said: I am accustomed to have my orders obeyed. Anyone who forgets this, I'll break.

He followed this up with his usual tirades, even though it was by then quite obvious that there was nothing more to be done than supervise the evacuation.

I told Lammers about this meeting, and added a few well-chosen words of my own. If anyone should have obeyed Bormann's order *Be victorious or die!*, it was this loud-mouthed *Gauleiter* of East Prussia.

When the battle raged in the streets of venerable old Königsberg, he was in Pillau. Yet when the commander capitulated, along with the remainder of his division, Bormann—obviously at Koch's instigation—decreed that the general be condemned to death by hanging for cowardice.

The *Gauleiter* had been completely taken by surprise, since he was at a different sector of the front. The assistant *Gauleiter* and the Kreisleiter were engaged in the life and death struggle for Königsberg. In the meantime, Koch boarded a fully loaded steamer in Pillau, and left his *Gau* post-haste. I know that he later was in Flensburg and thence fled to parts unknown. I did not see him. And since then I have heard nothing about him.[211]

---

[211] After the Second World War, Koch stood trial in Poland and was convicted in 1959 of "war crimes" and sentenced to death. The sentence was commuted to life imprisonment a year later. He died in 1986, of natural causes in prison at Barczewo, Poland.

Part Sixteen:
The End of the Reich

Hitler Made Same Mistake as Napoleon in Russia

In the beginning Hitler seemed not disinclined to accept my proposals that the East be ruled with three-quarters psychology and only one-quarter force.

But later he got entangled in other ideas, and lost all that feeling for space which he still had when I was appointed: the comprehension that the East was a continent in itself, in connection with which I was to counsel and help him.

In 1944, I read Coulaincourt's *Memoirs of Napoleon*, and was amazed to find that his attitude toward Russia was similar to mine. Coulaincourt warned Napoleon about the Russian winter, but Napoleon declared that by that time the war would be over. Coulaincourt said Alexander would not conclude a peace treaty. Napoleon replied that none of them understood politics, and he himself knew better. Once he was in Moscow, the Czar would soon enough make peace.

In both cases, luck went against them before Moscow. Just as Napoleon had refused to call upon the Russian peasants to revolt, so Hitler, applauded by his confidants, rejected my proposals regarding the political and cultural autonomy of all the peoples of Eastern Europe and their induction into the life of the continent.

End of the Third Reich—End of a Career

The great Soviet offensive carried the Red army to the Oder. A mighty battle for Berlin was imminent. I still went dutifully to my office, around which the bombs fell almost constantly. I went to the Michendorf office of the Ministry, where everything pertaining to the care of Eastern peoples had to be handled, together with matters of procedure, housing relatives escaped from Posen, and transferring sub-departments to Thuringia and Westphalia.

Often during the day, always throughout the night, bombs over Berlin, and the air-raid bunker a permanent abode for us and the families of the vicinity.

The Last Meeting with Hitler

I still made attempts to see the Führer, to whom I had last reported on November 16 and 17. I tried to reach him by way of the secretaries of a fellow-worker, with whom the Führer, after his military conferences, frequently spent the tea hour. I heard that he had said: *I would like to invite Rosenberg for tea, but what he wants is a technical discussion.* I asked my chief of staff: What is the head of a state for, if not for technical discussions?

At a *Reichsleiter* and *Gauleiter* rally held on February 24, 1945, the Führer spoke for the last time. He reiterated his hopes for success in the East, for the defensive measures in the West, and the revolutionary new U-boat warfare, and pointed with pride to the latest aeroplane models.

Of course, we wanted to have hope, but that had become increasingly difficult considering the type of men who constituted Hitler's sole retinue since 1941. Afterward a supper, without a chance to talk to him. That's the last time in my life I saw him.

Home is Bombed

During the night of March 21, 1945, there was another heavy bombing attack on our immediate vicinity. Several houses in the neighborhood burned down. The air pressure was so strong that our own roof caved in, and we had to move to the cellar. Only the kitchen and a corner room were still usable. That is how spring began. I did what seemed important. The garden was spaded, vegetables and potatoes planted, and trees transplanted.

My daughter, Irene, who had been looking forward to a small birthday party on March 22, had to spend the day in the midst of dust and rubble; she was quietly resigned. She sat in her cellar room in front of her small typewriter. What she wrote I don't know, but it was probably about life in Berlin, what she saw of destruction, and what she heard about death in the heart of the city.

Her young imagination had for a long time brought forth surprisingly good poems with impressive imagery and a rhythm all their own. Her fairy tales and short stories betrayed a talent that we intended to let ripen without interference. Then she went across the street to visit her girl friends. I still see her before me because I have made an effort to keep her picture in my memory: tall, young, with blond hair falling down over her shoulders, dressed in long slacks and a grey fur coat, carrying a handbag with long straps.

I often stood on the balcony, our Ingo beside me, his paws on the railing, both of us watching Irene, who would turn around frequently and smile. These visits were her last joy. My wife did her best to feed us as well as possible. It became ever more difficult, even though we did get occasional handouts from the commissary that was about to be discontinued.

Early in April I became bed ridden. On a walk in Dahlem, I strained my ankle, thus bringing about an inflammation and a hemorrhage. Lying on my couch, I received whispered reports about measures which were being taken: first of all, the evacuation of all ministries and party offices; contradictory orders, disapproval of the transfer of offices to Bavaria. In the offices themselves they knew nothing about it. Following instructions, I did send documents and supplies south, but considered the whole manner of proceedings unfair, and remained in Berlin myself.

Again I tried to reach the Führer to find out what his intentions were, but was referred to Bormann. Thereupon I wrote the Führer a personal letter—that must have been on April 13—to tell him that these contradictory orders made a bad impression; the way offices were being transferred looked like flight.

The reputation of many of his old coworkers was at stake. Our hearts told us to remain in Berlin. If reasons of state dictated otherwise, this would have to be announced clearly and frankly. I wanted to know what I was to do.

Thereupon word came from Schaub that I might as well stay on in Berlin. I informed my assistants accordingly, and left it to each of them to decide whether he wanted to go to Bavaria or remain in Berlin. In a short talk I went over our work for a last time and thanked each one individually. Two days later I learned that the friend of my youth, Arno Schickedanz, had killed his wife, his eight-year-old daughter and himself. He was a clear-headed politician, the only one with whom I had been able to discuss frankly the dangerous turn of events which neither one of us could prevent. Bormann and Himmler were to him what he called the megalomaniacal *Posemuckel*. His wife was ill, and he did not want to wait for the end. When Arno Schickedanz went I lost an old and true friend.

We, on our part, had inwardly prepared ourselves for a similar fate. I had managed to get hold of a sufficient quantity of cyanide, for it went without saying that neither I nor my family would voluntarily fall into the hands of the Soviets.

My pleas that they go to the Seehof[212] were emphatically rejected by both Hedwig and Irene. They wanted to share my fate, no matter what happened.

Ministers Ordered to Leave Berlin

On the night of April 20, another lengthy bomb attack. At 1:30 A.M. a call from the Reich Office: all ministers were to meet at Eutin. Departure on the morning of April 21.

We pack a few things; the driver says good-bye to his wife, who lives somewhere in the eastern part of Berlin. It is raining. I cannot put on shoes yet to walk for a last time through our once so beautiful garden. Only a last look from the window. There the paths where we used to stroll; in the back, Irene's swing and the half-demolished garden house. On the right the slender birch recently planted. Everything we still possess must remain behind, even the last few drawings I still have from my youth and from 1918.

I hand over keys, money, and so on, to the *Mannschaftsführer*[213] from the training school, and tell him that Ingo must not be allowed to fall into strange hands alive. I don't feel any too easy about leaving

[212] A resort near Berlin's Lietzensee Lake.
[213] Company sergeant.

others behind. Hedwig and Irene are worried about their friends. The man is quite calm: it is natural that the Führer should send his ministers away. I stroke Ingo's head. We have to leave our good dog behind. Then our car with a trunk trailer drives off toward the north. Outside of Berlin, fugitives from the East trying to get to the city. Alongside the road, camps of refugees. On the way, an aeroplane attack.

At last in Eutin, a stop before the government office. The driver asks for information. Hedwig is sad. She knows this ride means our separation. How shall I do it? I have lost my courage. Irene, we are losing a good friend and a comrade.

The sun shines bright into the car, I see Hedwig's grey hair with the old brown still showing through. Irene's delicate face haunts my memory. We spend a night at Eutin, then we go on to Flensburg.

Arrival in Flensburg

The *Kreisleiter* arranges for quarters with the family of a physician. The woman wants to settle Hedwig and Irene somewhere safely in the country. After a few bomb attacks near Flensburg, we make the trip. A small, very modest house, two tiny rooms, abandoned, isolated.

I move aboard the steamship *Patria* in Flensburg Bay to await rear Admiral Dönitz for the final decision.

The news of the Leader's death moves us deeply: he was our fate. One evening I hear that my wife is back; she will be with me shortly. I meet her in a freight car in Mürwik. She had been practically driven out of the village. She was attracting the bombers!

The returned husband of her landlady had been most antagonistic. This was repeated when Hedwig and Irene found shelter in a deaconess's home for the aged in Glücksburg. The physician in charge hunted for excuses. My wife: *Let's be frank. You want to get rid of us because I am the wife of Alfred Rosenberg!* But that I heard about only later.

In the meantime I went daily to the new government office of Dönitz. The atmosphere was ominous, capitulation inevitable, if at least a few things were to be saved.

Once I saw Himmler. I did not speak a word with him. I considered him one of the grave-diggers of the Reich, illusionary, arrogant, unscrupulous, underneath a smooth mask. I suppressed the desire to say that he and Bormann had brought Germany to this pass. Himmler disappeared. Word that Bormann might come to Flensburg prompted the decision that he would be arrested immediately. Even *Gauleiter* Wegener, whom Bormann had formerly helped, agreed to this.

I myself had to come to some sort of a decision, since I did not wish to be a burden to the Dönitz government, and since British papers had reported that I was still missing. I had taken leave of my wife and child in Glücksburg. We had talked of the good and the bad years, of all the decent things we had planned, of Germany's fate that now involved all of us.

Irene stood leaning against a tree, crying, when I drove off. On May 11 I walked along the seashore at Mürwik thinking about the future. Should I choose the way of Arno Schickedanz, or give myself up?

The harbor was crowded with ships. Toward the East, the open sea. Somewhere the old home town, Reval, with its towers and battlements. With the Red flag above the Lange Hermann. . .

On my return to the commander's headquarters, I stumbled and hurt my left ankle. A bad hemorrhage. Off to the Marine Hospital.

On May 12, I wrote Field Marshal Montgomery, putting myself at his disposal. The letter was handed to the British officer at Dönitz's quarters. I waited, but nobody called for me. My foot was heavily bandaged, but somewhat better.

Then Hedwig and Irene return, looking for shelter. Everyone in Flensburg is afraid to take them in. An official assignment card does no good. On May 17 they come to my room, very tired. The British military government has told the Lord Mayor that the wives of prominent National Socialists do not need cards. They are without shelter. Could they stay with me? They stayed in my room.

Arrested by the British

On May 18, at nine o'clock, quick steps outside. The door is torn open: British military police. Arrest. Ready in two minutes. I dress, putting only a sock on my foot.

Crying, Hedwig stares at the floor. I kiss her and Irene good-bye, and hobble out to where several cars with heavily armed guards are waiting.

In the Flensburg jail I am searched. I am moved very soon, probably by way of Rendsburg to headquarters.

Why did my wife carry a revolver and knuckle-duster? I explain: Years ago she was attacked on a street in Munich, and since then she has carried the knuckle-duster. She was supposed to turn in the revolver. Thus I know that my wife has also been searched. The Englishman tells me that she is under the surveillance of the German police, and can be reached through them. He also tells me that he knows nothing about my letter to Montgomery.

In jail an Englishman plays *Lili Marlene* on an ocarina. Another one tries to whistle the melody. Then I've got to go. When I come downstairs I see Hedwig and Irene sitting in a corner. Hedwig stares straight ahead; Irene, bent over double, is crying. The last picture of my family.

First to the jail in Neumünster. My things, a trunk full of suits and linen, together with a bag containing an overcoat and shoes, are delivered to the wrong house. I never saw them again.

Solitary confinement. Laughing soldiers. I hear them constantly mentioning my name, probably with appropriate comment. There is a lot of whistling; what, I don't know.

But then again, a few bars from *Lili Marlene.* Compulsory exercise in the yard. I point to my foot. The sergeant fingers his revolver: I am to go downstairs anyway.

One of the German prisoners, who is acting as orderly, fetches me an old slipper to put on my foot. In the yard I stand to one side; the others, National Socialists, police officers, and so on, alternately run and walk upon command.

British Sergeant Who Attended Nuremberg Rally

One evening a British sergeant comes in. He speaks German fluently. Could he have a personal talk with me? He had attended one of the party rallies in Nuremberg.

I tell him how I tried for years to bring about a German-British understanding and ask: Was it worth it to refuse Germany for twenty years any revision of an impossible treaty, just to have the Soviets on the Elbe, on the Atlantic, on the way to the Persian Gulf?

He replies that Hitler wanted everything too quickly; he should have waited. Something I don't deny, without knowing anything about the speech the Führer had made privately, and that was later read at the trial. Nevertheless, there has been a lack of wisdom on the other side, too. The sergeant takes his leave very politely.

On the fifth day, shackled, I am loaded into an automobile. The sergeant, accompanied by two heavily armed men, says something about Rendsburg or Flensburg which, I guess, means that we are not going to Rendsburg but to Flensburg.

In Flensburg the sergeant looks around for the place where he is to deliver me, but cannot find it. We crisscross the city. I keep looking out of the window, hoping I might catch a glimpse of Hedwig and Irene. By chance we stop in front of the house of the former *Kreisleiter,* to make yet another inquiry.

I notice his last few possessions are being loaded onto a truck. It turns out that we have made a mistake. It was to Rendsburg, after all, where we were supposed to go. Somewhat downcast, the sergeant sits beside the driver.

Evening comes, but the scheduled hearing does not take place.

Three days later I am again shackled. We bypass Rendsburg. Where to? Through the streets of Kiel to the airfield. After some time I am led over to an aeroplane, where a British captain receives me. The handcuffs are removed. A twin-motor ship. The two of us, the only occupants, other than the pilot.

We are heading in a south-westerly direction; in other words, towards Hamburg, I think, probably to Montgomery's headquarters. The captain asks me in German whether I still consider the theories expressed in my *Myth* to be right. He had read the book and speaks German quite well. I answer: some things in the book are naturally time-conditioned and outdated, but I still believe the essential contents are correct. Then I again describe my attempts to bring about an understanding: And this is the end!

We have long since left Hamburg behind; supposedly only the pilot knows where we are heading. Then below us I see Düsseldorf and Cologne, or rather what had once been Cologne. As if trampled down by gigantic beasts, Cologne's rubble lies heaped around the skeleton of the cathedral. Blown-up bridges in the river. A desert giving evidence of the terrible fate of people and Reich.

Now I believe that I will probably be set down on French soil. I try to see myself from outside, through the eyes of another person. Now we shall see, Alfred Rosenberg, how the adventure of your life will be concluded. But I am not very successful. Then we land and are met by Americans. We drive off in a small truck. I notice German street signs with arrows pointing in the direction of Trier. Luxembourg? Yes, we pass the town, keep on going, make a turn, and stop in front of a large building standing alone.

General Reinecke. That calms me down a bit. Americans are taking me over. It's the Palace Hotel at Mondorf in Luxembourg. Here I find Dönitz and all the men from Flensburg.

Then others are brought in: Schwarz, Frick and more. Surrounded by barbed wire three meters high, the Mondorf wait begins—until the material can be assembled by the prosecution to permit the opening of the trial at Nuremberg.

Part Seventeen:
My Political Testament

Only Hitler Could be Supreme Leader: Next in Line Would Have to Have Been Elected

The leadership of Hitler was the necessary result of a great national awakening, the Führer state an organically sound re-creation of the idea of the Reich.

Leadership is as different from rulership as it is from chaos. Tyrant and masses belong together just as much as do leader and follower. The two are possible only if they are paired, and are held together in a common bond of duty.

The ever greater power given Hitler was a temporary exception, permissible only after a fourteen-year-long test. This was not one of the goals of the National Socialist idea of state.

The first leader had to come into power as Hitler did. All others were to be elected to serve only for a limited period of time.

Thus it was provided, though no *Wahlgremium*[214] (electoral college) was founded. Before the *Ordensrat*[215] of sixty-one men from all walks of life, anyone could, and would have to, speak confidently and freely.

Before it every minister would have to defend his measures. It was the National Socialist plan to find a strong personality for every given task, and to give that individual all the authority he needed.

Adolf Hitler later broke this rule which he himself had made when, to all practical intents and purposes, he put the chief of police over the minister for the interior, when he allowed special appointees in ever increasing numbers to break into fields of activity that had been

[214] Electoral College.
[215] Literally, "Council of the Order," figuratively, a government executive council.

circumscribed by elections, and when he permitted several distinct functions to be concentrated in a single new office. Naturally, these may have been emergency measures, justified in times of revolution and war; but they should never be tolerated as permanent practices.

Thus the Minister for Culture of the liberal epoch was, in his day, more integral than the Reich Minister for Education of the National Socialist state.

Because art, science and education belong together, it is not necessary to turn science over to a musicologist.

In a great people there always will be a certain number of men, artistic in the best sense of the word, who really comprehend this unity.

A Propaganda Ministry is completely superfluous. An Information Department in the office of the Reich Chancellor is sufficient.

The Chief of Police must never have the rank of a minister, but must be subordinated to the Ministry for the Interior, nor may he hold any other political post.

Whether the Head of the State should also be Reich Chancellor, as in the United States of America, is something that can be decided later. In view of the proven tendency of the German to see everything basically, it seems safer to keep these two positions separate (in connection with which the matter of authority over the armed forces must be carefully weighed).

The Reich Chancellor, however, must never have the decisive voice in the government, but must confine himself, as long as he is in office, merely to directing policy.

The election of a body of so-called people's representatives appears to remain a necessity. Proportional elections, however, have led to chaos before. What is most evident is the need for finding a method of election which makes governing possible.

Nobody can govern a people if three parties form a coalition, and a fourth with only a few members holds the balance of power.

The so-called justice of not wasting a single vote is, in reality, evidence of the greatest neglect of duty toward the entire nation. Therefore, and without attempting to ape the English elections with their small election districts and personal campaigns in each, the method of election must insure that a majority wins, the others lose out.

The Reich Senate, chosen partially by election, partially by the appointment of selected men, must have as its function the confidential correction on the part of the government of open parliamentary discussions.

A one-party system was justifiable and historically even a necessity in 1933. But it was an historical mistake to attempt to perpetuate it for all eternity. This would have been impossible anyway, since, after Hitler's death, at least three distinct groups within the National Socialist German Workers' Party would have entered the political arena.

National Socialism at one time was, so to speak, a substitute nation, when the country was threatened with dissolution by thirty-two individual parties. The old parties of the class and religious wars were outmoded and had outlived their usefulness. They had in many respects become no more than hollow shells, and had to be remoulded.

This was as inevitable as the resignation of the twenty-three German dynasties in 1918. Thus it was the historic task of National Socialism to become the spiritual-political basis of life (Nationalism and Socialism) for the entire people.

With this national union no longer disputed, certain wing-groups could have been tolerated. But while this seemed desirable to a large number of people, it was never approved by Hitler who (together with Ley, Goebbels, and the rest) rode a good principle to death.

This new idea will somehow have to be the spiritual basis for the future. What experience taught us must never again be forgotten.

But since we will have to count on more than one political group, the National Socialist identification of party with state is automatically eliminated. In fact, between 1933 and 1945 this identity, never fully comprehended in its effect, jeopardized the most basic laws governing the very life of a people.

Not one of us can claim that we did not uphold the dictum, the party rules the state. For a while this was justified, for then it was not the state that created us, but we who had created the state.

True enough, but weren't we already living in a thousand year state—a state the party was to serve? This diffuse dualism could not be overcome by a personal union while the party office on the ministerial level worked towards the termination of this very union.

This would have simply meant the perpetuation of a dictatorship of the antechamber. In connection with the future multi-party system, the position of the representatives of the individual states which make up the Reich will have to be independent.

The creation of the office of *Reichsstatthalter* was basically sound. The sovereignty of the Reich was upheld while at the same time the various *Länder*[216] were permitted to govern themselves. That this required state governments (and perhaps even Chambers of Counsellors) though not necessarily *Landtage,*[217] is obvious, if for no other reason than the preservation of national strength. (The representatives elected to the *Reichstag* from a given Land could, incidentally, also make up the majority of these Chambers of Counsellors.)

National Socialism turned into legal centralism, but also to particularism in practice. Never was the unity of a central administration more of an obvious necessity than today, when the Reich is divided into four zones. This, then, could be the basis: the appointment by the Head of State of *Reichsstatthalter* (who also serve as Presidents of the State Governments), candidates to be suggested by the Reich Chancellor.

The special interests of the individual states to be safeguarded by Chambers of Counsellors, by representatives elected to the *Reichstag*, and by representatives in the Senate.

The shocking degeneration of police power in the Third Reich makes it mandatory that independent judges and due process of law once again guarantee the security of the individual.

Time-tested European methods must safeguard the community. Not even the most shrewdly conceived constitution can possibly guarantee permanent security. If a democracy tends toward chaos, the Führer principle on the other hand might lead to monocracy. Besides that, foreign political developments might lead to social conflicts, and human passions, despite all efforts to subdue them, might break through.

Fate will not be confined by paragraphs. Nevertheless it is important to build upon a foundation valid for all, though this is possible only when the character of a people is fully understood: its historical reaction to the world at large, its living space with its own inherent laws, and, as today, some immediate experience that necessitates, as never before, the examination of one and all existing problems.

National Socialism was both an ideal and an organization, but it had not yet taken on final form. This realization intrigued me long

---

[216] States.

[217] State Assemblies.

before the war, and I began work on a comprehensive book, tentatively entitled *Die Macht der Form.*[218]

The *leitmotiv* was that in any given historical situation revolutions are made victorious by ideas. Organizations are variable forms of utilitarianism. They can perpetuate a revolution only when they become forms, that is, natural habits, common psychological attitudes, characteristic general reactions to the surrounding world, and eventually spiritual disciplines.

This alone can guarantee an organic continuity if the creator of the idea is dead and fate has not provided an acceptable successor.

Only a general form of life—one might also call it type of life, though never scheme of life—can then serve the purpose. This holds good in every field of human endeavor. I had a draft of about four hundred pages ready—they disappeared during the war—which was a little sharp in the mode of expression and was to be rewritten completely and amplified at an older, riper age.

These writings on state, science, church, and art were lost (one copy in an air-raid shelter in Berlin, the second in a mine in Upper Austria, the third among the papers sequestrated in Castle Banz).

Seen even from this angle, a great accomplishment of the German nation—National Socialism—went to pieces before it had had a chance to become formed.

If I put down a few thoughts on the form of a state, I do this because I have experienced the birth, victory, and collapse of its auxiliary structure; for the party was never more than that, and the structure of the Reich itself had been taken apart without ever being put together again.

The following outline is purely theoretical in nature, since the present is too dark to analyze it fully.

Ideas on foreign policy cannot be discussed at all, as is obvious in the face of existing realities. Besides, this outline cannot possibly be couched in legal terminology. It is no more than an expression of my personal attitude, aims, and principles:

1. The Head of State (Reich President, Führer, Reich Protector, Reichsführer) is elected by the people as a whole. The majority of the ballots cast is decisive. In a run-off election only, the two candidates with the greatest number of votes can participate. The term is for five

218 "The Power of Form."

years. The Head of State is the Supreme Commander of the armed forces. A personal union with the office of Reich Chancellor is not possible. The Head of State can be re-elected any number of times.

Reasons: The position as Head of State presupposes a well-known personality, and therefore an election by the entire people seems justified, since under this system, character, feeling, and trust come directly into their own, something that must be taken into consideration in Germany if a real representative of the entire nation is to be elected. The German does not want a mere representative nonentity.

After the present collapse of confidence, a personal union between the offices of Head of State and Reich Chancellor is no longer possible. For the same reason the armed forces must be under the command of the Head of State. His title can be left for the future to decide.

A dynasty need not even be discussed, since personal reverence is unthinkable, considering the biological deterioration of a given family, quite apart from other dangers. If it were possible to conduct elections under the decimal system, the political rhythm would conform to the rhythm of the rest of life, something that must not be underestimated as a creative force.

2. Leadership, government, and representation of the people are in the hands of the Reich Chancellor, the *Reichssenat*,[219] and the *Reichstag*.[220]

The Reich Chancellor is selected by the Head of State, the Reich Ministers are appointed upon the proposal of the Reich Chancellor by the Head of State. The Reich Chancellor issues political directives, but does not have the decisive vote in the cabinet.

It is the duty of the *Reichssenat* to pass on the reports of the Reich Minister concerning important proposed measures. It has the right to submit propositions of its own to the Reich Chancellor. The *Reichssenat* consists of thirty elected and thirty-one appointed members. The minimum age of a Reich Senator is forty years.

Thirty senators are elected by *Nährstand*[221] (agriculture), *Städtetag* (Union of Cities), German labor unions, rectors of universities and churches. They require the approval of the Head of State. Thirty-one senators are appointed by him. The sessions of the Senate are secret, and no member is permitted to keep a diary or to make notes on them.

[219] Senate, or "Reich Upper House."
[220] Parliament, "Commons" or "Congress."
[221] Agriculture.

The Reich Senators hold office for five years, but the Head of State may reappoint them at the end of their terms. The Reich Senate cannot be dissolved. The *Reichstag* is elected by the people for five years. The territory of the Reich is divided into five hundred election districts in which each party can nominate its own candidates. The candidate getting the majority of votes is elected.

The Reich Chancellor and the Reich Ministers submit their planned political measures to the *Reichstag*. The latter is also permitted to initiate laws. If a bill submitted by the Reich government is turned down in three readings, the Reich Chancellor must submit his resignation to the Head of State. The Head of State may appoint a new Reich Chancellor, dissolve the *Reichstag* and announce new elections, or he can keep the Reich Chancellor in office until the end of the *Reichstag* term.

The Reich government must resign if the *Reichssenat* and the *Reichstag* demand it by a two thirds majority. In this case the Head of State must appoint a new Reich Chancellor, or else announce new elections for the *Reichstag*. The Head of State declares war only after consulting with the Reich Chancellor, the president of the *Reichssenat,* and the president of the *Reichstag*.

Reasons: Continental democracy with its proportional election system necessarily leads to party anarchy. Under the system outlined above it seems possible to achieve continuity, a really responsible government, the avoidance of majority demagogy, the attracting of men of really important achievements from all walks of life to responsible co-operation, the prevention of a splintering of the party.

This method of selecting the Reich Chancellor, of partly appointing the *Reichssenat,* and electing the *Reichstag*, guarantees the leadership both necessary rights and necessary controls.

3. The members of the *Reichssenat* and the *Reichstag* have the right and the duty of freely exchanging opinions. They must not be called to account for their political opinions or maligned in any way. In connection with any other delict provided for in law, they are held responsible just as is any other citizen. Their immunity is purely political.

Reasons: The immunity of politicians in the democratic Germany frequently had grotesque consequences, inasmuch as the members of the *Reichstag* were active in their professions, but could not be called to account for slander. This was as much a breach of law as were the irresponsible police arrests of the Third Reich.

4. To govern the individual German *Länder*, the Head of State upon proposal of the Reich Chancellor appoints *Reichsstatthalter* who are at the same time presidents of the provincial governments. The members of the *Reichssenat* and the *Reichstag* from his province are at his service in an advisory capacity. The Reich *Stadtholder* is bound by the directives of the Reich government. His term is for ten years.

Reasons: This assures the unity of the Reich in the field of politics and the principles of general conduct, but leaves the *Reichsstatthalter* every freedom for the cultural development of his home province. He is constantly kept informed by the senators and representatives, without being burdened with an assembly that in each province represents a tremendous squandering of energy. The title of *Staatsminister*[222] would have to be replaced by that of State Director.

5. Inhabitants are classified as citizens of the state or members of the state. Counted among the latter are all recent immigrants. The Reich Minister decides when citizenship may be granted. Only citizens have the right to active and passive election, and are eligible for appointment to state positions. In every other respect all state citizens and state members are equal before the law.

Personal freedom is guaranteed. Arrests can be made only by court order. In emergency cases the policy may deviate from this rule, but must take the case to court within three days. In principle, a judge cannot be unseated. He is independent in his judgments, and subject only to the dictates of the law and his conscience.

The Chief of Police is under the jurisdiction of the Minister for the Interior, and may not hold any post other than his office. The Reichsgericht[223] is the Supreme Court. In case of the death, absence or any incapacity of the Head of State, the President of the Reichsgericht takes over his responsibilities.

Reasons: The possibility of a differentiation between political rights must be newly incorporated into the constitution on the basis of what the experiences have been in various countries. It is an incentive for good behavior, makes the securing of citizenship a matter of achievement, and eliminates from the election of political leaders external, possibly financial, factors. On the other hand a uniform

[222] State Minister.
[223] The supreme criminal and civil court in Germany until 1945.

human evaluation precludes the possibility of any feeling of inferiority, and also guarantees the legal equality of all.

The election of a substitute for the Head of State seems undesirable. In case of his demise, the taking over of his duties by the president of the *Reichssenat* might be considered. The election of the president of the Reichsgericht, on the other hand, would permit law itself to assume its old honored position in German life.

6. The means of disseminating information are basically the property of the state, or are at least at its immediate disposal, particularly, the radio and the press. The official News and Information Bureau is under the jurisdiction of the Chief of the Reich Office. He allots the supplies to all government and private publishing enterprises.

The Reich *Stadtholder*s issue permits for the publication of newspapers, and engage the editors. The latter are contributors to the common weal. Articles must be published under the full names of the authors, or must be identifiable by initials.

Books and magazines can be freely published.

Reasons: The misleading of public opinion by private lust for sensationalism is a political cancer in all democracies and a crime against the self-respect of all people.

No reference to freedom of the press can justify what has been done by irresponsible journalists in world politics. On the other hand, the attempt to invest the profession of editor with a greater dignity eventually had quite the opposite effect, when the Propaganda Ministry kept them under constant surveillance, and prohibited the expression of any private cultural convictions.

It is suggested that all parties, according to their numerical strength, have licensed newspapers, the *Reichsstatthalter* to appoint editors from their respective ranks. Both the free expression of opinions and the interests of Reich and people would thus be safeguarded.

Simultaneously, less paper would be wasted. The German forests must not be further depleted, nor the imports burdened, for the sake of sheer sensationalism.

Every editor is obliged to treat the subjects under discussion with all seriousness, and the will to improve is to be his guiding light. Other provisos can be left safely to life itself to determine. In the cultural and scientific magazine field, private initiative has free reign. The Chief of the Reich Office seems the best possible impartial agent to direct and supervise the domestic and foreign news service.

The question as to whether or not the radio should be put entirely under his control must be carefully considered, since radio covers many fields. The same holds good for the film industry, especially in connection with its weekly news reels.

7. Our youth is the future generation of the people as a whole. It has the right to organize freely in bunds.

These bunds, however, must not be the youth organizations of political parties and social or confessional groups.

The central bund leadership, constituted by the representatives of the individual bunds, is under the supervision of the president of the Senate. He approves statutes and by-laws, and allocates funds for youth shelters, hikes, and so on.

Reasons: Youth groups of the old parties were frequently the original *foci* of dissension among the people. The same is true of confessional youth organizations within which the groundwork for the particularism of the Catholic Center or the Evangelical Bund was prepared.

In the Hitler Youth organization, exclusiveness, after the initial healthy spurt, led to a discipline unbearable to both youth and parents, and in the administration, to a conceit that had a most insalubrious effect on character.

However, the Hitler Youth as the successor to an outmoded youth movement must not be simply forgotten. What must be carried over into the future are self-discipline, the desire for unity, the recognition by the leaders of their responsibility for the physical and mental health of the young generation.

Supervision by the president of the Reich Senate seems desirable, inasmuch as he is not involved in everyday politics, though he is directly concerned with the guidance of growing life. The Head of State himself must not be burdened with organizational problems.

8. All Germans have the right to organize in political parties and to hold meetings. Presupposed is the recognition of the unity of Reich and people, and the absence of class and confessional discussion.

Reasons: This point merits careful consideration. How can we be assured there will never again be a historical necessity for another November 9, 1918, or another May 8, 1945?

How can division and unity exist side by side? How can ways and means be honestly fought over if there is no common goal to provide a basis for discussions?

Only after these questions are answered can social life be organized.

It is unthinkable that any party should take orders from outside the Reich, no matter what these orders may look like. By special law it should be expressly forbidden that parties train their own troops, except the regular *Ordnungsdienst.*[224]

Occasional orderly parades may very well be held without such detachments. The breaking up of any meeting must be severely punished by the banning of any provincial organization, or even entire party, whose leaders have been found guilty.

9. Economic and social organizations are united in the *Nährstand* and the *Arbeitysfront.*[225] Professional and cultural groups have the right to organize as they see fit.

Freedom of conscience and religious freedom are among basic rights of the Germans.

Reasons: The healthy union idea became a victim of party feuds. Class war and confessional war tried to turn unions into a reservoir of voters for their own purposes.

The German Labour Front was based on the sound idea of preventing this splitting into fragments and encouraging cooperation between employees and employers instead of antagonism.

A special law should guarantee the possibility of such co-operation, and a trustee of the Reich should be appointed to act as a neutral arbitrator. A commercial firm is just as much of a unit as a farm. Similar steps should be taken in connection with skilled labor or artisans.

Details must be worked out most carefully, and particular attention given to the fact that the farmer, his health and security, are the very foundation of the nation. It should also be decided whether the professions (attorneys, physicians, and so on) ought to be united in professional chambers.

The Kaiser Wilhelm Academy, the German Academy and other historic institutes, should be maintained. Universal freedom of conscience must be guaranteed. The problem of film censorship must be solved.

---

[224] Literally "Order Service," figuratively Municipal or Local Police.
[225] Labor Front.

This basic outline for a constitution appropriate to the German character and historic situation naturally demands that a great deal of thought and study be devoted to a great many problems. For example, the powers to be granted the Head of State in case of a national emergency, corresponding to Paragraph 48 of the Weimar Constitution, the organizational structure of the *Nährstand* and the *Arbeitsfront,* the various professional chambers, and so on.

Today all this is mere *theorizing;* but all the constitutions prepared during the occupation are not testimonies of a free will, but merely involuntary adaptations to that of the occupying powers. Considering the position of the German nation, this is not an accusation but merely a statement of fact.

Any constitution presupposes national sovereignty and an extraterritorial area in which a provisional government, headed by the legal Chief of State, can begin the work of reconstructing the German Reich. This idea of a national and governmental unity cannot, must not, and will not be given up by a nation that has fought two world wars, nor by the young men of 1939–1945.

It is true that times are dark, that terrible possibilities threaten to relegate even the best of theories into the distant field of hypotheses.

The Communist world revolution was repulsed by the advent of energetic passionate men without the aid of the bourgeoisie of the 18th century, which alone was incapable of this accomplishment and which quickly forgot its own salvation.

In fact this bourgeoisie even attacked its saviors, safe on the soil of satiated nations where this world revolutionary movement had never been able to take root.

Above all these trials of National Socialists,[226] serve no other purpose than to becloud an event of world historical importance, towers this social-philosophical, and truly tremendous, problem.

National Socialism called the attention of Great Britain (and thus also of the United States of America) to the necessity of an alliance with a strong Germany in her own interest.

To be sure, Great Britain rejected Communism, but since 1933 no man of real stature has guided the destiny of the British Empire. London failed to understand the traditional concept of a balance of power on the continent of Europe as it applies to the new historic

---

[226] A reference here to the then ongoing Nuremburg Trials.

situation, according to which Soviet Russia stands on the one side, and on the other, the rest of Europe. With true bourgeois conceit they refused to listen to us. There would not be any reason to complain if, after 1933, they had thought and acted in a modern farsighted fashion. Great Britain would be standing firmer than ever, Europe would be strong and invulnerable, if only a competent statesman in London had strengthened and broadened the Four Power Pact, and the wrong done Germany had been righted by extensive revisions in the East and the return of at least one colony.

That Adolf Hitler lost patience and hope is the second tragedy in this development which, so far, has brought about only a great accusation, not a new decision.

Because of the attack upon Germany's back by the Western powers, the Soviet Union was able to spread out so far that today all Slavic peoples are under her sway, and the territories Russia now rules represent the glacis for plans of conquest in the oldest Czarist tradition: the Persian Gulf, the Atlantic, the Dardanelles.

Today there are, beyond all this, Communist parties active in the democracies, and threats of revolt among the colored peoples. Compared with these threats the atom bomb is a mere firecracker.

True, in the East the Soviet Union is more vulnerable than the Western powers (especially the United States of America); but Great Britain is well within the range of Soviet atom bombs, since England by her victory has enabled the Russians to advance as far as Lübeck and Magdeburg.

Thus western Germany is no more than a bridgehead for the Anglo-Saxons, and it is definitely within the realm of possibility that this bridgehead might be overwhelmed, that the Russians might appear on the Channel and hoist the Red Rag over Paris.

Naturally general staffs of every country are even now diligently studying this very problem which, during the Nuremberg trials, is being condemned with a great deal of moral suasion as criminal in principle.

But, on the one hand, is an American army which wants to go home and does not feel that it is defending its own country in Europe; and on the other is the dictatorially led Red Army whose members are living better than ever before at the expense of the conquered countries.

The officers of the Western powers must look with wrath in their hearts upon these frenzied prosecutors who are bent upon killing off the last vestige of manhood in a Germany which alone could furnish a fanatical army, but instead is subjected to defamation every day.

No doubt in many German heads the thought has cropped up that it might be best, now that they are proletarians anyway, to turn their backs on everything, to proclaim a German Soviet Republic, and thus preserve at least the unity of people and land, no matter on what wretched terms.

However, what is happening behind the iron curtain has definitely put a damper on these thoughts which were, no doubt, also entertained by many National Socialists. Thus Germany finds herself spiritually and politically in the most terrible situation, which may actually grow far worse if the great conflict everybody sees approaching should be fought out on her blood-soaked soil.

Hitler Experienced Wotan's Tragedy

Adolf Hitler, the fascinated disciple of Richard Wagner, listened to the *Nibelungenlied* in the Linz Theatre. I had someone point out to me the pillar where he used to stand.

Now, like Wotan, he wanted to build a Valhalla, but when the will to power and right broke asunder, this castle fell to dust. Hitler experienced Wotan's tragedy in his own person without being warned by it; and he buried Germany under the ruins of his Valhalla.

Yes, we must never disdain agreements, nor ever suffer a Loki to whisper ill counsel into our ears.

The Nuremberg show trials will presently be over and our fates decided.

Let my confession stand behind them: National Socialism was the European answer to a century-old question.

It was the noblest of ideas to which a German could give all his strength. It made the German nation a gift of unity, it gave the German Reich a new content.

It was a social philosophy and an ideal of blood-conditioned cultural cleanliness. National Socialism was misused, and in the end demoralized, by men to whom its creator had most fatefully given his confidence.

The collapse of the Reich is historically linked with this.

But the idea itself was action and life, and that cannot and will not be forgotten. As other great ideas knew heights and depths, so National Socialism too will be reborn someday in a new generation steeled by sorrow, and will create in a new form a new Reich for the Germans.

Historically ripened, it will then have fused the power of belief with political caution.

In its peasant soil it will grow from healthy roots into a strong tree that will bear sound fruit.

National Socialism was the content of my active life. I served it faithfully, albeit with some blundering and human insufficiency. I shall remain true to it as long as I still live.

Index

A

Ahenerbe 114
America, racial problems of 72
Austria 27, 35, 36, 48, 49, 99, 115, 167, 191
Axmann, Artur 123, 126, 128

B

Balticum 1, 34, 174
Balts 1, 3, 4, 5, 6, 14, 15, 16, 41, 134
Barbarossa 166
Bavaria 20, 25, 30, 34, 37, 43, 50, 51, 55, 59, 95, 97, 137, 149, 166, 180, 181
Bavarian Soviet Republic 20, 25, 27
Bayreuth 22, 62
Berchtesgaden 54
Berlin 18, 19, 22, 23, 25, 43, 44, 55, 78, 87, 91, 92, 100, 101, 102, 103, 104, 107, 109, 110, 114, 118, 125, 129, 137, 145, 151, 153, 167, 168, 169, 170, 173, 174, 178, 179, 180, 181, 182, 191
Bismarck 10, 16, 42, 108, 159
Bolsheviks 13, 16, 135
Bormann, Martin 66, 67, 112, 123, 124, 125, 126, 127, 129, 133, 145, 168, 169, 170, 171, 174, 175, 176, 177, 180, 181, 183
Bürgerbräu 101

C

Cathars 65
Catholic Church 44, 65, 73, 116
Chamberlain, Houston Stewart 7, 57, 80, 161
Charlemagne 3, 42
Christianity 31, 57, 58, 59, 72, 75, 79, 82, 114, 121, 124, 145, 158, 159
Class war 35, 36, 144
Coburg 38, 43, 44
Cologne 92, 93, 107, 185
Council of Trent 75
Crimea 12, 13, 172
Czar Peter 1, 15

D

Darré, R.W. 105, 114, 167, 168, 169
Democracy 84
Deutsche Arbeiterpartei 27, 28
Deutsch Völkische Freiheits Partei 49
Dönitz, Admiral Karl 155, 156, 174, 182, 183, 186
Dostoyevski 10
Drexler, Anton 23, 28, 33
Düsseldorf 185

E

Eckart, Dietrich 21, 22, 23, 24, 25, 26, 28, 29, 30, 31, 39, 40, 41, 43, 45, 48, 54, 55
Educational Office of the S.S. 116
Eisner, Kurt 20, 25
Estonia 1, 2, 14, 16, 23
Euthanasia 82
Externsteine 114

F

Feder, Gottfried 23, 24, 33, 48
Feldherrnhalle 48, 49, 86, 150, 152
Finland 1, 84, 87
Flensburg 177, 182, 183, 184, 185, 186
Four Power Pact 59, 199

G

German nationalism 17, 36, 174
Goebbels, Joseph 69, 91, 92, 99, 100, 101, 102, 103, 104, 105, 106, 107, 108, 109, 110, 111, 112, 113, 123, 126, 127, 131, 133, 140, 144, 157, 189
Goethe 7, 9, 22, 57, 71, 75, 94, 101
Göring, Hermann 40, 47, 92, 110, 111, 163, 169, 174, 175
Grossdeutsche Zeitung 51, 53
Günther, H.F.K. 47, 78

H

Hedwig Rosenberg 181, 182, 183, 184, 185
Henry the Lion 166
Heydrich, Rheinhard 60, 65, 66, 115, 118, 119
Himmler, Heinrich 60, 63, 65, 66, 69, 70, 87, 88, 112, 113, 114, 115, 116, 117,

118, 119, 120, 121, 125, 127, 128,
133, 162, 163, 164, 167, 168, 170,
171, 172, 176, 181, 182, 183
Hindenburg 42, 132, 138, 141, 142, 143,
145
Hitler and art 148
Hitler, and Christianity 158
Hitler, first meeting with 29
Hitler, first speech Rosenberg heard 32
Hitlerjunge Quex 144
Hitler, last meeting with 179
Hitler, on principled politics 132
Hitler, on private property 132
Hitler, on South Tyrol 133
Hitler, permitted misuse of power 134
Hitler, seeks alliance with England 133
Hitler, Wagnerian end 200
Hofbräuhaus 32
Homosexuality 137

I

India 25, 73, 75, 77
Irene Rosenberg 180, 181, 182, 183, 184,
185

J

Jabotinsky, Vladimir 71
Jesuits 42, 44, 80
Jewish Question 70
Jewish Terrorism 72
J. F. Lehmann 30

K

Kapp Putsch 42, 43
Kerenski 13
Kristalnacht 110

L

Landsberg 52, 53, 140, 158
Leadership 187
Ley, Robert 64, 93, 94, 95, 96, 97, 98, 99,
105, 124, 189
Lloyd George 33
Lord Moyne 72
Lüdecke, Kurt 37, 38
Ludendorff 41, 42, 52, 53, 151

Luther, Martin 32, 57, 75, 82, 153
Luxembourg 99, 143, 156, 186

M

Marienplatz 26
Mein Kampf 21, 43, 152, 158
Meyer, Alfred 64, 90, 91, 170
Mjölnir (cartoonist) 103
Moscow 7, 9, 10, 11, 14, 15, 29, 31, 89, 171,
178
Mosley, Oswald 84, 85
Mulattoisation 81
Munich 19, 20, 21, 23, 25, 26, 27, 28, 29, 30,
32, 37, 38, 39, 41, 43, 44, 47, 49, 50, 52,
73, 79, 92, 97, 101, 102, 103, 113, 115,
121, 123, 125, 131, 135, 136, 137, 147,
148, 150, 151, 153, 155, 167, 184
Mussolini 69, 85, 163
Mutschmann, Martin 87, 88, 89, 108, 113
Myth of the Twentieth Century 57, 58, 60,
79, 86, 167

N

Napoleon 43, 135, 153, 178
National Socialism 24, 35, 57, 70, 84, 85, 96,
110, 115, 134, 135, 143, 144, 189, 190,
191, 198, 200, 201
Nietzsche 4, 116
Nordic Society 84, 86, 87
Nordland Verlag 116
Norway 96, 163
NSDAP 21, 23, 25, 27, 28, 33, 38, 41, 46, 47,
48, 53, 54, 56, 63, 95, 99, 103, 107, 118,
119, 127, 137, 140, 150, 163, 169, 170,
174
Nuremberg 27, 60, 64, 94, 99, 110, 117, 118,
119, 121, 151, 153, 157, 184, 186, 199,
200

O

Odeonsplatz 19
Ordensburgen 95

P

Palestine 71, 72
Peter the Great 1, 4, 6

Pravda 12
Prince Lvov 11
Propaganda Ministry 157, 188, 195
Prussia 16, 34, 53, 66, 77, 95, 134, 142, 167, 169, 173, 174, 177
Pulverturm 17

R

Racial History 75
Racial respect 70
Reval 2, 4, 5, 13, 14, 15, 17, 19, 43, 45, 74, 183
Rhineland 34, 93, 101
Riga 5, 8, 12, 14, 17, 177
Röhm, Ernst 47, 93, 103, 115, 117, 137, 138, 139, 141, 143
Rosenberg, Hilda 4, 6, 7, 12, 13
Röver, Carl 63, 64, 138
Ruskoye Slovo 9

S

Schirach, Baldur von 106, 128, 157
Sicherheitsdienst 125
Speer, Albert 149, 151, 169, 170
S.S. 63, 88, 113, 114, 115, 116, 117, 118, 119, 120, 122, 125, 126, 163, 168
Stahlhelm 71, 141, 144
Stennes-Putsch 103
Storm Troopers 40, 43, 103, 115, 117, 136, 137, 138, 139, 141
St. Petersburg 7, 10, 11, 12, 13, 21, 29, 31
Strasser, Gregor and Otto 47, 53, 56, 91, 92, 93, 103, 113, 140

Streicher, Julius 56, 140
Strength through Joy 96, 98
Swastika 152

T

Tannenberg 41, 142
The Myth of the Twentieth Century 58, 61, 68, 74, 80, 83, 86, 107
Todt, Dr. Fritz 169, 170
Tolstoy 4, 10
Troost, Paul Ludwig 148, 150

U

Ukraine 12, 169, 172, 174, 175, 176

V

Vatican 59
Versailles 33, 131, 142, 157
Völkischer Beobachter 38, 39, 40, 45, 48, 54, 55, 56, 63, 101, 102, 103, 127, 130, 142, 151, 158
Volkswagen 96, 97
Vörwarts 12, 20

W

Wagner, Richard 22, 55, 63, 64, 71, 143, 200
Wehrmacht 66, 67, 69, 127, 134, 141, 143, 145, 156, 159
Weimar 15, 16, 19, 77, 87, 132, 142, 144, 157, 167, 198
Weizmann, Chaim 71, 72